The Harm Paradox

Tort Law and the Unwanted Chil
in an Era of Choice

Can a healthy child resulting from negligence in family planning procedures constitute 'harm' sounding in damages, when so many see its birth as a blessing? Can a pregnancy constitute an 'injury' when many women choose that very event? Are parents really harmed, when they choose to keep their much loved but 'unwanted' child? And why don't women seek an abortion if the consequences of pregnancy are seen as harmful?

These questions constitute *The Harm Paradox*. Offering the first comprehensive theoretical engagement with actions for wrongful conception and birth, the author examines the significance of these questions in explaining the recent retraction of liability for claims of 'unsolicited parenthood' in the UK. Centralising gender as a critical axis of enquiry, the author argues that the concept of autonomy, though an important value for promoting women's reproductive *freedom*, is transforming into a reproductive *expectation*. Not only has autonomy become central to the law's response that enforced parenthood is a harm*less* outcome, but as Priaulx reveals, similar discourses have come to inhabit the reproductive landscape generally. Seeking to challenge such accounts and pernicious assumptions that inform them, the author questions: 'Just what is it that we *value* about the concept of autonomy?'

Nicolette Priaulx is a lecturer in law at Keele University. Her research interests include tort law, medical law and feminist legal studies. She has published work on the reproductive torts in a series of journals and edited collections including: *Studies in Law, Politics & Society*.

Biomedical Law and Ethics Library
Series Editor: Sheila A.M. McLean

Scientific and clinical advances, social and political developments and the impact of healthcare on our lives raise profound ethical and legal questions. Medical law and ethics have become central to our understanding of these problems, and are important tools for the analysis and resolution of problems – real or imagined.

In this series, scholars at the forefront of biomedical law and ethics contribute to the debates in this area, with accessible, thought-provoking, and sometimes controversial ideas. Each book in the series develops an independent hypothesis and argues cogently for a particular position. One of the major contributions of this series is the extent to which both law and ethics are utilised in the content of the books, and the shape of the series itself.

The books in this series are analytical, with a key target audience of lawyers, doctors, nurses, and the intelligent lay public.

Forthcoming titles:

Horsey and Biggs, *Human Fertilisation and Embryology* (2007)
McLean and Williamson, *Impairment and Disability* (2007)
Gavaghan, *Defending the Genetic Supermarket* (2007)
Downie and Macnaughton, *Bioethics and the Humanities* (2007)
McLean, *Assisted Dying* (2007)
Huxtable, *Euthanasia, Ethics and the Law* (2007)
Elliston, *Best Interests of the Child in Healthcare* (2007)

About the Series Editor:
Professor Sheila McLean is International Bar Association Professor of Law and Ethics in Medicine and Director of the Institute of Law and Ethics in Medicine at the University of Glasgow.

The Harm Paradox

Tort Law and the Unwanted Child
in an Era of Choice

Nicolette Priaulx

Taylor & Francis Group
LONDON AND NEW YORK

First published 2007
by Routledge-Cavendish
2 Park Square, Milton Park, Abingdon, Oxon OX14 4RN, UK

Simultaneously published in the USA and Canada
by Routledge-Cavendish
270 Madison Ave, New York, NY 10016

Routledge-Cavendish is an imprint of the Taylor & Francis Group, an informa business

© 2007 Nicolette Priaulx

Typeset in Times New Roman by
RefineCatch Limited, Bungay, Suffolk
Printed and bound in Great Britain by
MPG Books Ltd, Bodmin, Cornwall

All rights reserved. No part of this book may be reprinted or reproduced or utilised in any form or by any electronic, mechanical, or other means, now known or hereafter invented, including photocopying and recording, or in any information storage or retrieval system, without permission in writing from the publishers.

British Library Cataloguing in Publication Data
A catalogue record for this book is available from the British Library

Library of Congress Cataloging in Publication Data
Priaulx, Nicolette, 1973–
   The harm paradox : tort law and the unwanted child in an era of choice / Nicolette Priaulx.
     p. cm.
   Includes bibliographical references.
   ISBN-13: 978–1–84472–107–8 (hbk)
   ISBN-13: 978–1–84472–108–5 (pbk)
   1. Wrongful life—Great Britain. 2. Wrongful life. 3. Autonomy (Psychology). 4. Medical personnel—Malpractice—Great Britain. I. Title.
   KD2960.M55P75 2007
   344.4104′121—dc22

                            2006031946

ISBN10: 1–84472–107–8 (hbk)
ISBN10: 1–84472–108–5 (pbk)
ISBN13: 978–1–84472–107–8 (hbk)
ISBN13: 978–1–84472–108–5 (pbk)

Contents

Acknowledgements	vii
Introduction	ix
Table of cases	xv
Table of legislation	xix

1 The beginning of the decline — 1

Characterising harm 4
Loss of autonomy? 8
Defining the problem 11
Notes 14

2 Injured bodies — 15

Natural born reproducers 18
Wrongful pregnancy as a personal injury 24
Orthodox *injuries* 31
Harmed minds, harmed bodies 38
Paradigm shifts 43
Conclusion 47
Notes 49

3 Health, disability and harm — 53

Emerging dichotomies 56
The 'disability' exception 59
Parental autonomy 64
The importance of context 68
Rees *in the House of Lords* 71
Conclusion: What kind of autonomy? 78
Notes 82

4	**The harm paradox**	**85**

The mitigation ethic 90
Mitigation is dead . . . 91
. . . Long live choice! 101
My family and other animals 105
Conclusion: A harm paradox? 109
Notes 110

5	**Constructions of the reasonable woman**	**113**

On being responsible 115
Responsible women 121
Self-regarding woman: 'Still a choice' 122
Natural woman: 'She had no other choice' 128
The 'Woman in Need' 132
Conclusion: Not a choice? 136
Notes 139

6	**Reproductive choice, reproductive reality**	**141**

A (wo)man's right to choose 144
Reversing nature's discrimination 149
'In practice abortion is not a choice' 150
'Women do not experience abortion as a choice' 151
'Women are conforming, not choosing' 154
Conclusion 156
Notes 159

7	**The moral domain of autonomy**	**161**

What kind of person? 164
Beyond personhood 166
'Autonomous choice': A relational approach 170
Being responsible beings 173
Concluding remarks 178
Notes 184

Bibliography   185
Index   197

Acknowledgements

This book, which started out as a doctoral thesis, would not have come about but for the love and patience of my immediate family – Bob, Hilary and Ady Priaulx – my friends and the support of my amazing colleagues at Keele. Of my colleagues, particular thanks go to Matthew Weait. I have enjoyed many hours of thought-provoking discussion with Matthew, and consider myself extremely fortunate to have such dear friends in him and his partner, Robert Hanwell. I remain grateful to Beverley Brown for her input at the very earliest stages of this book, as well as Emily Jackson, whose *post viva* comments have proved invaluable. And finally, I wish to extend my very warmest thanks to Hazel Biggs and my partner, Russell Hardy – both of these individuals have been critical supports for my work over the years and the *most* indispensable sources of intellectual stimulation.

This book contains revised material from my earlier published work including: (2002) 'Conceptualising Harm in the Case of the "Unwanted" Child' *European Journal of Health Law* 9: pp 337–59 (with permission of Koninklijke Brill NV); (2004) 'That's One Heck of an "Unruly Horse"! Riding Roughshod over Autonomy in Wrongful Conception' *Fem LS* 12: pp 317–31 (Reprinted with kind permission of Springer Science and Business Media); (2004) 'Joy to the World! A (Healthy) Child is Born! Reconceptualizing "Harm" in Wrongful Conception' *SLS* 13: pp 5–24 (Reprinted by permission of Sage Publications Ltd); (2005) 'Health, Disability and Parental Interests: Adopting a Contextual Approach in the Reproductive Torts' *European Journal of Health Law* 12: pp 213–44 (with permission of Koninklijke Brill NV); (2006) 'Beyond Stork Delivery: From Injury to Autonomy in Reconceptualising Harm in Wrongful Pregnancy' *Studies in Law, Politics & Society* 38: pp 105–49 (with permission from Elsevier); (2006) 'Beyond Health & Disability: Rethinking the "Foetal Abnormality" Ground in Abortion Law' in Hazel Biggs and Kirsty Horsey (eds) *The Human Fertilisation and Embryology Act 1990: Reproducing Regulation*, London: Routledge-Cavendish (with kind permission from Routledge-Cavendish): pp. 205–29.

Introduction

> Alice looked round her in great surprise. 'Why, I do believe we've been under this tree the whole time! Everything's just as it was!'
> 'Of course it is', said the Queen. 'What would you have it?'
> 'Well, in *our* country,' said Alice, still panting a little, 'you'd generally get to somewhere else – if you ran very fast for a long time as we've been doing.'
> 'A slow sort of country!' said the Queen. 'Now, *here*, you see, it takes all the running *you* can do, to keep in the same place. If you want to get somewhere else, you must run at least twice as fast as that!'
> (Carroll, 1998: 143)

The issues explored in this book relate to a narrow, but controversial, species of case arising within the law of negligence, involving clinical mishaps in the realm of family planning. Sitting within a class of actions known as the 'reproductive torts', my focus is upon two specific actions – wrongful conception and wrongful birth – whereby women seek compensation (and in many cases, their partners), typically against health authorities, following the setback of their reproductive plans. In the case of wrongful conception, claimants had sought to avoid conception entirely by methods such as sterilisation, while in wrongful birth cases the effect of negligence was to deprive the claimant of the ability to terminate a pregnancy under the Abortion Act 1967. While wrongful conception cases typically involve allegations of negligence in the performance of sterilisation procedures or the provision of advice (e.g. about the woman's or her partner's sterility), in the case of wrongful birth, by contrast, the negligence may have involved the failure to diagnose a pregnancy, or the failure to diagnose or inform of the risk, that if born, the child would suffer from a serious disability. Yet while these actions are deserving of their different labels, the crux of the complaint is ultimately the same: the unwanted processes of reproduction, culminating in fresh parental responsibilities that these claimants sought to avoid.

These actions can be viewed as the products of 'medical progress' and 'increased choice' in the field of reproduction. While relatively new to the UK courts, what these actions demonstrate is the law of tort's ability to embrace a widening ambit of harms under its cloak. Bringing fresh promises for claimants whose reproductive decisions are destroyed through negligent treatment, these cases have also required the courts to address difficult ethical and legal questions. At the heart of the dilemma lies a tension between two constructions of 'harm'. Is the experience of unsolicited parenthood simply part of the vicissitudes of life, or is it a harmful event that should be the subject matter of litigation, sounding in damages? Reference to changing reproductive norms might be thought capable of providing a decisive answer. The promotion of family planning services in the UK has certainly given rise to a variety of familial forms, postponement of parenthood and childless women, indicating that traditional domestic activities such as child-rearing are no longer seen as 'central unifying roles' (Clarke and Roberts, 2002: 165). Normal expectations of life therefore may include the decision to limit family size, to abstain from parenthood altogether or to avoid parenthood when the conditions are not 'right', for example where there is a risk that if born, the child would suffer from a disability. But these expressions of reproductive choice frequently depend on the medical profession. And when such expectations are defeated through negligence, individuals must confront a different life plan, one that arguably holds inescapable parenting obligations, including financial, emotional and social implications.

Affording legal recognition of this type of harm has not been straightforward. The actions of wrongful conception and birth do not sit easily within the paradigm of the conventional negligence claim, and clearly involve more than the 'run-of-the-mill features to be found in other areas of medical negligence' (Symmons, 1987: 298). The claim that under some circumstances 'a new life amounts to damage in the law of tort' (Donnelly, 1997: 10) ultimately requires the courts to recognise a new wrong. And perhaps for these reasons the courts have struggled to reconcile their position within the law of tort. Nor is the related question, 'Can parenthood constitute an injury?' decided within a legal vacuum. Policy factors such as the value of life, the promotion of family stability and the consequences of attributing liability to the medical profession have deeply affected the nature and existence of the case law.

Yet, as the most fleeting glance of the now numerous comments and articles exploring the case of the 'unwanted child' reveal, in the UK these are actions in decline. Departing from the principles of corrective justice, the courts have determined that parents complaining of the unwanted repercussions following a negligently born child should no longer be entitled to full compensation. Although causative of celebratory cheers from some scholarly corners, this book takes a very different stance. From a feminist perspective, one rooted in protecting and promoting women's reproductive freedom, the demise of these actions is viewed as a cause for great concern. While not discounting the importance of men's contribution to child-rearing, it is nevertheless women who experience the biological processes of reproduction, and despite shifting (rather than shifted) attitudes towards women's role in public life, it remains the case that the responsibility of caretaking for children and others in society falls, more often than not, upon women. For these reasons, my exploration of these cases centralises its concern with the reproductive experiences of women and their lives before the law of tort. Changes in legal policy as to the injuries and harms the law is willing to acknowledge and protect when relating to matters of reproduction cannot be properly viewed or understood without specific reference to women – this is *not* an area of law that warrants a gender-neutral stance.

My examination of this area, though not entirely limited to the law of tort, nevertheless places much emphasis on the need for law to fully acknowledge the injuries and harms that women sustain in matters of reproduction. Some, however, might see this as offering a very limited view, and suggest that such an analysis places too much faith in tort to resolve issues that might be better dealt with *outside law*. And there is some truth in this assertion. In his detailed critique of legal intervention in the field of obstetrics, John Seymour concluded that many of the problems within that field could not be wholly resolved by resorting to the law; rather, he suggested that, 'legal concepts and techniques can impede the search for appropriate solutions' (2000: 375). None of this is denied. Indeed, a broader exploration reveals just *how* limited the law of tort is as a means for resolving social problems. Among the apocalyptic talk of the UK being immersed in a 'blame culture' where virtually any 'adverse experience is readily blamed on someone else's negligence' (Furedi, 2003: 11) lies the stark truth that the law is simply not prepared to respond to any adverse life event; only a small number of people will become the recipients of damages under the civil justice system. Among the filtering mechanisms of negligence, one must point to the fault of another to become one of the deserving few. Therefore, for the vast number of those suffering injuries and disablement, the loss will lie where it fell. There is no doubt that tort law offers less than a fair, effective or efficient system as a means of dealing with social ills; nor indeed is that its current aim. Arguably, what the law of tort does best is tort law.

Recognising the limits of tort, some of which are perhaps most ably demonstrated by the cases that this book examines, I do nevertheless think that there are good reasons for scrutinising these claims in the light of how tort law *does* tort law, what harms and injuries it recognises and why this might be important and to *whom*. After all, a system of law that cannot illustrate why it deserves its place is not a system worth having at all. In the context of the reproductive torts then, why should it be important to recognise the kinds of harms and injuries sustained through negligence in the reproductive realm? As this book considers, there are very practical reasons, most obviously concerning the existing responsibility that women currently undertake for dependency work. Not only does this impose very clear financial limitations upon life, but can hinder a woman's aspirations for a career, or education, among other opportunities open to men and childless women. While this imbalance is not something that can be generally tackled through the law of tort, it is a different matter when those responsibilities are thrust upon women by negligence. In this context, it is therefore of critical importance that the law of tort handles constructively, rather than reflects, the unequal nature of society (Peppin, 1996). However, alongside this, the law of tort also holds significant symbolic power, in three interlinked ways. First, these actions hold the potential to *reinforce* that the negligent failure to protect women's reproductive choices constitutes a *real harm*, with significant and enduring repercussions upon their lives. The law can articulate that the harms that women suffer, as women, *really matter*. Second, the reproductive torts could *enhance* women's reproductive freedom by enforcing higher standards of medical care – liability for the frustration of women's choices sends out a strong signal that the medical profession should take greater care in their facilitation. Third, the law also plays an important role in reflecting the reality and diversity of women's lives. Although 'choice' is a term inclined to mislead, in bespeaking an array of unlimited choices that is rarely there, it is nevertheless important to *take seriously* a woman's choice to avoid, or indeed delay, parenthood to pursue other avenues, which she regards as more fulfilling in her life. The law does play an essential role in articulating that these interests are ones worthy of protection, and the importance of reproductive autonomy in the diverse lives of women (and of course, men) as a means of leading a fulfilling and chosen life.

Given these points, how then do we assess the demise of the reproductive torts? To what extent have these considerations been taken (or not taken) into account in shaping the law's response that no longer should women harmed through negligence resulting in pregnancy, childbirth and the responsibilities of parenthood become the recipients of full compensation? What assumptions have informed legal principle that these kinds of injuries should be assessed as less deserving, less worthy of recognition than other kinds of harms sustained in the clinical arena? Are these harms so different in nature from other kinds of injuries? How does the law understand those harms specifically sustained by women? What factors inform what counts as compensable harm? As this book considers, the explanations offered by the courts, and others commenting on this development in the reproductive torts leave many questions begging as to *why* the injuries sustained in these actions have been singled out and largely transformed from compensable harm into the mere vicissitudes of life. And it is a search for a fuller explanation that this book embarks upon.

The flow of the book

As the foregoing suggests, this book seeks to unravel a puzzle – one which, for the author, remained despite the growing interest in these specific torts and the voluminous literature now available in the field. Each chapter is structured so as to focus the reader on specific aspects of these reproductive torts, as a means of unravelling the question as to why and how these actions have met their demise and, ultimately, *how* the law thinks about injuries and harms specific to women in the reproductive domain. To achieve this, rather than providing a full history or picture of the reproductive torts, the chapters take up very specific questions. I seek to shed light on the meaning of the concept of harm within the law of tort, to think about how concepts that might seem fruitful for enhancing women's reproductive freedom, such as the concepts of autonomy, choice and bodily integrity, are being invoked within the narrative of the judgments. My central argument and sustained critique, one might think, quite oddly, does not truly emerge until Chapter 2; the first chapter is put forward as the beginning of a dilemma, a puzzle that is in need of a solution; there I very briefly set up the context, and set out the different questions, which we might ask in light of a decision that marked the beginning of the decline of the reproductive torts. From Chapter 3 onwards, my claims and the thrust of my argument become quite apparent. My view is that the law of tort has presented women seeking recovery of damages in these suits with a Harm Paradox – where in all but the most *exceptional* circumstances, the consequences of pregnancy, no matter what way the claim is put, are always constructed as chosen, wanted and harm*less*. This paradox, I claim, is premised upon very particular constructions of women and a very particular construction of the concept of autonomy – these constructions, I argue, live not in the real world, but in the law's imagination and serve to fundamentally misrepresent women's sexual and reproductive lives. To challenge the law's current *thinking*, this book raises the question as to what it is that we value about the concept of autonomy, and my claim is that its value, for each and every one of us, must reside in our care for people, the moral concern we show towards others and hope will be extended towards us. This richer, broader understanding of what is *valuable* about autonomy, I argue, is one that reveals that despite some of the contradictions thrown up by these cases, the repercussions of enforced reproduction and parenthood are undoubtedly harmful and deserving of a full legal response.

This book does not attempt to provide a working knowledge of the law of tort or a primer as to the mechanics of negligence; however, two points may allay the fears of a reader who feels that they are in need of such instruction. The first is that in the majority of these cases, for the purposes of the judgments, negligence was assumed. So on the ordinary application of the rules of negligence, these claimants would have recovered (if negligence were subsequently made out) full compensation to place them, as far as money could do it, into the position they would have been in had the tort not occurred. Rather, the question arising in many of the cases explored here was whether and to what extent the repercussions of the birth of an unwanted child, *should* be recognised as capable of amounting to damage that could found an action in the law of negligence. Relating to this is the second point – insofar as that latter question does involve issues of legal doctrine, in my view, the reader without a specific knowledge of doctrine may be in a *better* position by which to adjudge the case law in this field and question the different positions the courts have taken in recent years. To some degree, a legal education can rather blind us to what is going on in cases, given the tendency to see law through law (Conaghan, 2002), rather than to ask broader questions about whether the policy of the law is *fair* or sustainable outside the operation of legal rules. On this basis the non-legal eye has a great advantage, for what becomes apparent through a reading of these cases is that what is at work here is not strict legal doctrine, but exceptions to doctrine – in other words, what underpins the various outcomes of all these decisions is policy. And it is on that important note that we now turn to consider the questions that are raised by the first part of the puzzle – and this begins with the wrongful conception case of *McFarlane v Tayside Health Board* [2000] 2 AC 59.

Table of cases

A (Children)(Conjoined Twins: Surgical Separation), Re [2000] 4 All ER 961 164
AD v East Kent Community NHS Trust [2002] EWHC 1890;
    [2002] EWCA Civ 1872 .... 83, 130–1, 139
Adams v Bracknell Forest Borough Council [2004] UKHL 29 50
Allen v Bloomsbury Health Authority [1993] 1 All ER 651 .... 2, 24, 49, 50
Andersson and Kullman v Sweden (application no 11776/85) 46 DR 251
    (European Commission) 184
Attorney-General's Reference No 3 of 1994 [1996] QB 581 23

Barnett v Chelsea & Kensington Hospital Management Committee [1969]
    1 QB 428 50
Bolitho v City and Hackney Health Authority [1997] 4 All ER 771 139
Bradford v Robinson Rentals Ltd [1967] 1 All ER 267 139
Bravery v Bravery [1954] 1 WLR 1169 112
Buck v Bell 274 US 200 (1927) (United States) 67

C v S [1987] 2 WLR 1108 149
Caparo Industries plc v Dickman [1990] 1 All ER 568 14
Cattanach v Melchior [2003] HCA 38 (Australia) 72, 77, 96, 176–7
CES Superclinics (Australia) Pty Ltd (1995)
    38 NSWLR 47 (Australia) 81, 105, 108, 140
Chester v Afshar [2004] UKHL 41 139

Dulieu v White [1901] 2 KB 669 32

Emeh v Kensington, Chelsea and Westminster Area Health Authority [1985]
    QB 1012 .... 1, 14, 92, 94, 95, 96, 99, 137
Evans v Amicus Healthcare Ltd & Others [2004] EWCA Civ 727;
    Evans v UK (Application 6339/05, 7 March 2006) 146–9

Fairchild v Glenhaven Funeral Services Ltd [2002] 3 All ER 305 179
Finlay v NV Kwik Hoo Tong [1929] 1 KB 400 116
Flynn v Princeton Motors [1060] 60 SR (NSW) 488 (Australia) 95

Glasgow Corporation v Muir [1943] AC 448 113
Gold v Haringey Health Authority [1988] QB 481 2
Goodwill v British Pregnancy Advisory Service [1996] 1 WLR 1397 26–7
Greenfield v Irwin [2001] 1 WLR 1279 .... 28–30, 35, 50, 83, 127, 131, 179

Groom v Selby [2001] EWCA Civ 1522 83
Gwilliam v West Herfordshire NHS Trust [2002] EWCA Civ 1041;
    [2003] QB 443 120

Hardman v Amin [2000] Lloyd's Rep Med 498 .... 68, 83
Hedley Byrne & Co. v Heller & Partners Limited [1964] AC 465 32
HL Motorworks v Alwahbi [1977] RTR 276 116
Hunt v Severs [1994] 2 AC 356 139

Jones v Berkshire Area Health Authority (1986) 2 July (unreported) 1–2, 132

Lee v Taunton and Somerset NHS Trust [2001] (October 2000 unreported) ... 57, 83
London & South of England Building Society v Stone [1983] 1 WLR 1242 116

McCamley v Cammell Laird Shipbuilders Ltd [1990] 1 All ER 854 132
McFarlane v Tayside Health Board [2000] 2 AC 59 .... 2–4, 5–8, 11, 13, 14,
        27–8, 29, 30, 33, 34, 35, 36, 38, 44, 46, 50, 56–7, 58, 59, 60, 61, 62,
            63, 64, 70, 71, 72, 73, 75, 76, 77, 78, 79, 80, 81, 88, 89, 99, 100,
            101–4, 105, 106, 107, 108, 119, 121, 130, 132, 133, 137, 138, 179
McKay v Essex Area Health Authority [1982] 2 All ER 777;
    [1982] QB 1166 .... 14, 96–7, 111
McKew v Holland & Hannen & Cubitts (Scotland) Ltd [1969] 3 All ER 1621 92
McLouglin v O'Brien [1983] AC 410 .... 24, 36
Mohr v Williams (1905) 104 NW 12 (United States) 49
Murphy v Brentwood District Council [1991] 1 AC 398 14

N v Warrington Health Authority (unreported, 9 March 2000) 83
Nance v British Columbia Electric Railway Co Ltd [1951] AC 601 111
Nettleship v Weston [1971] 2 QB 691 120

Parkinson v St James' & Seacroft University Hospital NHS Trust [2002]
    QB 266 .... 13, 39, 44, 45, 46, 59, 60, 61, 62, 69, 70, 74, 75, 80, 100
Paton v BPAS Trustees [1996] 1 QB 276 .... 22, 149
Paton v UK (1981) 3 EHRR 408 149
Penney v East Kent HA [2000] Lloyd's Rep Med 41 50
Phelps v London Borough of Hillingdon [2001] 2 AC 619 50
Pilkinton v Wood [1953] Ch 770 116
Planned Parenthood of Southeastern Pennsylvania v Casey,
    120 L Ed. 2d 674 (1992) (United States) 118–19
Practice Statement (Judicial Precedent) [1966] 1 WLR 1234 72

R v Blaue [1975] 3 All ER 446; [1976] Crim LR 648 117
R v Bourne (1939) 1 KB 687 150
R v R [1991] 4 All ER 481; [1991] 3 WLR 767 21
R v Raby (Unreported, Supreme Court of Victoria, Teague J,
    22 November 1994) (Australia) 184
R (on the application of Pretty) v DPP [2002] 1 All ER 1 184
Rand v East Dorset Health Authority (2000) 56 BMLR 39 .... 57, 68, 83
Re B (Adult: Refusal of Medical Treatment) [2002] 2 All ER 499 184
Rees v Darlington Memorial Hospital [2002] QB 20 (CA);
    [2003] UKHL 52 (HL) 56, 62–3, 69, 71–8, 80, 88, 89, 99,
                                              100, 105, 121, 132, 133, 139, 179
Richardson v LRC Products (2000) 59 BMLR 185 .... 111, 112

Royal College of Nursing of the United Kingdom v Department of Health
    and Social Security [1981] AC 800 86

Sabri-Tabrizi v Lothian Health Board (1997) 43 BMLR 190
    (Court of Session, Outer House) 94
St George's Healthcare NHS Trust v S [1998] 3 WLR 936 ....9, 49
Salih v Enfield Health Authority (1991) 7 BMLR 1; [1991] 3 All ER 400 134
Schloendorff v Society of New York Hospital 105 NE 92 (NY, 1914)
    (United States) 22
Scuriaga v Powell (1979) 123 SJ 406 111
Selvanayagam v University of the West Indies [1983]
    1 All ER 824 (Privy Council) 87

Thake v Maurice [1986] QB 644; [1985] 2 WLR 215 ....1, 49, 50, 111
Troppi v Scarf, 31 Mich App 240, 187 NW 2d 511 (1971) (United States) ...117, 184

Udale v Bloomsbury Area Health Authority [1983] 1 WLR 1098;
    [1983] 2 All ER 522 ....1, 7, 49

Vowles v Evans [2003] EWCA Civ 318; [2003] 1 WLR 1607 120

Walkin v South Manchester Health Authority [1995] 1 WLR 1543;
    [1995] 4 All ER 132 25–6

Table of legislation

Abortion Act 1967 ......22, 50, 64, 85,
    86, 93, 96, 97, 110, 111, 116
    121, 122, 136, 150, 151
  s 1(1)(a) 86, 110, 150
  s 1(1)(d) 55, 58, 59, 64,
    66, 82, 83, 135
  s 1(2) 86
  s 4 97
  s 4(1) 112

Child Support Act 1991 ....145, 149
Children Act 1989 117
Congenital Disabilities
  (Civil Liability) Act 1976
  s 1(5) 14

European Convention for the
  Protection of Human Rights and
  Fundamental Freedoms 1950 31
  Art 2 146
  Art 8 ....146, 179
  Art 8(1) 184
  Art 8(2) 148
  Art 12 146
  Art 14 ....146, 179, 184

Family Law Act 1996 145

Human Fertilisation and Embryology
  Act 1990 ....146, 147, 148
  s 13(5) 67
  s 28(3) 147
  s 37 ....55, 111
  Sch 3 146
  s 4(1)–(2) 147
  s 6(3) 146–7
Human Fertilisation and Embryology
  (Disclosure of Donor Information)
  Regulations 2004 159
Human Rights Act 1998 ...31, 179, 184

Law Reform (Contributory
  Negligence) Act 1945 31
  s 1(1) 111
Law Reform (Miscellaneous
  Provisions) Act 1934 31
Limitation Act 1980 ....30, 37, 43
  s 14 49
  s 38(1) 24, 25

Mental Health Act 1983 130

NHS Redress Act 2006 ....90, 110

Protection from Harassment
  Act 1997 31

Unfair Contract Terms Act 1977 31

Chapter 1

The beginning of the decline

> She pondered. 'Androids can't bear children', she said, then. 'Is that a loss?'
> He finished undressing her. Exposed her pale, cold loins.
> 'Is it a loss?' Rachel repeated. 'I don't really know; I have no way to tell. How does it feel to have a child? How does it feel to be born, for that matter? We're not born; we don't grow up; instead of dying from illness or old age we wear out like ants. Ants again – that's what we are. Not you – I mean me. Chitinous reflex-machines who aren't really alive.'
>
> (Dick, 1968: 165)

The stories of parents bringing wrongful conception actions against health authorities render familiar allegations – clinical mishaps ranging from negligently performed vasectomy or sterilisation, to the provision of incorrect test results following postoperative testing. Claiming that in the absence of such negligent treatment the child would not have been born, parents have typically sought to claim damages for the pain and suffering of the physical events of pregnancy and childbirth *and* for the costs of child-rearing. While English law has traditionally permitted both claims, the question of whether parents should be entitled to the costs of child-rearing has proved controversial. The initial reaction to such a claim was outright rejection. In *Udale v Bloomsbury Area Health Authority* [1983] 2 All ER 522, Jupp J denied damages under this head on the grounds of public policy, observing *inter alia*, that the birth of a child 'is a blessing and an occasion for rejoicing' (p 531). Although not repudiating the 'child as a blessing', *Udale* was soon overruled by *Thake v Maurice* [1985] 2 WLR 215. In allowing damages for child-rearing, Peter Pain J preferred to address the issue in economic terms: '. . .every baby has a belly to be filled and a body to be clothed' (p 230). And this more pragmatic line of reasoning was followed by the Court of Appeal in *Emeh v Kensington, Chelsea and Westminster Area Health Authority* [1985] QB 1012. Despite occasional expressions of 'surprise' that English law should permit such recovery (see for example, *Jones v Berkshire Area Health Authority* (unreported, 2 July 1986), *Gold v Haringey Health Authority* [1988] QB 481, and *Allen v Bloomsbury* [1993] 1 All ER 651), it seemed that *Emeh* had settled the matter. As Mary Donnelly considered at the time, 'in the unlikely event of the House of Lords overruling any of these decisions, the policy debate in England appears to be concluded' (1997: 16); but the gates of policy were about to reopen in the case of *McFarlane v Tayside Health Board* [2000] 2 AC 59.

In 1999 the House of Lords were faced with two claimants, Mr and Mrs McFarlane, who had been assured by doctors that the husband was no longer fertile following his vasectomy operation. Having dispensed with contraceptive methods, Mrs McFarlane became pregnant and gave birth to their fifth child, Catherine. Mrs McFarlane claimed damages for the pain and inconvenience of pregnancy and birth, and both pursuers claimed for the costs of rearing their healthy child. Despite the Health Board's contention that the processes of conception, pregnancy and childbirth were natural events, thereby pure economic loss,[1] the majority of the House found relatively little difficulty in construing such events as actionable physical harm to the mother. Therefore, while reaching little agreement as to the extent of damages, their Lordships found that Mrs McFarlane should be entitled to recover for the pain and inconvenience of the pregnancy and for those expenses arising as a result of the pregnancy. However, in relation to damages for the cost of raising a healthy child, all their Lordships were in agreement – this part of the claim should be denied – although they employed a variety of techniques in reaching this conclusion. Lords Slynn and Hope typified this part of the claim as pure economic loss. In severing the child maintenance claim from the duty of the doctor to prevent pregnancy, no justification was provided as to why a doctor should be liable for the economic loss consequential on the personal injury of pregnancy and childbirth, yet not the maintenance of the child. One would seem to flow inexorably from the other – well recognised by Lord Millett, who rejected that the question should turn on whether economic loss was *pure* or *consequential*.

> The distinction being artificial if not suspect in the circumstances of the present case, and is to my mind made irrelevant by the fact that . . . conception and birth are the very things that the defendant's . . . were called upon to prevent.
>
> (p 109)

To hold a doctor liable for such economic losses, Lord Slynn considered, would not be 'fair, just, and reasonable',[2] reasoning that while the doctor is under a duty to prevent pregnancy, he does not assume responsibility for the costs of child maintenance. Lords Hope and Clyde, noting that this was a minor procedure, suggested that the loss suffered was disproportionate to the wrongdoing. Lord Millett rejected this line of reasoning, noting that it is commonplace that 'the harm caused by a botched operation may be out of all proportion to the seriousness of the operation' (p 109). Lord Clyde, while categorising the loss as purely economic, rejected recovery on the basis that an award enabling parents to maintain their 'welcome' child free of cost would not accord with the idea of restitution. And, although their Lordships had already rejected a 'set-off' argument, the benefits of having a child being incalculable in monetary terms, Lord Hope reiterated that it would not be 'fair, just or reasonable' to leave such benefits out of account, otherwise the parents would be unjustly enriched. Is this not obviously engaging in a set-off exercise?

Similarly, in declaring the set-off exercise as capable of producing 'morally repugnant' results, Lord Millett also engaged in the same process, finding that *society* must take the blessing of a healthy baby to outweigh the disadvantages of parenthood. A rather odd conclusion one might think, having earlier described the benefits as 'incalculable and incommensurable' (p 111). On this reasoning, parents could not make it a matter for compensation because 'it is an event they did not want to happen' – they cannot 'make a detriment out of a benefit' (p 113). Such reasoning, Lord Millett found, led to the rejection of both claims. Pregnancy and delivery were the inescapable preconditions of the child's birth, and raising the child was an inevitable consequence – 'the price of parenthood' – unaltered by the fact that 'it is paid by the mother alone' (p 114). Instead he suggested a conventional award of £5,000 to reflect their loss of freedom to limit their family size.

While both Lords Millett and Steyn sought to reject the 'formalistic techniques' of duty, foreseeability, causation and reasonable restitution employed by the remainder of the House, Lord Steyn suggested that this process of categorisation acted to 'mask the real reasons for the decisions' (p 82). Noting that on the normal principles of corrective justice, such a claim would succeed, Lord Steyn preferred to regard the case 'from the vantage point of distributive justice' (p 82). Echoing sentiments expressed in each judgment in *McFarlane*, he concluded that it would be contrary to the moral ethos of society to compensate parents for the birth of a healthy child:

> [I]t may become relevant to ask commuters on the Underground the following question: 'should the parents of an unwanted but healthy child be able to sue the doctor or hospital for compensation equivalent to the cost of bringing up the child for the years of his or her minority, i.e. until about 18 years?' My Lords, I am firmly of the view that an overwhelming number of ordinary men and women would answer the question with an emphatic "No" . . . Instinctively, the traveller on the Underground would consider that the law of tort has no business to provide legal remedies

consequent upon the birth of a healthy child, which all of us regard as a valuable and good thing.

(p 82)

Lord Steyn readily admitted that the principles of distributive justice were grounded on moral theory. Alert to the fact that some may object to the House acting as a court of morals, rather than of law, he noted that the 'judges' sense of the moral answer to a question . . . has been one of the great shaping forces of the common law' (p 82). Denying that such conclusions were the 'subjective view of the judge', he noted that these views were ascertainable by what the judge reasonably believes that the ordinary citizen would regard as right. The differing approach of the judges has not provided a straightforward judgment, or one that is defensible on the ordinary rules of tort. But irrespective of the various legal techniques employed, the issue central to *McFarlane* is policy. As Baroness Hale asserts:

[A]t the heart of their reasoning was the feeling that to compensate for the financial costs of bringing up a healthy child is a step too far. All were concerned that a healthy child is generally regarded as a good thing rather than a bad thing.

(Hale, 2001: 755)

It is undeniable that *some* might regard a healthy child as a joy, but what does this perspective miss? If one decides to undergo invasive medical procedures to remove the prospect of parenting responsibilities, can the failure of that procedure be properly described as a 'joy' or 'good thing'? Herein lies the notion that the parents have, as a matter of law, suffered *no harm* from a child's birth, even when that 'joy' is thrust upon them.

Characterising harm

The concept of 'harm', though seemingly self-evident, is thoroughly ambiguous. In defining our understanding of 'harm', we might initially allude to broken bones or other types of obvious injuries; injury in this sense clearly constitutes 'harm'. Nevertheless, the further we stray from the corporeal paradigm, the more difficult it becomes to refer to 'injury' (Feinburg, 1984); for example, a stolen wallet – we would hardly refer to the owner as being 'injured', but we could conceptualise this through a customary understanding of harm, notably the 'setting back, or defeating of an interest' (Feinburg, 1984: 33). On this view, 'harm' is a broader notion than 'injury'. Nevertheless, individual notions of harm can both overlap and be quite distinct from legal conceptions of harm. As Joanne Conaghan and Wade Mansell (1999) point out, 'While some kinds of harms are easily assimilated within the traditional corpus of law, others do not lend themselves so easily to tortious characterisation' (1999: 16). Considering the doctrinal limitations of tort and the construction of harm it is worth considering what interests, and, more particularly, *whose* interests, tort law serves. In this respect, Conaghan argues that tort law, 'while quick to defend and protect interests traditionally valued by men, is slow to respond to the concerns which typically involve women, for example, sexual harassment or sexual abuse' (1996: 48). It is only since the late 1970s that sexual harassment has transformed from behaviour widely regarded as a 'harm*less*' part of normal human engagement to behaviour constituting sex discrimination, deserving of a legal response (Conaghan, 2002).

In examining the array of harms that women predominantly suffer, some have deployed the concept of 'gendered harm' in rendering visible the harms that women suffer, as women (Graycar and Morgan, 2002). Therefore, in the context of wrongful conception, it should be relevant that the experience of pregnancy and childbirth is not universal, and that, as actual mother and carer of an unintended child, women will be most affected by decision making in this area of tort law. Seen in this light, the principles of distributive justice, directed towards the 'just distribution of burdens and losses among members of a society' (p 165 per Lord Steyn), certainly fall under suspicion; the 'losers' will always be women. Therefore, one must question why 'harm' in wrongful conception does not translate into cognisable legal 'harm', where significant policy considerations militate against such a finding.

In *McFarlane*, 'harm' is legally constructed in two principal ways. First, a healthy child is a blessing and its existence cannot be injurious. Second, the 'harm' claimed in wrongful conception is wholly economic and in the absence of a duty of care to protect the claimants' ecomonic interests, damages are not available. Yet, Lord Millett recognised that the contention that the birth of a healthy child 'is not a harm', was not 'an accurate formulation of the issue', but that it would only constitute a harm if its parents chose to regard it as such (p 112). It can be a harm, but not at law? Alternatively, claimants are wrong to assert a child constitutes harm because society regards a child as a blessing? Akin to Lord Millett's view that 'society must regard the balance as beneficial' (p 114), Lord Steyn was equally certain that the commuter on the Underground would consider those in society unable to have children and find it morally unacceptable to compensate parents for rearing a non-disabled child in these circumstances. Of course, the commuter is nothing more than a fictitious character of the legal imagination used as a doctrinal obstacle to recovery – but to pernicious effect. He carries with him the 'sting of societal condemnation' (Meyer, 2000: 565) and has only served to limit a fundamental right and exclusion from protection. This commuter, J. K. Mason suggests, is a 'tough person, inured to the slings and arrows of outrageous conditions' (2000: 205). He speculates that the traveller on the Strathay Scottish Omnibuses would provide a different view: 'these people find themselves in a position which they sought to avoid' (Mason 2000: 205).

The assumption that the parents have suffered no 'harm' through the blessing of a child is erroneous and conveniently overlooks the fact that here a 'blessing' has been forced upon them. The experience of parenthood in wrongful conception is clearly different from the situation where parenthood has been planned. The fundamental distinction is that in the former, medical negligence led to the birth of a child. Even if society does hold the assumption that a healthy child is a good thing, it seems unlikely that many commuters would be quick to assume that the parents have suffered no harm in this factual setting. Children may well be valued, but the inevitability of procreation has lost contemporary significance to many in society. Peter Pain J expressed the importance of this countervailing policy factor in *Thake*, stating:

> By 1975, family planning was generally practised. Abortion had been legalised over a wide field. Vasectomy was one of the methods of family planning which was not only legal but was available under the National Health Service. It seems to me to follow from this that it was generally recognised that the birth of a healthy baby is not always a blessing.
>
> (p 230)

As Symmons (1987) remarks, judicial 'Gallup polling' of society's sentiments will be 'both speculative and subjective' (1987: 280). Public policy considerations can point in either direction, from the unqualified goods of children on one hand, to the value of family planning on the other; either can constitute the will of the people.[3] Therefore, the question of whether a child is a blessing loses its validity in answering the question of damages because 'for every "policy" factor . . . thrown onto the scales to *deny* liability' another exists to 'redress the balance' (Symmons 1987: 305).

The principle criticised here is not the assumption that a child is a blessing but rather that this fact can only be determined by those who have gone to great lengths to put an end to their reproductive capacity (Jackson, 2002). In making this decision, an intricate network of values and subjective preferences will determine what importance a child will hold in their lives; it should not be the role of the court to trivialise those values by reference to the abstract goods of children in society. Following invasive surgery to avoid a child, it should be obvious that the prospect of a baby will not herald the sense of joy expounded in *McFarlane*. It is a source of concern that their Lordships thought to utilise such a line of reasoning in denying damages to the McFarlanes. One possibility is that the courts have searched for *any rule* that will deny recovery in these cases, simply because the wrongful conception claim requires judges to address difficult questions (Ryan, 1994). The clearest method of escape is to provide a basic moral framework that assumes that the birth of a child is a blessing and is an occasion for joy as a matter of law to its parents, but the moral foundation is unstable.

Pervasive throughout *McFarlane* are notions of 'sanctity of life'. Lord Steyn suggested that his decision to deny recovery was 'reinforced by coherence' expressly relying on English law's rejection of wrongful life claims (p 83). However, given that actions for wrongful life are brought by a disabled child born as a result of negligence, where s/he puts forward the somewhat difficult claim that but for the negligence his/her parents would have aborted the pregnancy, the parallels are less than apparent.[4] As Jennifer Mee contends 'wrongful conception is a cause of action based on the negligent invasion of an individual's interest in *preventing* conception, it does not raise the abortion issue or implicate "sanctity of life" concerns' (1992: 899). If Lord Steyn has approached this question on the basis of moral theory, then as Alisdair Maclean (2000) suggests, the substance of the moral answer is both questionable and unconvincing. In this vein, Bernard Dickens comments that such celebration of children 'denies the compatible social and legal reality that many conscientious, responsible couples do not want children either at all or at particular times' (Dickens, 1990: 87). He transposes the false logic of the 'moral answer', noting that no court would entertain the argument from a putative father that he should not be required to provide financial support for a child on the grounds that he has conferred a priceless blessing on the mother (Dickens, 1990). So, in alternative contexts, the courts rigidly take the view that the joys of parenthood fail to outweigh the costs, yet in wrongful conception, claimants are not permitted 'by a process of subjective devaluation, to make a detriment out of a benefit' (p 112 *per* Lord Millett). What kind of moral theory produces the astonishing, if not absurd, conclusion that parenthood is 'objectively' more joyous, beneficial and welcome precisely when it is unwanted? If parenthood were *always* beneficial, why would anyone wish to undergo procedures designed to avoid that very consequence (Jackson, E., 2005: 669)?

Perhaps we should look more closely at what the *McFarlane* court is saying, or is *not* saying here. As Reg Graycar (1998: 32) notes, we might 'learn something from the "stories judges tell" if we think about the epistemological content of each of them'. In earlier case law, the representations of women were most visible. In *Udale*, Jupp J. referred to the claimant in the following terms: 'She is not only an experienced mother but, so far as I am able to judge, a good mother, who has all the proper maternal instincts' (p 526). However, in relation to the child-rearing claim in *McFarlane*, rarely does one see *any* reference to the mother or her *role* as mother; but she *is* very much there. For example, should it be significant that their Lordships repeatedly referred to the fact that Catherine was 'loved', 'accepted' and 'welcomed'? Or, that their Lordships thought it 'absurd to distinguish between the claims of the father and mother' (p 79, *per* Lord Steyn)? Might it also be relevant to our enquiry that the court focused on the benefits and financial costs of parenthood alone? It seems that only Lord Millett recognised that the burden of raising the child was 'paid by the mother alone' (p 114). The concern which preoccupied the House is well demonstrated by Anthony Jackson who suggests that: 'every burden, such as the financial cost of the child's life, his feeding, clothing and education would shift firmly onto the medical profession' (1995: 598). Significantly, Alisdair Maclean (2000) comments that this raises doubts about their conclusions on fairness in having only considered one dimension of the moral argument:

> Perhaps from the skewed masculine viewpoint of a father whose almost exclusive role lies in economic provision, they have failed to take into account the considerable non-pecuniary detriments that come with parenthood.
>
> (Maclean, 2000)

Or indeed, those that come with motherhood. Here judicial techniques denying recovery through set-off exercises, unjust enrichment or 'distributive justice' all proceed from the assumption that the 'blessing of a healthy child' outweighs the cost of raising the child – an argument that will leave either the burden of caring or the financial losses unaccounted for. Remarking on the belief that a child is a blessing, Susan Atkins and Brenda Hoggett (1984) suggest that this provides:

> [A]n excellent illustration of how easy it is for the law to perceive the financial loss to the father who has to provide for an unplanned child, but not to the mother, who has to bring [the child] up . . . The law is not used to conceptualizing the services of a wife and mother as labour which is worthy of hire.
>
> (1984: 90)

Therefore, in comparing non-pecuniary benefits with pecuniary detriments, this approach reflects a narrow definition of harm, failing to recognise that not all the burdens will be financial. And, having characterised unwanted conception as actionable physical harm – reasoning that has been employed in a consistent line of authority before *McFarlane* in permitting the recovery of child maintenance costs – can maintenance costs be correctly characterised as 'pure economic loss'? If pregnancy is a personal injury, then surely the economic loss suffered by the mother is immediately *consequential* on that injury? It seems that their Lordships have inadvertently recognised that wrongful conception is a harm, but have just declined to provide the complete remedy.

Loss of autonomy?

An alternative, albeit tentative, construction of the harm(s) resulting from unsolicited parenthood is presented here. In endeavouring to locate a balanced approach, the principle of autonomy most obviously arises as an interest capable of being defeated through wrongful conception. Legally characterised in other areas of medical law as a fundamental principle (*St George's Healthcare NHS Trust v S* [1998] 3 WLR 936), its relevance to the wrongful conception action is clear. While autonomy is not a 'univocal concept' (Beauchamp and Childress, 1994) in the context of respect for reproductive choice, it holds a specific meaning. At a minimum, this requires respect for an individual's right to make choices, and to take actions based upon their personal values and beliefs. Emily Jackson's 'enthusiasm for autonomy as an organising principle' (2001: 2) is justified upon the conviction that a broader and richer understanding of reproductive autonomy may be normatively desirable. She suggests that autonomy is 'not just the right to pursue ends that one already has, but also to live in an environment which enables one to form one's own value system and to have it treated with respect' (2001: 6). Social norms may shape the character of our choices, but it is nonetheless important to recognise the exceptional value of being the author of our actions, particularly in an area as personal as reproduction. Similarly, the acknowledgement of this value has 'served to discredit paternalism ... reflected in the legal regime by which medical treatment is regulated' (Mason and McCall Smith, 1999: 6). The value of autonomy within medical law therefore encapsulates the notion that the right to physical integrity and the ability to make voluntary decisions must be respected (Morgan, 2001). While this liberal conception of autonomy may present *some* answers within medical contexts, Robin Mackenzie (1999) notes that it is impossible to reconcile with the everyday realities of women's lives in pregnancy and motherhood. Susan Sherwin contends that the model of personhood under the liberal autonomy ideal constructs a false ideology that decisions can be isolated from their social environment, when in fact 'so much of our experience is devoted to building or maintaining personal relationships and communities' (1998: 34). Nor does this liberal idea seem to permit room to question differences among people, or the effects that 'oppression ... has on a person's ability to exercise autonomy' (1998: 35). By contrast, a relational view of autonomy squarely addresses these issues. In the healthcare context, not only are the social and political contexts of decision making questioned, but also the options really available to women – and those who control those options (Sherwin, 1998). Therefore, in the context of reproduction, this relational approach to the value of autonomy highlights the increasing medicalisation of women's lives, their social positioning within the familial unit and the resulting impact on their 'choices'.

Clearly this approach holds considerable weight in the context of wrongful conception and birth suits. From this perspective, the characterisation of 'harm' in wrongful conception as being purely economic must be seen as deeply problematic. Through an economic lens, the creation of the parent–child dyad is conceived of as a relationship rendering purely financial obligations – and financial repercussions – should parenthood be brought about as a result of negligence. Nevertheless, as will be clear at this stage, the relationship is not conceptualised as wholly fiscal. Indeed, when assessing the benefits emerging from parenthood their Lordships turn to consider purely non-financial considerations;[5] yet, how many of us quantify or calculate the profits or joys of parenthood? Since this aspect of parenthood is hardly amenable to financial calculation, what then, of the losses, which also fail to translate readily into the language of dollars or pounds? What of other interests, such as planning the size/timing of the family, potential harm to other family members, and the significant disruption of one's future plans? Why are these not assessed as deserving of protection? Quite simply, a child is not a trouble-free consumer product, thereby comparable to 'unordered goods' or the 'mundane transactions of commercial life' (p 114 *per* Lord Millett),[6] which can be returned or sold on the market. In the realm of family life, parenthood demands an active response to a relationship of dependency that holds considerable and enduring responsibilities for those concerned. Other losses are consequent upon the birth of an unplanned child. As Amy Bernstein observes, whereas pregnancy and childbirth occur during defined episodes, motherhood is 'chronic' (2001: 173); it spans throughout the woman's lifetime and evolves as mother and child age. So, from a relational perspective the losses entailed with motherhood endure past childbirth; and motherhood involves more than just biological capacity. And for men who embrace caring responsibilities, this 'chronic' experience will be almost identical. If parenthood is chronic, what of those who have chosen to reject that very state? Parenthood involves considerable responsibility and will not always carry positive connotations, but the courts assume that these responsibilities are outweighed by the joy that *non-disabled* children naturally bring. In this context, restricting injury within the economic sphere results in a narrow view of what constitutes harm. It is not doubted that economic motivations will influence reproductive decision making; this possibility is fully embraced. But financial concerns may not have been the primary motive and therefore any assessment of harm needs to take into account a series of intangible, non-pecuniary and relational harms. Refusal to acknowledge the fuller range of interests that individuals seek to protect both excludes and misrepresents the reality of their motivation (Norton, 1999: 826).

The loss central to the wrongful conception case must be seen as one of reproductive autonomy. In choosing to avoid parenthood, the failure of that decision will impact on individuals in myriad ways and to differing degrees. The individual's power to decide whether or not to become a parent has been irrevocably lost, and inevitably faces a profound change of lifestyle as a direct result of the fresh parenting responsibilities that they now confront. If we accept that individuals should have the right to choose the type of life they find subjectively meaningful, providing it causes no harm to others' interests, then the individual is best placed to determine their reproductive choices.

The belief in autonomous control over whether and when to reproduce, Laura Purdy (2001) contends, is the linchpin of women's equality in the context of reproduction. Depriving individuals of such control interferes with their capacity to live in accordance with their own beliefs and can involve infringing bodily integrity.

The courts have traditionally failed to view unsolicited parenthood in this manner. One must therefore question the courts' adherence to the principle of autonomy and consider to what extent conflicting principles are at play. Few would find difficulty in accepting Derek Morgan's proposition that there are areas of medical law 'where the goal comes closer to the enforcement of moral notions' (2001: 53) and the wrongful conception action demonstrates exactly this tension between law and ethics. Other values have been accepted into the ambit of the courts' decisional framework, such as the role of the family, the value of life and societal expectations of women. These have been used to generate an outcome that deeply misrepresents the harm experienced through unsolicited parenthood. Denying legal recognition of the consequent harm communicates negative signals to claimants about the value of their lives, autonomy and the nature of the harm following wrongful conception. The law should now acclimatise its treatment of such individuals and place greater emphasis on care, dignity and respect, providing a force that promotes a more expressive characterisation of autonomy.

Defining the problem

In the context of wrongful life suits, Mackenzie has noted that, 'the judiciary seem to prefer medical paternalism over patient autonomy, male dominance over reproductive choice and a legal forum for the resolution of medical ethics issues' (1999: 181). These comments have equal application here. Concepts of 'duty' or 'distributive justice' have themselves served to 'mask the real reasons' for decisions, but what do those 'real reasons' consist of? While these concepts have been used to limit the legal responsibility of practitioners towards women, why were they not formulated so as to *extend* the duty of the medical profession to take greater care in facilitating the reproductive choices of their patients? In a society that promotes the good of family planning, such medical immunity communicates dangerous signals. The current approach suggests that negligence resulting in the birth of a healthy child is an inevitable and harm*less* part of life, for which individuals must now be prepared to bear the costs.

All in all, the *McFarlane* judgment poses rather a puzzle; after over a decade of the courts recognising that parents do suffer compensable harm as a result of the responsibilities of caring for a healthy child, the House of Lords has taken the view that these repercussions can no longer count as compensable harm. And the judgment certainly provides a battery of reasons for departing from the ordinary principles of the law of negligence based on notions of distributive justice, duty ('fair, just and reasonableness'), reasonable restitution, and let us not forget the trusty commuter's view that the healthy child is a blessing and a joy to all of us, even if the claimants do not share that view. In addition we are presented with the comparison between these fortunate parents so blessed with a healthy child and those who experience the sorrow of raising a disabled child, alongside the plight of couples who have long desired the fortune that these claimants unsuccessfully sought to avoid. True it is that we may feel on comparison that the burden of raising a disabled child may be greater than in the case of raising a healthy child, but does that provide a good reason for denying *these* claimants compensation? Does this mean that their Lordships would have permitted damages in the case of a disabled child – if so, would it then be considered fair, just and reasonable to do so, would the commuter on the Underground agree with that course of action, and wouldn't that risk expressing the view that a disabled child was *not* a blessing? While no doubt our hearts go out to those who might struggle to care for a disabled child, as well as those unable to have children, what of those who do not wish to have children yet confront that very outcome as a result of negligence? Do we not feel some measure of sympathy for them? Are these individuals not harmed? And what precisely does 'love' and 'acceptance' of a healthy child have to do with the recovery of tortious damages? Raising further questions as to the basis of the decision is the judgment of Lord Slynn, who comments:

> I do not find real difficulty in deciding the claim for damages in respect of the pregnancy and birth itself. The parents did not want another child for justifiable, economic and family reasons; they already had four children. They were entitled lawfully to take steps to make sure that did not happen, one possible such step being a vasectomy of the husband. It was plainly foreseeable that if the operation did not succeed, or recanalisation of the vas took place, but the husband was told that contraceptive measures were not necessary, the wife might become pregnant. . . . It is not contended that the birth was due to her decision not to have an abortion which broke the chain of causation or made the damage too remote or was a *novus actus interveniens*. If it were suggested I would reject the contention and I see no reason in principle why the wife should not succeed on this part of the claim.
>
> (p 161)

But why should she not also succeed in her claim for child maintenance damages? Why should the line be drawn at birth? Why are the losses that foreseeably result from the 'personal injury' of pregnancy, not adjudged as *consequential* losses rather than purely economic ones? Is it true that no judge would scrutinise the mother's failure to terminate her pregnancy? Would it be wrong to do so?

Such questions, I suggest, are absolutely critical to gaining an understanding of the basis of *McFarlane*, and all of these will be addressed in the chapters that follow. And what we are searching for is a fuller explanation for the outcome in the *McFarlane* case, and in particular to locate the *unifying strand* that links the diverse legal and policy responses of judges who spoke 'in five different voices' (*per* Brooke LJ p 277 in *Parkinson v St James' & Seacroft University Hospital NHS Trust* [2002] QB 266). Of course, one might point to the assertion that the birth of a healthy child is an occasion for rejoicing, not sorrow; yet given that the claimants in this case sought to avoid that very occasion, and damages would otherwise have been forthcoming prior to *McFarlane*, the healthy child rationale, in itself, does not tell us why parents should be denied damages.[7]

For the time being, however, we will leave issues surrounding the healthy but unwanted child alone. In the immediate aftermath of *McFarlane*, there are, I think, two issues that should form our starting point for thinking about the reproductive torts. The first concerns the sustainability of my tentative account as to the value of reproductive autonomy; this does raise difficult questions, the most pressing of which must be: Is it not arguable that through recognising the mother's claim for pain and suffering attendant upon pregnancy, their Lordships *did* recognise the value of autonomy? The concept of autonomy is by no means absent from the judgment; Lord Steyn, for example, suggests that 'the law does and must respect these decisions of parents which are so closely tied to their basic freedoms and rights of autonomy' (p 165); and Lord Hope in his assessment of the mother's claim similarly argues that 'the law will respect the right of men and women to take steps to limit the size of their family' (p 167). Nor are they alone in these assessments. Indeed, it is plausible that their Lordships considered that while autonomy must be valued, in the context of the wrongful conception action its value has *limits*. So on that account, would this mean that a woman's reproductive autonomy is only set back insofar as it affects her physical integrity? The second and clearly related issue, given my attempt to offer an alternative account as to the nature of the loss(es) suffered, concerns the concept of harm itself. What counts as compensable harm, as actionable damage for the purposes of negligence? What factors serve to transform compensable harm into the vicissitudes of life? To gain an insight into the nature and meaning of the damage concept, as well as challenge their Lordships' view that claimants suffer no setback to their autonomy interests consequent upon childbirth, the analysis which follows asks one seemingly simple question: In what way might an unwanted pregnancy – a normal, biological function, although unwanted – be conceptualised as actionable physical damage?

Notes

1 Note that numerous losses resulting from tort are describable as economic; however, these are categorised into consequential and purely economic losses. The law of negligence takes a restrictive approach towards the latter, which by contrast with *consequential* losses, constitute financial damage that neither results from personal injury nor property damage.
2 The term 'fair, just and reasonable' constitutes one of the three *Caparo* criteria for establishing a duty of care, notably: (1) the damage must be foreseeable; (2) there must be a sufficiently proximate relationship between the parties; (3) it must be 'fair, just and reasonable' for the court to impose a duty of care in the circumstances (*Caparo v Dickman* [1990] 2 AC 605). For an interesting critique of the development of the duty concept culminating in the three-stage approach in *Caparo*, see Conaghan and Mansell (1999).
3 Of interest, their Lordships firmly rejected that they were stepping into the 'quicksands' of public policy. Considering the House reversed case law spanning some 15 years, could this be indicative that this was an issue best left for legislators, who do enter such 'quicksands', rather than judges?
4 Note that the action for wrongful life has been barred since the case of *McKay v Essex Area Health Authority* [1982] 2 All ER 777 and is excluded under s 1(5) of the Congenital Disabilities (Civil Liability) Act 1976.
5 Indeed, had this been the case, the court would have struggled to defend its claim that the economic benefits of parenting outweigh the economic detriments. As Anthony Giddens (1999b) comments, 'Having a child is no longer an economic benefit and the family is no longer an economic unit.'
6 As Lord Millett states: 'In the mundane transactions of commercial life, the common law does not allow a man to keep goods delivered to him and refuse to pay for them on the ground that he did not order them. It would be far more subversive of the mores of society for parents to enjoy the advantages of parenthood while transferring to others the responsibilities which it entails.'
7 And others might point out the significance of the shift in legal policy since the decision in *Emeh*. As Lord Steyn noted in *McFarlane*, *Emeh* predated the House of Lords' reformulation of the test for the existence of a duty of care in *Murphy v Brentwood District Council* [1991] 1 AC 398, and since then 'a judicial scepticism has prevailed about an overarching principle for the recovery of new categories of economic loss' (p 163). Nevertheless, as later chapters explore, the concept of 'duty' fails to provide any coherent legal justification for the decision of *McFarlane*, or later appellate decisions.

Chapter 2

Injured bodies

> 'When I use a word,' Humpty Dumpty said, in rather a scornful tone, 'it means just what I choose it to mean – neither more nor less.'
> 'The question is,' said Alice, 'whether you can make words mean so many different things.'
> 'The question is,' said Humpty Dumpty, 'which is to be master – that's all.'
>
> (Carroll, 1998: 186)

Pregnancy is women's work. It is the one experience that 'inevitably differentiates women from men' and thus forms a 'crucial part of our identity which we cannot ignore, even supposing we would wish to do so' (Atkins and Hoggett, 1984: 83). The fact that *most* women hold the capacity to bear children, Anne Morris and Susan Nott (1995) reflect, has had adverse consequences for the treatment of women in society. The dominant ideology of reproduction positions and defines women in terms of their *potential* mothering role (Morell, 2000) and thereby exercises a regulatory role over *all* women's lives. Nor has the increasing incidence of infertility and deliberate childlessness displaced this view. Childless life is not perceived as being a 'viable or appealing choice' and 'women who purposefully do not have children are not taken on their own terms, but are measured by the idealized standard of motherhood' (Morell, 2000: 314). While pro-natalist norms hold a powerful influence on the way that women are viewed, *non*-pregnant women are nevertheless assumed to have the capacity to make valid self-determining choices about their lives and destinies in a way that the *pregnant* women rarely are. The pregnant woman's body is no longer her own; it labours now for another – she is not one person 'but two – mother and foetus – and society may expect, even demand, that her freedom is curtailed in the interests of the foetus' (Morris and Nott, 1995: 54–5). Under an ideology whereby 'the foetus is something to be protected from its mother' (Diduck, 1993: 471), the rational and sane mother must willingly accept treatment by medical professionals; however, 'no normal mother-to-be' would persist with a course that would cause serious harm to her foetus. As a result, pregnant women are confronted with a law that speaks 'loudly of care and protection of children, and less loudly but perhaps more profoundly, of control of women' (Diduck, 1993: 465).

It is in this context that this chapter explores wrongful pregnancy in the tort of negligence. This becomes important when considering that the law has been more involved in conceptualising women as a 'harm' to foetal health, than as harmed through the experience of pregnancy itself. Therefore, while society values motherhood for its product – a healthy child – and is one that construes motherhood as naturally involving sacrifice, the law rarely speaks the language of the care and protection of the rights, health and integrity of pregnant women. But in confronting the action of wrongful pregnancy, this is the language demanded of it. Does wrongful pregnancy constitute a personal injury or merely a harm*less* biological function that cannot constitute 'damage' or 'harm'? The significance of this question lies at the heart of the tort of negligence.

A number of torts, such as trespass or libel, are actionable *per se* – without evidence of damage.[1] The absence of damage is not germane to such actions since tort law operates here to 'vindicate private rights and not necessarily to compensate the victim' (Markesinis and Deakin, 1999: 18). By contrast, in the law of negligence, 'damage' holds a central role and is said to form the 'gist of the action' (Stapleton, 1988: 213). Therefore, a claimant will not only need to establish a duty of care, a breach of that duty, and that the breach caused the damage complained of – she must also show that the *type* of harm she has suffered is one that is accepted by the law as 'actionable'. This proves unproblematic in the case of the 'straightforward results of many physical acts of negligence' (Atiyah, 1997: 52). Beyond the broken bones and personal injuries obvious to the human eye, it is well recognised that 'damage can be recovered for any physical harm' (Atiyah, 1997: 53). Therefore, gastroenteritis suffered through swallowing parts of a snail in a bottle of ginger beer, cancer or lung diseases suffered through exposure to asbestos in the workplace, will most certainly constitute physical harms for the purposes of negligence (Witting, 2002). The question is, in what way might an unwanted pregnancy – a normal, biological function, although *unwanted* – be conceptualised as actionable physical damage for the purposes of negligence? It is undeniable that there are salient differences between an unwanted pregnancy and broken bones, but what do they consist of? What is a 'personal injury', and importantly, *who* defines it? Does it matter for these purposes that while some pregnancies are unwanted, others are not? Or in determining this issue should we merely be content with the weaker view that pregnancy should be treated as *analogous* to a personal injury, so as to avoid the difficult arguments that pregnancy gives rise to (Mullis, 1993)? And indeed, if wrongful pregnancy does constitute 'damage', what rights/interests are being implicated and how do such conceptualisations of harm intersect or conflict with alternative representations of the processes of pregnancy and childbirth? As Morris and Nott highlight, understanding how the law engages with pregnancy and constructs the 'Pregnant Woman' demands 'more than a consideration of single issues' (1995: 55).

There is a growing body of literature relating to wrongful conception; however, remarkably little addresses the mother's claim for pain and suffering consequent upon the *injury* of pregnancy.[2] In fact, this element of the claim is more often than not dismissed as either unproblematic or uncontroversial. Possibly the main reason for the 'pregnancy-as-damage question' being speedily dismissed is simply because it has not *yet* suffered rejection by English law. Undergraduate texts on medical law often reflect this unproblematic status: 'so far as we know, such damages have never been denied in any jurisdiction' (Mason *et al*, 2002: 116). Or could it be because this question is considered to be less philosophically *interesting* than the contention that the birth of a 'healthy' child causes harm to its parents? It is true that the child maintenance claim raises a series of difficult legal and ethical considerations, and constitutes the more substantial compensation claim made by parents.

Nevertheless, what this chapter seeks to illustrate is first, that the mere fact the 'pregnancy-as-damage' question has not attracted a similar level of analytical enquiry by no means denotes ready acceptance of its status as 'damage'. Second, the issue of 'pregnancy-as-damage' I argue, is by far the *more* interesting question – here we gain a greater insight into the law of tort's response to those harms unique to women, the extent to which the law expresses concepts of harm, responsibility and autonomy resonant with women's experiences and, importantly, to offer possible strategies for their articulation in the law.

Developing some of the themes identified in the last chapter, the analysis that follows explores in greater detail the English judiciary's engagement with the characterisation of harm in relation to the mother's claim for pain and suffering attendant upon the personal injury of pregnancy and childbirth. Illustrating that there are problems and promise to be found in such accounts, this chapter calls for a different construction of harm. The thrust of the argument is that the courts must seek to reject the traditional 'personal injury' framework that is currently applied to this discrete area of law – the current construction of pregnancy as a breed of 'physical injury' is not merely fraught with difficulties, but from a feminist perspective, it is deeply *harmful*. Therefore, in seeking to forward an alternative account of reproductive harm, the latter part of this chapter draws in particular upon the work of Robin West (1997) and the inspiring judgments of Baroness Hale, and argues for an approach that embraces a deeper and richer notion of reproductive autonomy. This, it is argued, not only offers the potential to provide a more authentic conceptualisation of harm in wrongful pregnancy, and an approach that will better resonate with women's diverse experiences of conception, pregnancy, childbirth and *motherhood* – but significantly, this richer characterisation powerfully expresses what is *valuable* and *important* about the concept of autonomy in the sexual and reproductive domain: women gaining control over their moral, relational and social lives.

Natural born reproducers

> The body has been made so problematic for women that it has often seemed easier to shrug it off and travel as a disembodied spirit.
>
> (Rich, 1976: 40; cited by Rúdólfsdóttir, 2000: 338)

Through discourse, both law and medicine construct bodies. Bodies that are deviant, diseased, injured, autonomous, inviolable, private – medico-legal metaphors that give rise to bodies that are constituted as property or machine – all constitute discursive social constructions of the body. The body in western culture is traditionally conceptualised 'as something apart from the true self (whether conceived as soul, mind, spirit, will, creativity, freedom) and as undermining the best efforts of that self' (Bordo, 1993: 5). Rúdólfsdóttir explains that the dominant idea is that the 'truly liberated and disciplined self cultivates rational thought, the instrument of the self, on the basis of its freedom from the impulses of the body' (2000: 338). In law, this mind/body dualism finds its expression in dominant liberal conceptions of individual autonomy, the notion of the rational, self-determining and self-owning individual. This notion of the person as property, or as 'self-proprietor', Ngaire Naffine suggests, has become 'a convenient way of highlighting the freedoms enjoyed by the modern individual . . . which serves to accentuate the fullness of the rights enjoyed by persons in relation to themselves and to others' (1998: 194). In healthcare law, this paradigm of autonomy holds a pivotal role. The giving of valid consent provides the authority for medical procedures, and therefore underpins this Lockean notion of self-governance where the *competent* individual is free to do with his body whatever he chooses, providing he does not cause harm to others. This notion of self-ownership however, Naffine suggests, implies that the property owner is something separate to the body:

> [T]he important thing for self-ownership is that the subject 'I' – the person as mind – should retain control of its object body; no one else should exercise this self-possession or self-control. The divided self must operate in this manner if personhood is to be retained.
>
> (Naffine, 1998: 202)

Therefore, under such conceptions of liberal autonomy, the 'true subject self' is the rational mind, which takes control of and governs the 'object' body and therefore self-ownership translates into body ownership – and demands 'self-control and the ability to repel the encroachments of others' (Evans, 2001: 20). Such constructions of the body as property can also be seen to underpin the provision of compensatory damages for personal injury. As Alan Hyde comments, the law recognises a market value for intact and attractive bodies, and hypothesises the body 'as property "had" and "lost" ', even though neither lost attractiveness or pain-free existence are open to market value quantification (1997: 62). Therefore, notions of bodily autonomy and bodily privacy all imply bodily boundaries and an internal division of the person – 'the owner and the owned' (Naffine, 1998: 201). While legal analysis has proceeded in conceptualising man's rights to civic freedom through distinguishing the mind from the body, this Cartesian dualism has also been highly influential in scientific disciplines where the body is reconstituted under the medical gaze as machine. Here the mind is reduced to a spirit or ghost that directs the disconnected body – the machine, representing the mindless body. The patient under this reconstruction is reduced to nothing more than *a body*, a passive medical object, rather than an experiencing subject. The body is observed and understood through its machine-like functionality – 'it works or fails to work' (Evans, 2001: 20). The medical body is a biological organism, 'entirely discoverable and convertible to information', and rendering a set of facts about physical status and functionality (Evans, 2001: 20).

As 'heirs of Cartesianism' (Grosz, 1994: 8), both the legal and medical constructions provide an impoverished view of personhood. The machine body is reduced to mere physical existence, while the property body neglects the significance of the human body, as if this 'autonomous subject is not possessing a body', but is 'an instrument through which the subject is interacting with the world' (Editorial, 1998: 104). Whether or not we think it makes sense to construct bodies in these ways, both representations are productive of cold and inhuman bodies that fail to account for the variety of ways in which we *experience* our lives through bodies as human beings. One is either a 'body', or a 'thinking and choosing' agent, but never 'a feeling and being agent' (Budgeon, 2003: 37). But it is not just this impoverished view that opens up Cartesian methodology to criticism – these ways of seeing are highly gendered. Such dualism is characterised by (and productive of) sex difference: the male body, free from the burdens of pregnancy and menstruation, while women are constructed as being essentially *bodily* beings, 'unable to transcend [their] corporeality' (Keywood, 2000: 325). Femininity is tied to corporeality, and associated with the non-rational: emotion, passion, care and partiality, while 'reason and masculinity are co-defined in opposition to the body' (Colebrook, 2000: 28). This opposition between reason and the body, Claire Colebrook comments, 'not only harbours a hierarchy, it constitutes an axiology through which the very categories of thought are produced as sexed' (2000: 34). And this sexing in western culture has been posited as a 'necessary consequence of an irreducible biological difference' (Mullin, 2002).

That men are to mind/reason, as women are to body/emotion, holds deep philosophical foundations. The radical distinction between 'material' or physical pregnancy and 'spiritual' pregnancy, with primacy given to the latter, as Mullin (2002) comments, is illustrated by Socrates' comparison of his art of 'giving birth to thought', with that of midwifery:

> My art of midwifery is in general like theirs; the only difference is that my patients are men, not women, and my concern is not with the body but with the soul that is in travail of birth. And the highest point of my art is the power to prove by every test whether the offspring of a young man's thought is a false phantom or instinct with life and truth.
> (Plato, 1961; as quoted by Mullin, 2002: 29)

Spiritual pregnancy is strongly associated with man, for it is only those 'who are physically incapable of giving birth who can become spiritually pregnant' (Mullin, 2002: 29); physical pregnancy in Nietzsche's (1990) view would exhaust a woman of all her psychic energy, removing her ability to become intellectually creative. But, such creativity, according to Nietzsche, comes at a price; since when a woman has scholarly inclinations, 'there is usually something wrong with her sexuality' (1990: 101; quoted by Mullin, 2002: 29). While this would appear to suggest that both women and men *can* become spiritually pregnant – women will only achieve this by virtue of malady. As Mullin suggests, the use of philosophical metaphor drawn from women's experiences of pregnancy and childbirth not only acts to deny any spiritual or philosophical significance to the physical pregnancy, but reinforces that it is a process 'valuable or interesting only for its result, the physical or spiritual child' (2002: 30).

This view of pregnancy as a merely physical event resonates in modern medical practice, in which we see two body constructs emerging – the pregnant body as passive and as pathological. In the first, Hyde explains that if a woman's body is a machine with different parts, only her reproductive organs are the active agents; women would merely be 'the passive instruments of nature's purposes, their agency appearing only as they *interfered* with the purposes nature intended for their bodies' (1997: 38). This passive body can be clearly illustrated by ultrasound scanning, which, as Mullin comments, diminishes 'the importance of a woman's bodily knowledge during pregnancy, and also . . . increase the sense of the foetus as an independent agent that just happens to be temporarily contained within a pregnant woman's body' (2002: 36). Within this construal, the body is a passive machine, the physician a technician and pregnancy is merely 'a solely physical event in which a woman's participation is limited to patiently waiting for (and not harming) the foetus within her' (Mullin, 2002: 37). While this construction of pregnancy positions the body as passive, the second typification renders the pregnant body as a site of risk and pathology – by contrast with the healthy (male) body, which is posited as unchanging, the female body falls outside this criterion of health. Because such 'natural life processes are ... perceived as deviant where they differ from men's' (Purdy, 2001: 251), pregnancy is rendered abnormal, pathological and problematic – as a disease in need of medical treatment and control (Rúdólfsdóttir, 2000: 339).

The connecting of women more closely to their bodies than men, through a biological specificity, Elizabeth Grosz contends, has served to restrict women's 'social and economic roles to (pseudo) biological terms' and confined women to the biological role of reproduction (1994: 14). Furthermore, this biological account of women as *essentially* corporeal has been problematic in terms of justifying women's legal subjectivity and agency. As Lacey notes, only 'subjects with normal bodies can claim full legal privileges, including on occasion, the privilege of corporeal invisibility' (1998: 107). In other words, having a 'normal' body allows a subject to fit the culturally privileged model of the rational choosing individual' (Naffine, 1998: 204). Therefore, while women have been conceptualised through biological accounts as surrendered to the flesh through reproduction, and their bodies differentiated to men, women would be deemed under this mind/body split, to be 'insufficiently individuated to own themselves' (Naffine, 1998: 204), and therefore excluded from the framework of self-ownership – the domain of rationality. Indeed, from a historical perspective, women's essentially sexual and reproductive identity has permitted possessory rights to be exercised *over* women. Ngaire Naffine notes how a woman within marital relations became an 'object of sexual property, a physical being over which the husband exercised exclusive rights of use and possession' (1998: 208). At one time, a man could not be charged with the rape of his wife; however, if his 'cold-blooded' wife denied him of pleasant intercourse – and children – husbands would be received sympathetically by the divorce courts (Atkins and Hoggett, 1984: 84). Furthermore, the law of consortium, which provided remedies for the loss of affection and companionship, was never premised as a female right, but was a husband's cause of action. Similarly, in the medical domain, Susan Atkins and Brenda Hoggett (1984) comment, there was not only the belief that a husband could prevent his wife from being sterilised or provided with contraception, but that when she had conceived he was entitled to choose between her life and the child's.

These are, of course, historic accounts. The action for loss of consortium was abolished in 1952, and despite the continuing centrality of sex in marriage (Naffine, 1998), a husband can now be charged with rape of his wife (*R v R* [1991] 4 All ER 481). And the ability of a man to determine what happened to his wife's body in matters of reproduction was put firmly to an end in the UK, one judge commenting that:

[N]o court would ever grant an injunction to stop sterilization or vasectomy any more than it would use the old decree of restitution of conjugal rights to compel matrimonial intercourse.
(*Paton v BPAS Trustees* [1996] 1 QB 276)

Although no longer the property of their husbands, what then of a woman's self-ownership? These ways of constructing 'femininity' have traditionally influenced the regulation of women's bodies where, 'female sexuality and women's powers of reproduction are the defining (cultural) characteristics of women, and, at the same time, these very functions render women vulnerable, in need of protection or special treatment' (Grosz, 1994). Female bodies are different, and it is this bodily difference in the capacity to procreate that has posed a particular dilemma for law. Arguably, this is why matters of equality and self-determination become peculiarly messy when the law is required to deal with pregnant bodies. Are pregnant bodies comparable to *men's* sick bodies? Pregnancy is not comparable to an 'illness' as such, but for years this was exactly how English law approached pregnancy discrimination claims (Morris and Nott, 1995).

While the experience of pregnancy is hardly a new phenomenon to women, the law has traditionally struggled to find the language to conceptualise it. For instance, what language is appropriate for decisions to terminate a pregnancy or refusals of invasive treatment where this may place a healthy foetus at risk? How, for example, can the classic expression of self-determination that 'Every human being of adult years and sound mind has a right to determine what shall be done with *his* own body' (*Schloendorff v Society of New York Hospital* 105 NE 92 (NY, 1914)), apply to pregnant bodies, which are 'Not-One-But-Not-Two' (Karpin, 1992: 329)? And, in relation to abortion, rather than this being conceptualised as a matter of self-determination, the Abortion Act 1967 explicitly *avoids* according substantive rights to women, but rather divests decisional powers to the medical profession. The conceptual basis of the 1967 Act, Sally Sheldon (1997) comments, perpetuates the view that the decision to abort in itself is not an acceptable one for a woman to make. Rather, it stands as 'the exception to the norm of maternity' and only those women who have *good* reasons – the wrong type of foetus, existing obligations to children, poor social and living conditions – will be permitted to terminate a pregnancy (Sheldon, 1997: 42). Abortion, then, is not a matter of self-ownership and self-determination, but is one that concerns the regulation and control of women. Here, we find that the rhetoric of body ownership has threatened, rather than facilitated, women's rights to control their bodies, where such arguments have been 'deployed, through the use of medical knowledges ... to facilitate the construction of the foetus as a separate, rights-holding "being" ' (Stychin, 1998: 223). The foetus is positioned as a patient in its own right, the medical profession as its protector. Autonomy in this context 'continues to be defined in terms of a separate self, in need of protection from the (m)Other, now constructed as both a potential threat to the innocent and a perversion of the natural' (Stychin, 1998: 224). Moreover, this medical model of foetal separation and abstraction from the woman's body has highly influenced the law. When a pregnant woman and her foetus are injured, is the foetus part of the mother like 'her arm or her leg' or 'a separate organism from the mother' (*Attorney-General's Reference No 3 of 1994* [1996] QB 581: 593)? As Carl Stychin comments, the application of the liberal ideal of autonomy to the foetus has had the consequence of constructing the female body as a passive object 'which must be controlled and regulated to protect the autonomy of the foetus' (1998: 224), rather than situating the woman as an autonomous self.

From a feminist perspective then, it is biological difference that has formed the source of oppression, rendering women as connected, dependent and subordinate to men. While this has served to undermine women's involvement in the public sphere, it has also affected their capacity to act autonomously in relation to matters of reproduction. Of course, there has been a conceptual shift in the law's engagement with women, and in the reproductive field, most significantly in relation to the courts' articulation of women's claims to autonomy in enforced caesarean cases.[3] Despite this, however, the law still defers considerable power to doctors, regarding access to both abortion and infertility services, and the extent of power that doctors hold more generally in the management of childbirth holds serious practical implications for women's autonomy in reproduction. While competent women hold the right to self-determination, doctors still hold control over the determination of incapacity, which is often accepted by judges as an 'incontestable question of fact' (Jackson, 2001: 139). This, coupled with the 'prevailing assumption . . . that every right-minded pregnant woman will eagerly comply with her doctor's requests for cooperation' (Jackson, 2001: 135), means that there are more subtle ways of undermining a woman's self-determination in practice. As Emily Jackson maintains, there is a need for the law to spell out more clearly 'when a patient will be judged incapable of making her own decision', and the 'circumstances in which a caesarean section will be deemed to be in her best interests' (2001: 136).

So where does this leave us? In practical terms, reproduction remains a matter of medical control, and the law has certainly been permissive of this. However, a more optimistic reflection upon reproduction as a significant part of healthcare provision would suggest that medical law is undergoing a 'conceptual metamorphosis'. By no means is this a fresh observation; Derek Morgan's (2001) work has provided a detailed and insightful view of the 'metamorphosis' of medical law in a multifaceted sense. My interest in this notion is particularly focused on the central stance now afforded to considerations of patient autonomy in the courts' deliberations in the healthcare forum – and the action for wrongful pregnancy, I suggest, forms part of this 'conceptual metamorphosis', in more ways than one. The law's acceptance of the 'mother's claim' in the action for wrongful conception, and its recognition that an unwanted pregnancy brought about by negligence can be a real harm, invites a different perspective in relation to the debate on women's autonomy in reproduction – and an altogether more promising one. Such claims have been met by a greater judicial willingness to construe pregnancy under some circumstances as harmful to the woman rather than a state that gives rise to a conflict between foetus and mother. And significantly, the case law here signals a willingness to characterise women as *subjects*, rather than the passive *objects* of legal and medical control. But, that is *not* to say that the characterisation of the harm offered by the English courts is free of problems; there remains an obvious tension in the way that the courts have constructed the 'harm' individuals suffer in raising negligently born children. However, this specific (and separate) head of damages opens up a space in which to consider how pregnancy impacts upon women's lives and identity, and of significance, it provides an important standpoint from which to challenge the notion that pregnancy is merely a corporeal and episodic event with a line drawn at childbirth.

Wrongful pregnancy as a personal injury

Babies do not arrive as the result of a painless and uneventful stork delivery. Recognition of this fact in the wrongful conception action is found in the first head of damages for the pain and suffering and loss of amenity attendant upon pregnancy.[4] For pregnancy and childbirth to attract such damages, these may only be awarded if they are treated as forms of 'personal injury' (*McLoughlin v O'Brian* [1983] 1 AC 410). In *Allen v Bloomsbury Health Authority* [1993] 1 All ER 651, Brooke J was willing to conceptualise pregnancy and childbirth in this way, when considering the claim of a mother who was negligently deprived of the opportunity to have a pregnancy terminated. He awarded damages for:

> [T]he discomfort and pain associated with the continuation of her pregnancy and the delivery of her child [as] a claim for damages for personal injuries . . . *comparable to*, though *different from*, a claim for damages for personal injuries resulting from the infliction of a traumatic injury.
>
> (pp 657–8; my emphasis)

Just how might pregnancy and childbirth be 'comparable to, though different from' other injuries? Brooke J failed to expand on this point. Failing to commit one way or the other merely leaves unwanted pregnancy as a 'sort of injury'. In the absence of a 'conclusive judicial definition' (Mullis, 1993) authors grappling with this question have been inclined to refer to the definition of personal injury under section 38(1) of the Limitation Act 1980: 'any disease or any impairment of a person's physical or mental condition'.

Indeed, this broad definition certainly permits scope for suggesting that wrongful pregnancy can constitute a personal injury. WVH Rogers submits that it should not be difficult to regard pregnancy as an impairment of a woman's condition since it involves 'an element of danger, certain discomfort and possibly severe disruption of the woman's employment and pattern of life' (1985: 310).

This 'pregnancy as impairment' perspective resonates with the Court of Appeal's holding in *Walkin v South Manchester Health Authority* [1995] 1 WLR 1543, in which a more detailed consideration of the issue was offered. At what point could it be said that an injury was sustained? Here the Court considered three possible periods: the failure of the sterilisation, the conception and the birth. The failure of the attempt to sterilise, Auld LJ considered was not itself a personal injury: 'It did her no harm; it left her as before' (p 1550). Rejecting the birth as the injury, albeit with no justification as to why this could not be the originating point, Neill LJ was 'persuaded . . . that the better view is to treat the "wrongful" conception as the moment of injury' (p 1554). Despite this, Neill LJ was not entirely satisfied with the conclusion, noting that in most cases the cause of action arises at the time of the negligent act. This is doubtful, bearing in mind that in *all* personal injury cases time only starts to run from the date of the injury or from the date of the knowledge of such injury.[5] Nor did Neill LJ consider that this might well be inappropriate in the context of a wrongful conception suit, since knowledge of the failed sterilisation 'may not occur until some weeks later, especially where the plaintiff does not realise that there is a possibility that she may be pregnant' (Comment, 1995: 238). Taking conception as the moment of injury, and expressly relying on section 38(1) of the Limitation Act 1980, Auld LJ considered that an unwanted conception, whether as a result of negligent advice or surgery, would constitute a personal injury in the sense of 'impairment'. He added that the 'resultant physical change in her body resulting from conception was an unwanted condition which she had sought to avoid by undergoing the sterilisation operation' (p 1550). As this had been accepted by both parties, Roch LJ conceded the point, although expressed his reservations that:

> I have some difficulty in perceiving a normal conception, pregnancy and the birth of a healthy child as 'any disease or any impairment of a person's physical or mental condition' in cases where *the only reasons for the pregnancy and subsequent birth being unwanted are financial*.
>
> (p 1553; my emphasis)

A somewhat unlikely state of affairs considering that Mrs Walkin had taken deliberate steps to avoid conception, pregnancy *and* birth, all of which hold more than merely financial repercussions.[6] This does, however, raise an interesting point. The identification of conception as the point of injury, Adrian

Whitfield suggests, 'depends upon whether or not the mother wanted to conceive', adding that 'this presents the conceptual difficulty of the plaintiff's right to damages being dependent not upon the defendant's acts but upon the plaintiff's *attitude* to the defendant's act' (1998: 690). One of the practical difficulties Whitfield considers to emerge from this conceptualisation of injury is that of the woman who does not wish to be pregnant at the time of conception, but later changes her mind, when she finds out that she is pregnant. Surely, as in the majority of cases, this woman would not then bring a claim? Questioning the attitudes of those who do bring claims is to trivialise the importance of the decision to undergo sterilisation, and moreover, seems to suggest that any woman who wavers in her view towards pregnancy is more likely than not to fall down in favour of *wanting* it. If indeed conception following a failed sterilisation is an injury, then it should be treated *as an injury*. The court would be unlikely to question in any other context a claimant's state of mind towards his injury caused by negligence, to determine if indeed it really is an injury.

The *Walkin* definition of injury, however, has other implications. The Court of Appeal having ruled out the failed sterilisation itself as the point of injury, on the basis that 'it left her as before', must also eliminate any possibility of a man claiming personal injury where his fertility remains following a vasectomy. Is it sensible to speak of an ineffective vasectomy in terms of personal injury? Many think not (Whitfield, 1998; Jackson, 2001; Mullis, 1993). Professor Rogers (1985) suggests that as a failed vasectomy merely maintains the status quo, that is maintains the normal condition, a 'state of fertility, albeit undesired' cannot constitute actionable damage (1985: 310). Unless the claimant can illustrate that he has suffered mental disturbance – nothing short of psychiatric harm – his claim will be one of economic loss through raising an unwanted child, therefore parasitic to the mother's claim. Therefore, in this alternative situation, the woman will need to establish that her partner's doctor owed her a duty of care to prevent physical injury. In a continuing relationship where the partner's doctor knows of her existence, this should be straightforward,[7] since it would be readily foreseeable that if a vasectomy fails the woman will become pregnant as a result of sexual intercourse. Where this is not the case, a doctor will not owe a duty to every woman that a man impregnates. In *Goodwill v British Pregnancy Advisory Service* [1996] 1 WLR 1397, Ms Goodwill claimed damages for the costs associated with pregnancy, as a result of her partner's vasectomy having spontaneously reversed. Her partner, Mr Mackinlay, however, had undergone the vasectomy procedure three years *prior* to his (extra-marital) sexual relationship with Ms Goodwill. The Court of Appeal struck out the claim as 'vexatious', holding that at the time her partner was told that he could dispense with contraception the claimant was:

> [M]erely like any other woman in the world, a potential future sexual

partner of his, that is to say a member of an *indeterminately large class of females* who might have sexual relations with Mr MacKinlay during his lifetime.

(p 1405)

Therefore, providing that a duty is owed, the personal injury suffered through wrongful conception is one that is sustained by the woman who conceives, carries and gives birth to the child – and this is so, whether conception results from a failed sterilisation or vasectomy. As Mason comments, 'the fact that the claim can be a real one is demonstrated by the acceptance of the mother's claim in *McFarlane*' (2002: 48). The House of Lords in *McFarlane v Tayside Health Board* [2000] 2 AC 59 unquestionably accepted that the mother had suffered an actionable physical wrong – although the judgment is littered with varying accounts as to how this natural, biological process could be conceptualised – as 'injury', 'harm', 'damage' or 'invasion of bodily integrity'. Lord Slynn, for example, commented that it was unnecessary to consider:

> [T]he events of an unwanted conception and birth in terms of 'harm' or 'injury' in its ordinary sense of the words. They were unwanted and known . . . to be unwanted events. The object of the vasectomy was to prevent them happening.
>
> (p 74)

Not a harm or injury in its ordinary sense of the words – therefore in an *extraordinary* sense? Lord Hope, by contrast, considered that the mother's claim *could* be described in 'simple terms' as one 'for the loss, injury and damages which she has suffered as a result of a harmful event' although noting that it 'may seem odd to describe the conception as harmful' (p 86). His Lordship noted that in normal circumstances this would not be the case, as the 'physical consequences to the woman of pregnancy and childbirth are, of course, natural processes'; however, in these circumstances 'it was the very thing which she had been told would not happen to her' (p 86). Refusing to take account of any possible 'relief and joy' following childbirth, Lord Hope observed that 'pregnancy and childbirth involve changes to the body which may cause, in varying degrees, discomfort, inconvenience, distress and pain'. The fact that these consequences flowed naturally from the 'negligently-caused conception' would not remove them from the proper scope of an award of damage. Underpinning this point, Lord Hope raised examples from the field of personal injury where the natural consequences of an initial injury, such as the development of arthritic changes, are taken into account. An alternative analogy might have been suitable here, since these particular natural consequences emerge *after* the (unnatural) infliction of an injury – but the point is clear. What might constitute natural processes in the course of ordinary life (for example, illness and eventual death) do not remain 'natural' and thereby harmless events, if negligently *inflicted* upon an individual. Also rejecting the 'natural not injurious' proposition, Lord Steyn remarked that 'the negligence of the surgeon caused the physical consequences of pain and suffering associated with pregnancy and childbirth. And every pregnancy involves substantial discomfort' (p 81). In similar vein, Lord Clyde suggested that natural as the mechanism may have been, 'the reality of the pain, discomfort and inconvenience of the experience cannot be ignored. It seems to me to be a clear example of pain and suffering such as could qualify as a potential head of damages' (p 102). Even Lord Millett, having commented that conception and childbirth were the 'price of parenthood', thereby dissenting from awarding damages under this head, found no difficulty in conceptualising pregnancy in these circumstances as a harm: 'This was an invasion of her bodily integrity and threatened further damage both physical and financial.' In his view, the injury and loss was one of personal autonomy and the decision to 'have no more children is one the law should respect and protect' (p 114).

Could these characterisations leave lower courts in any doubt that wrongful pregnancy constitutes anything other than an actionable physical harm? In *Greenfield v Irwin* [2001] 1 WLR 1279, a case following *McFarlane*, the claimant was treated with a course of contraceptives.[8] She alleged that the defendants negligently failed to diagnose that she was pregnant at the time, with a *healthy* child that she did not want; as such that their negligence deprived her of the opportunity to have the pregnancy terminated. Having given up work to look after the child, she brought a claim for lost earnings. The main factual difference between *McFarlane* and *Greenfield* was that in the former, the negligence led to the wrongful conception, while in *Greenfield*, the negligence consisted of a failure to diagnose pregnancy, depriving the claimant of the opportunity to terminate. Providing the leading judgment in the Court of Appeal, Buxton LJ stated:

> I am unable to accept that the damage suffered here was 'physical' in any way that makes a relevant distinction between this case and *McFarlane*. It may or may not be right . . . that what happened here is to be characterised as an interference with the plaintiff's body, even though it was a failure to interrupt a physical process already in operation rather than the initiation of a process. But there is no difference between this case and *McFarlane* which, in my judgment, makes any distinction that is relevant in law between the two cases.
>
> (p 1283)

This can be interpreted in two different ways. In isolation this might appear to reject that an unwanted pregnancy is a type of physical harm at all. In attempting to demonstrate the difficulties courts have encountered in conceptualising pregnancy as an injury, Christian Witting comments of Buxton LJ's statement that, 'His Lordship appears to have assumed that the House of Lords in *McFarlane* had found that the claimant suffered *no* physical injury' (2002: 195). Indeed, others have also interpreted Buxton LJ as 'initially' rejecting that the primary injury is the mother's condition of being pregnant (Radley-Gardener, 2002: 13).

Such interpretations, however, are misconceived. Both Buxton and May LJJ *expressly* acknowledged the basis of the decision in *McFarlane* to allow the mother's claim: 'which was a claim for discomfort from the pregnancy and the injury and stress of the act of giving birth. A ruling that she could recover in that respect was upheld in the House of Lords' (*per* Buxton LJ p 1282 in *Greenfield*). And May LJ, reflecting on the determination of the claim for loss of earnings due to pregnancy and birth in *McFarlane*, commented: 'That might readily have been characterised as a claim for damages consequential on, or parasitical to, a personal injury claim, the personal injury being that associated with the pregnancy and birth itself' (p 1291). Once one examines the context of this judgment, and the arguments raised by counsel in *Greenfield*, it is abundantly clear that Buxton LJ's response does *not* reject that pregnancy is a personal injury, but merely indicates that there is no 'relevant' difference arising in this case to justify deviating from *McFarlane*.

To make this clearer, in *Greenfield*, counsel for the claimant argued that the personal injury Mrs Greenfield suffered was no different to those cases where injuries, diseases or other conditions were not properly diagnosed and treated – notably as the result of a negligent act. A good example of this is where the defendant fails to detect the early symptoms of a treatable cancer.[9] By contrast, in *McFarlane* the negligence consisted of a *misstatement*, notably that the claimant's vasectomy operation had been successful and that the couple could now dispense with contraception. Where the distinction lies is that the first is a negligent act (negligence *simpliciter*), while the latter consists of negligent words.[10] The significance being that the common law tended to take a cautious approach in imposing loss caused by statements, on the basis that *words* are more likely than *deeds* to give rise to only financial loss, than physical harm. That this seems to be the driving force of Buxton LJ's concerns is further reinforced:

> The attraction of the analysis [to counsel] was to seek to argue that there was a strong, indeed stark, distinction in the law of negligence between the rules applying to a case that can be characterised as one of advice or causing of economic loss; and to a case that can be characterised as one of physical damage. That, however, is not now the law.
>
> (p 1283)

Perhaps the most interesting aspect of *Greenfield* is that this claim actually went as far as the Court of Appeal, since in *McFarlane*, Lord Steyn ruled out such a distinction in these actions:

> [I]n regard to the sustainability of a claim for the cost of bringing up the child it ought not to make any difference whether the claim is based on negligence *simpliciter* or on the extended *Hedley Byrne* principle ... the latter is simply the rationalisation adopted by the common law to provide a remedy for the recovery of economic loss for a species of negligently performed services.
>
> (pp 83–4)

This, as Hoyano (2002) suggests, is to conflate 'pure' and 'consequential' economic loss. On this basis, it appears that the claimant's counsel in *Greenfield* had hoped to encourage the Court of Appeal to distinguish between consequential and pure economic loss, so that the loss of earnings claim would be regarded as economic loss consequential on personal injury. Therefore, contrary to Witting's interpretation, the Court of Appeal on this reading was not casting any doubt as to whether pregnancy was a physical injury. Indeed, this issue did not seem to unduly preoccupy the court at all – nor ought it to have.[11] Rather, the Court was more concerned as to whether a distinction could be drawn between *McFarlane* and *Greenfield* as to the *manner* by which the injury was caused and was simply rejecting counsel's argument that this should be conceptualised as a single cause of action in respect of personal injury. Indeed, if any question arose concerning pregnancy as an injury, this centred on the fact that *Greenfield* concerned a 'failure to interrupt a physical process already in operation rather than the initiation of a process' (p 1283). Certainly the *Walkin* definition of injury, which posits the precise point of injury at the point of conception – a view also echoed by Lord Hope in *McFarlane*: 'the harmful event was the child's conception' (p 86) – must fail to apply in this situation. Nevertheless, in *McFarlane*, their Lordships' review of the case law relating to such claims appears to provide, at least, tacit approval that the continuation of an unwanted pregnancy owing to negligence would entitle such a claim to succeed.[12] No doubt, this view underpinned the reasoning of the Court of Appeal in *Greenfield* that such damages should be recovered.

Leaving these more technical points behind, there is no doubt that for the purposes of the law, an unwanted pregnancy brought about by negligence *is* a compensable harm. This is the case, whether justified by reference to 'impairment' under the Limitation Act 1980, the 'unwanted' nature of the condition, the frustrated purpose of sterilisation or vasectomy, the invasion of a woman's bodily integrity, and the pain and suffering that these events entail. For some, however, these accounts are deeply problematic; as has been contended, the language of 'harm', 'injury' or 'invasion of bodily integrity' used variously in such cases merely indicates that these are types of harms that, in an *orthodox* legal sense, cannot be said to be harm at all. Here sits the contention that the law is being 'stretched' to give effect to a 'social conception of harm'.

Orthodox injuries

The law of tort, it is said, is being stretched 'in half a dozen different directions' (Atiyah, 1997: 32). Concepts of fault, causation, harm – the 'very concept of negligence' – have been stretched out of all recognition in the 'favour of injured accident victims' (Atiyah, 1997: 32). Whether owing to sympathetic judges, greedy lawyers (who might be seen as the ultimate beneficiaries of 'law stretching'), or the product of living in a 'blame culture', the result is that 'the whole system is shot through with absurdity and unreality' (Atiyah, 1997: 94), or so Atiyah maintains, lamenting that 'at one time damages for injury, especially for personal injury, were almost entirely confined to cases where the victim suffered a plain and obvious physical injury' (1997: 52). Whether one should regard the recognition of merely 'plain and obvious' physical injuries as constituting the *good old days* of tort law, is to be doubted, but no doubt it was a great deal simpler.

Over the decades, the legislative and common law development of tort, in general, has been nothing short of astonishing. In the legislative realm, numerous pockets of liability have opened up. As Tony Weir's (2001) delightfully succinct appraisal of developments in the law of obligations illustrates, one can now take a claim for harassment, even where no immediate violence is threatened (Protection From Harassment Act 1997), a claim against a tortfeasor who specifically excludes such liability (Unfair Contract Terms Act 1977), or indeed a claim where one is partly at fault for his injuries (Law Reform (Contributory Negligence) Act 1945) – not even the grave will shield a dead tortfeasor from liability (Law Reform (Miscellaneous Provisions) Act 1934). This is to name just a few of the legislative developments, but of the most significant has been the enactment of the Human Rights Act 1998, which allows claims to proceed against public authorities for the invasion of, or failure to protect against invasion, the rights under the European Convention on Human Rights. While such legislative hyperactivity might be partly explained by the refusal of judges to modify a rule 'even though it had become unacceptable' (Weir, 2001: 3), as Weir comments, the common law has been far from complacent:

> In 1789 [the courts] held that a liar was answerable for the harm caused by his deceit although he obtained nothing by his false pretences. In 1862 they held it tortious knowingly to persuade a person to break his contract with the plaintiff. In 1866 they held the occupier of premises liable for failing to make them reasonably safe for people who came there on business. In 1891 they allowed injured workmen to sue for breaches of

safety legislation. In 1897 they held it tortious to play a nasty practical joke which made the victim ill. In recent years the courts have increasingly held defendants liable for failing to protect people against third parties, or even themselves...

(Weir, 2001: 3–4)

And the list of instances where the courts have opened up liability continues to grow, not only through recognising new types of harm, for example, pure economic loss (*Hedley Byrne & Co. v Heller & Partners Limited* [1964] AC 465)[13] or purely psychiatric damage (*Dulieu v White* [1901] 2 KB 669), but the variety of *ways* that such harms, whether physical, psychological or economic, might be inflicted.[14] Therefore, for those who have been harmed, this snapshot of the development of torts might well appear an entirely *positive* and promising one – after all, is it not the case that the law of torts is increasingly willing to extend its protection? Or rather, should we, like Weir, regard this development in more *negative* terms: 'it is undeniable that the progressive socialization of harm diminishes the responsibility, indeed the autonomy, of the individual' (2001: 6). Whether one is inclined to view the growth of tort law and its increased recognition of harms in either positive or negative terms much depends on one's perspective and, of course, the questions one asks. As Joanne Conaghan comments, 'from a feminist perspective, it is difficult to see how the autonomy of women is diminished by developments which facilitate legal redress in the contexts of acts of sexual violence and abuse, raising a question as to *whose* autonomy Weir perceives to be threatened' (2003: 186). This is a valuable point. Some might, for example, cast a suspicious eye on this rather generalised talk of growth and stretching when considering those areas where the law is *not* in favour of expanding liability, but rather retracting it (Conaghan, 2002). It is undeniable that the increased recognition of different harms must also bring with it the burden of increased responsibilities. Therefore, the individual in this context – the teacher, doctor, employer or policeman – will need to be on their guard to prevent the occurrence of harms that, at one time, would not have been regarded as harmful at all (Conaghan, 2002).

In this sense, while Conaghan quite correctly seeks to bring a feminist perspective to bear here, we shouldn't be too dismissive of the general point that Weir is attempting to make – notably, that the greater the responsibility to avoid causing harm, the greater the impairment of *that* responsible agent's ability to move freely in society. Frank Furedi neatly encapsulates this view:

> The most negative consequence of compensation culture is not the amount of money paid out in frivolous cases. It is the extension of formalised liability into areas that were hitherto considered to be the domain of personal responsibility [which] contributes towards relieving

the burden of responsibility from the individual by reinterpreting misfortune as by definition the responsibility of others.

(Furedi, 1999: 36)

But, of course, there are two faces of autonomy. It is one thing to deny burdening individuals with responsibility where harms are spread equally, but quite a *different* matter where those harms are spread 'unequally and if some persons or classes of persons bear them to a considerably greater degree than others' (Murphy, 1994: 210). Such liberal conceptions of autonomy, responsibility, harm and risk then merely become a mask for substantive and procedural inequality. Therefore, whether the growth of tort law and the transfer of responsibility are considered as autonomy *enhancing* or *diminishing*, must certainly depend on what values are at stake, *whose* interests are at stake, and whether these are considered in society as worthy of protection. So, if the law is being stretched, in what areas and in what way is it being stretched? A number of commentators have pointed specifically to one action within the law of negligence as constituting a piece of 'English folly' (Weir, 2000), in awarding damages for the unexpected physical consequences of medical procedures, 'even where they cannot be said to be injuries at all' (Atiyah, 1997: 54). In Weir's view,

[T]he proper answer to the question whether reluctant parents of a healthy unwanted child can claim the cost of bringing it up is to say that to have a healthy child cannot be counted as 'damage', even though parenthood involves considerable expense.

(Weir, 2001: 186)

In this context, Weir complains, if 'damage is the proper object of compensation, it is surprising how little attention courts and lawyers have paid to the concept' (2001: 186). He suggests that, 'In the normal case, damage consists of having fewer good things to enjoy or more bad ones to put up with than one would otherwise have had' (2001: 186). If the courts apply this definition, can it be any surprise if the concept of harm is being stretched? Others, however, have undertaken a more detailed consideration of the concepts of 'harm' and 'damage' within the tort of negligence, and of particular interest here, Christian Witting has done so within the context of the wrongful pregnancy claim. Questioning whether an unwanted pregnancy can constitute *physical damage*, and echoing Atiyah's sentiment that, 'giving birth is hardly a physical injury' (1997: 54), Witting claims that: 'We find that what constitutes physical damage for one purpose in the law of negligence might not constitute physical damage for another purpose' (2002: 190). His thesis is *not*, however, that pregnancy and childbirth should not be treated as actionable damage, conceding that the reasoning employed by their Lordships in *McFarlane* was the 'product of an inherent logic' (2002: 194). Rather, his claim is that the alleged injuries to the mother 'are not describable as deleterious physical changes' (2002: 192), and therefore do not constitute physical injuries 'in the orthodox sense', but those of a 'socially constructed kind' (2002: 194). Considering the claim for pain and suffering in *McFarlane*, Witting comments:

> [T]he mother's conception was an entirely natural event that her physiological constitution was designed to induce and to accommodate . . . The development of her baby restricted her movements and resulted in physical confinement towards the end of the pregnancy. This was undoubted interference with the mother's autonomy. . . . But the fact remains that the mother's physiological integrity was not compromised. Her organs continued to function in the way that 'nature intended' and her body returned after delivery to its pre-conception state. It is difficult, as such, to describe the changes that took place within the claimant's body as *deleterious changes* or as having impaired their functioning.
>
> (Witting, 2002: 192–3)

Equating wrongful pregnancy with injury because of its *unwanted nature* or the risks of something going wrong, Witting rejects as fallacious, on the basis that threatened injury is not actual injury, as negligence does 'not compensate for risks arising in the air' (2002: 193). Similarly, while one might imagine that the bodily changes involved in a pregnancy could easily satisfy notions of impairment or deleteriousness, for Witting, this is simply not enough. Juxtaposing the woman who is desirous of children against the woman who is not, he comments that, 'the fact that minds could differ over the question' (2002: 194) indicates that no physical injury has been suffered in the *orthodox sense*. Therefore, on what basis did the House of Lords in *McFarlane* permit recovery if no physical damage has been suffered? Witting suggests that their Lordships clearly took:

> [S]ocial views into account in determining the answer to the question whether the law *should* treat the kind of claim in question *as if* it were a claim for physical injury or damage. The question they answered was a normative one, dependent upon social perceptions, not a positive one, dependent upon the proof of deleterious changes in the body of the claimant.
>
> (Witting, 2002: 194)

Significantly, Witting creates a story of judges at a complete loss in conceptualising this manifestation of injury in orthodox legal terms, to the extent that they are forced to resort to the ordinary bystander (commuter) test – a social conception of harm – in order to justify recovery. That their Lordships could not properly found the claim on the basis of orthodox physical damage, he suggests, also left the Court of Appeal in *Greenfield* confirming an award upon this 'wider notion of physical injury' (Witting, 2002: 196), since (in his view) there was great doubt as to what *McFarlane* had determined on this issue. Earlier analysis certainly illustrates that Witting's view of *Greenfield* is misconceived; however, of greater concern is how gendered assumptions appear to strongly inform Witting's views on this subject. After all, is it possible to reach any other conclusion when considering his view that, 'most women are only too glad to avail themselves of the opportunity to conceive and to give birth to children at some stage during their reproductive lives' (2002: 192–3)?

Despite significant evidence to the contrary,[15] and the fact that women are 'increasingly asking themselves whether they actually want to be mothers' (Bartlett, 1994), the main thrust of Witting's argument is founded upon this premise. Moreover, his presentation of unwanted pregnancy as 'natural' and therefore not 'deleterious', sustains a view that would only retain its cogency in a physical world completely untouched by human intervention – one where life is lived as fate. As a product of scientific and medical endeavour, mankind can now intervene to prevent the *natural* occurrence or *natural* progression of diseases that would otherwise have been undetectable. Would we be as calmly accepting of the view that the negligent failure to detect the early signs of cancer really did no harm, since it is 'natural' for humans to become diseased and to eventually die? And, when transposed into the field of reproduction, can it really make sense to refer to anything as 'natural' in a biotechnological world that facilitates artificial means of reproduction such as *in vitro* fertilisation and gamete intrafallopian transfer (GIFT)? Surely these are instances where both 'nature and tradition release their hold' (Giddens, 1999a: 5)?

Much related to this is the apparently pre-social conception of 'orthodox physical damage', which Witting presents as existing separately from any social conceptions of harm. Against this idea of law as an autonomous and self-referential system, the stronger view must be that the legal and the social are inextricably intertwined. Peter Fitzpatrick, for example, underpins this point, commenting that society 'depends every bit as much on law for its identity as law depends on society', and that the two coexist in a relational or constitutive 'theory of mutual determination' (1997: 148–9). Also critical of Witting's thesis is Joanne Conaghan, who questions how, in the absence of 'social values or attention to context, notions of nature or deleteriousness are to be determined' (2003: 191). Indeed, this portrayal of 'physical damage' as an immutable, fixed category becomes highly contentious when we consider that, 'of all the conceptual elements of the tort of negligence . . . *damage*, is by far the least developed' (Markesinis and Deakin, 1999: 77), and that the concept is 'relative, dependent on the circumstances of the occasion' (Fleming, 1992: 216). Even if the law determines concepts of 'damage' by reference to the 'commuter on the Underground', does this really implicate a *new* conception of harm, when historically 'the common law has been strongly associated with the concept of community . . . giving institutional expression to strongly consensual views of the community' (Mullender, 2003: 312)? And on those occasions where a decision 'may require the extension or adaptation of a principle or in some cases the creation of new law to meet the justice of the case' (*McLoughlin v O'Brian* [1983] AC 410 *per* Lord Scarman), and the recognition of different harms, is this always explicable through a social conception of harm? However, of greater importance, can we be confident that law has even identified an authentic 'social conception of harm', when the judge's articulation on any given issue is one that the judge 'reasonably believes that the ordinary citizen would regard as right' (*McFarlane*, 82 *per* Lord Steyn)? At best, judges grounding their decisions on an 'empirical community' (Mullender, 2003: 313) are simply second-guessing. After all, would a society that 'demands that parents should have the ability to limit the size of their families' (Witting, 2002: 194), be so quick to assume that while an unwanted pregnancy *was* a compensable harm, maintaining a child for 18 years *was not*?[16]

But, more contentious still, is Witting's conceptualisation of unwanted pregnancy as a harmless, non-injurious event, in *orthodox* terms. As Conaghan suggests, the injury is located 'in a woman's *perception* of her state in a way which divorces that perception from her "naturally" pregnant (and thereby harm-less) body, which Witting manages to present the injury as non-physical in origin' (2003: 191). The 'unwantedness' of the pregnancy is rendered completely separate to the experience of the pregnancy itself and in so doing displaces the 'embodied and affective aspects' (Lacey, 1998: 114) of an unwanted pregnancy. Elsewhere the law reflects this Cartesian tradition of a dualism between mind and body, and the privileging of the mind over body. Take, for example, the criminal law of rape with the notion of consent at its heart. As Lacey comments in this context, where the law locates the harm as a 'particularly mentalist, incorporeal one', this serves to 'block the articulation of the inextricable integration of mental and corporeal experience' and deny 'any expression of the corporeal dimension of this violation of choice' (1998: 112). In this respect, the law of rape might form an analogous wrong, since many would argue that the injury of an unwanted pregnancy lies precisely in the absence of consent (McDonagh, 1996).[17] While this is resonant of a weaker and particularly 'mentalist construction of the wrong' (Lacey, 1998: 112), even this perspective is disarmed by Witting who constructs the woman's perception as too unreliable (irrational) to constitute an injury. Her autonomy is denied once placed within a framework of varying attitudes towards the desirability or otherwise of pregnancy – quite simply, if this is an injury, it is one which most women invite – how then can this constitute '*orthodox* physical harm' (Witting, 2002: 203)?

So, what is this orthodox physical damage? While Witting concedes that unwanted pregnancy is 'so closely *analogous* to orthodox kinds of damage that one would be splitting hairs to attempt to draw a line between them' (2002: 203), others are less generous in their view:

Doctors would be puzzled by this talk of injury. This appears to have been a normal pregnancy, a physiological process no different in substance to a filling and emptying of the bladder or bowel. No doctor would equate a normal pregnancy followed by the birth of a healthy child with any kind of injury.

(Mahendra, 1995: 1375)

Until we can define what physical damage consists of, surely it must be impossible to confidently assert that an unwanted pregnancy is, or is not, a personal injury? But this is far from straightforward. Any attempts to provide a definition by reference to the Limitation Act 1980 of 'any disease and impairment of a person's physical or mental condition', merely throws up more questions – what is disease or impairment? That the search for such definitions have 'occupied so many good minds for so long with so much continuing contention', Randolph Nesse suggests, perhaps illustrates that the question of what 'disease' is, might either be 'miscast or unanswerable' (2001: 37). Of course, to some, this might seem surprising, perhaps even intuitively wrong – we *know* what disease is, what impairment is – the body is not functioning properly, it deviates from the norm. Then what is the norm? How do we decide what concepts of normality are, in the absence of complete knowledge about the body?

What constitutes disease or normality is an entirely slippery matter. In the context of mental illness, Ian Kennedy (1981) demonstrates this point, noting how homosexuality transformed overnight from an illness to a *not*-illness in 1974 following a vote of the American Psychiatric Association. As he suggests, it is not the *objective facts* that changed, since homosexuality remains as much a part of social life after 1974 as it was prior to that date. What *has* changed however 'is how the particular doctors *choose* to judge it' (Kennedy, 1981: 2). The significance of this is clear. Rather than being immediately ascertainable as a matter of scientific exactitude, what we know as disease, illness and impairment are 'themselves fabrications of powerful discourses, rather than discoveries of "truths" about the body and its interaction with the social world' (Annandale, 2001: 35). Therefore, what constitutes a personal injury is not 'some static objectively identifiable fact' (Kennedy, 1981: 4), but instead must be viewed as a concept that varies and changes in its meaning and application.

The circularity of arguments that rely on the false premise of 'most women do, some women don't' in relation to the experience of unwanted pregnancy, coupled with a confident reliance upon some self-evident notion of 'personal injury', must be seen to cast doubt on Witting's claims. Rather than blindly accepting the view that concepts of 'damage' and 'personal injury' are self-evident, objective and gender-neutral categories, we come to engage with the question of *what harm is* when we examine their distribution, recognition and quantification. For example, why does lost attractiveness in the case of women generate considerably higher awards than for men? Or in the context of female harms, why does the law provide generous damages for injuries causing *infertility*, yet only modest awards for wrongful pregnancy?[18] And tellingly, could it be significant that Witting contends that wrongful pregnancy is *not* a personal injury, while judicial consensus holds that it is? The 'fact that minds could differ over the question' (Witting, 2002: 194) might well indicate that what *physical injury is*, is most certainly not set in stone.

Despite such criticisms, Witting's characterisation of unwanted pregnancy as an injury sustained to the (differing) mind rather than the (unharmed, pregnant) body sets the stage for a further mode of enquiry. There are obvious differences between the outcomes of the courts and Witting's deliberations, but just how different are they in substance? As earlier analysis illustrates, western metaphysical thought has been pervasive, and continues to reflect the law's mechanistic treatment of bodies in personal injury. Furthermore, dualistic thought continues to resonate with liberal conceptions of autonomy and body-ownership. Bearing in mind the gendered history of dualistic thought, and its tendency to exclude women's perspectives, it must be essential to question to what extent this informs the construction of harm in wrongful pregnancy. Therefore, the questions that we must ask at this stage are, how is wrongful pregnancy constructed and by reference to what values? And, importantly, what aspects of the experience of unwanted pregnancy are encapsulated (or excluded) through a personal injury framework?

Harmed minds, harmed bodies

> The law of torts values physical security and property more highly than emotional security and human relationships. This apparently gender-neutral hierarchy of values has privileged men, as the traditional owners and managers of property, and has burdened women, to whom the emotional work of maintaining human relationships has commonly been assigned. The law has often failed to compensate women for recurring harms – serious though they may be in the lives of women – for which there is no precise masculine analogue.
>
> (Chamallas and Kerber, 1989: 814)

It is beyond question that the courts' acceptance of unwanted pregnancy as a recognised head of damages constitutes an important step in the field of reproductive law. Conceptually, this constitutes a significant shift away from viewing women as irrevocably tied to their reproductive functions, and indeed, the *legal* recognition that 'harm' has occurred is a key societal signifier, since perceptions of harm 'are closely linked to law' (Conaghan, 2002: 322). From early case law that exhibits judicial expressions of doubt, if not considerable discomfort, in describing unwanted pregnancy as injurious, later case law such as *McFarlane* provides a much stronger account. Contrary to the view that pregnancy is natural, therefore non-injurious, the law provides that, 'this is an area of family life in which freedom of choice may properly be exercised' and will respect 'the right of men and women to take steps to limit the size of their family' (p 86, *per* Lord Hope).

But – *there is a but*. A striking feature of *McFarlane* is that despite their Lordships' firm acceptance of unwanted pregnancy as actionable physical damage, we are presented with a variety of models of personal injury rather than a unitary vision as to what that injury precisely consists of. Moreover, each way of seeing the pregnant body perpetuates a dualistic view of the experience of unwanted pregnancy. Lord Slynn, for example, proceeded from a 'mentalist' perspective of injury, grounding his decision on a consent-based framework where the events that happened were simply 'unwanted' and known to be unwanted. Similarly, Lord Hope embraced this framework, but shifted his analysis of the injury as holding a strong physical dimension, detailing that the bodily changes might cause 'discomfort, inconvenience, distress and pain'. For Lord Steyn, the injury is situated precisely in these physical consequences of pregnancy, commenting that every pregnancy involves 'substantial discomfort'. Certainly, pregnancy holds a strong physical dimension. As Eileen McDonagh comments, 'pregnancy is a massive, ongoing set of processes, caused by a fertilized ovum, which keeps a woman's body physically operating and changing every second, minute, hour, day, week, and month for nine months' (1996: 71). While the physical changes to a woman's body are unquestionably a strong element of the harmful experience of unwanted pregnancy, the inherent weakness of this approach is that it fails to recognise that pregnancy is 'rarely, if ever, experienced by women as solely bodily significance' (Mullin, 2002: 33). By contrast, however, a much stronger thesis was put forward by Lord Millett who conceptualised the injury as consisting of the invasion of a woman's bodily integrity, and the threat of future physical and financial risk.

So, is the injury 'physical', or 'mental', in the sense that the event was unwanted, an invasion of bodily boundaries, or does it consist of something else? Broadly speaking, each judgment presents the harm as an invasion of the fundamental right to bodily integrity, although each is expressed differently, without any 'detail about what is entailed' (*per* Hale LJ p 285 in *Parkinson v St. James and Seacroft University Hospital NHS Trust* [2002] QB 266). Significantly, while these accounts of injury are premised upon the traditional tort framework, in treating the body as something to be controlled by the mind, and the bodily boundaries to be protected from outside invasion, how do these fail to capture the experience and impact of an unwanted pregnancy? Is not a pregnancy something more than just a physical and biological event? While the courts have rejected child maintenance damages, thereby severing the harm at the point of birth, does this not posit the harm as peculiarly *episodic* and *fleeting*, rather than what must be perceived in these cases as an *enduring* responsibility? Might it be significant that these ways of describing the harm could be as easily deployed to describe an injury that a man might sustain (and speedily recover from)? Is there not some sense that the uniquely female experiences of pregnancy and childbirth have been 'squeezed through a masculine interpretative sieve' (Bridgeman and Millns, 1998: 390) in order to provide legal recognition of this harm?

In daily life, Robin West (1997) suggests that women sustain physical, emotional, psychic and political harms that have little or no counterpart in the lives of men. Unwanted pregnancy, whether brought about by negligence or not, is itself a harm, and the aspect of this experience, which holds no correlate in men's lives, is that a woman finds herself in 'an *involuntarily nurturant* position' (West, 1997: 105). When the pregnancy is wanted, West maintains that this constitutes an uncomplicated act of altruism. However, when the pregnancy is *involuntary and unwanted*, the pregnant woman is undertaking nurturant work against her will, the consequence of which is that a woman's:

> [M]oral, relational life is thus as fully invaded as is her physical body. She nurtures, but without the preceding act of will and commitment that would engage her moral, choosing self. She becomes a nurturant but *unchoosing* creature – a little more like the spreading chestnut tree that gives without choosing to give, and a little less like an autonomous individual whose selfhood is strengthened rather than threatened by altruistic acts.
>
> (West, 1997: 105)

West's emphasis on this relational and psychic dimension is one that the various accounts of the harm of unwanted pregnancy as physical, merely unwanted, or an invasion of bodily boundaries fail, *by themselves*, to capture. That this dimension is so often overlooked, West suggests, is perhaps because it is so deeply gendered (1997: 106). While both men and women will be *causally* responsible for pregnancy, a woman's bodily connection with the foetus means that she also holds an inescapable 'decision responsibility' – a responsibility that men can 'choose not to assume' or acknowledge by virtue of their bodily *alienation* from the consequences of their actions (MacKenzie, 1992: 141). Furthermore, conceptualising the pregnant woman as involuntarily undertaking a nurturant position in relation to the foetus directly challenges liberal conceptions of 'possessive individualism, in which a free, self-determining and self-responsible identity is constituted as property' (Lury, 1998: 1). Instead, the nurturant self is the 'self that does not choose' and 'does not engage her will with her actions' in which selfhood is further undermined (West, 1997: 106). Also highlighting the psychic and bodily connections between the foetus and the woman in the context of abortion, Catriona MacKenzie comments:

> To think that the question of autonomy ... is just a question about

preserving the integrity of one's body boundaries, and to see the f[o]etus merely as an occupant of the woman's uterus, is thus to divorce women's bodies from their subjectivities. Ironically, it comes close to regarding women's bodies as simply f[o]etal containers . . .

(MacKenzie, 1992: 150)

Female personhood in pregnancy cannot be understood by reference to the merely biological, as these 'processes are always mediated by the cultural meanings of pregnancy, by the woman's personal and social context, and by the way she constitutes herself in response to these factors through the decisions she makes' (MacKenzie, 1992: 141). Although rooted in biology, the significance of pregnancy – whether something that we hope for, deeply fear, or experience as a wanted or unwanted state – cannot be appreciated by focusing on the physical manifestation of pregnancy. Rather, the significance of *being* pregnant is inextricably intertwined with the considerable responsibility and enduring consequences which pregnancy heralds. From a relational perspective, a woman's expectations of her life, her stability, her security, her hopes for the future have been irrevocably changed by virtue of that physical state and it will be the woman alone who holds the responsibility for determining whether she will commit or not to the existence of a future child. Furthermore, an unwanted pregnancy can seriously disrupt important aspects of a woman's life, including family relationships, work, education and finances, which may result in enduring demands and burdens upon her life (Orr and Miller, 1997). Significantly, none of these are corporeal harms. Acknowledgement of only the physical impact perpetuates a medical model of pregnancy, which as Marie Ashe observes, 'informs legal discourse as well as medical theory and practice', and emphasises 'the separability of the pregnant woman and the fetus' defining 'the female reproductive process in terms of discontinuity rather than continuity' (Ashe, 1988: 539). Only when we acknowledge both the physical and *emotional* feelings of the mother and her connection with the foetus, can we begin to address important aspects of a woman's subjectivity and the extent of the harm of an unwanted pregnancy. And this will never be a merely physical event that ceases at childbirth. For many women, this may be viewed as an enduring, continuing source of responsibility and connection – a process that has a beginning, but no end. As Bergun and Bendfeld comment, by engaging with the 'feeling body' of the pregnant mother, 'another scene unfolds before us that allows us to acknowledge the primacy and full subjectivity of the mother, the potential of the fetus, and the environment within which the relation must survive and flourish' (2001: 90). How does this 'feeling body' impact upon dominant conceptions of harm and autonomy? And if the body in this area of tort law is too Cartesian, thereby jettisoning the affective, relational and emotional dimensions of an unwanted pregnancy, what strategies might be employed to challenge this? As a starting point, because pregnancy is a uniquely female experience, an experience shared by many women, then it will be important for the law to conceptualise notions of harm, autonomy and responsibility by reference to *women's* perspectives.

The concept of autonomy, as I suggested earlier, is absolutely central to matters of reproduction and clearly must be fully embraced within any conceptualisation of the harm in the reproductive torts. But the tension here is that the liberal discourse of autonomy positions the harm of unwanted pregnancy in a way that many women might not readily accept. The language of lived subjectivity, of embodied existence, is denied, reducing bodies to property, and injuries to merely physical pains. This is not to say that the law doesn't recognise harms that are non-physical, non-pecuniary, intimate and relational, but that these are often devalued and diminished. So, is there room for emotions, intimacy and affect within the language of autonomy? And in the context of wrongful pregnancy, by highlighting this as a unique experience, is there not an inherent danger in reconstructing harm in order to embrace emotional and relational losses? This strategy could well act to position women as being in need of special treatment, as weaker and emotional (in opposition to reason), thereby serving to merely perpetuate dualistic thought rather than challenge it. But, as Jennifer Nedelsky's (1997) work illustrates in the context of judicial decision making, emotion is an essential part of reasoning – rather than a binary opposition between mind and body, reason and emotion, the partnership between reason and emotion requires 'a responsiveness to the reasoner's body states' (Nedelsky, 1997: 102). The significance of this in the context of our discussion is that it acts to challenge dualistic thought, and importantly to particularise autonomous decision making as connected to affect and the body. Therefore, rather than rejecting the significance of the body in challenging metaphysical thought, Nedelsky (1989) reconstructs the concepts of autonomy and rights so as to encompass it. Nedelsky fully embraces the centrality of autonomy to feminism, but illustrates that *liberal* conceptions of autonomy are simply illusory in denying the self that is psychically and relationally connected and constituted by relationships with others. In this sense, the capacity to self-govern can only develop in the context of intimate and social relations with others – it is not isolation that is necessary for the development and experience of autonomy, but relationships (Nedelsky, 1989: 12). In reconceiving autonomy then, the task 'is to think of autonomy in terms of the forms of human interactions in which it will develop and flourish' (Nedelsky, 1989: 21).

This re-envisioning of autonomy is essential to the characterisation of harm in unwanted pregnancy. It emphasises an embodied, feeling, relationally connected human being – those aspects central to the pursuit and attainment of autonomy. On this view then, our conceptualisation of harm in unwanted pregnancy shifts well beyond the merely physiological aspects of reproduction, and considers the relational and social impacts that result from disrupted relationships, the involuntariness of a woman's nurturant position, her fears and anxieties for the future, the significant moral and decisional responsibilities that she finds herself holding, which endure well past childbirth and develop as mother and child age. Reproductive autonomy then takes on a richer meaning – it is more than merely bodily autonomy, the right to control our bodily boundaries – the definition of personal integrity takes on a broader characterisation to integrate a feminist conceptualisation of harm.

Paradigm shifts

Having spoken of a 'conceptual metamorphosis' much earlier on, perhaps some will wonder at what point it is suggested that this shift actually took place in the context of the wrongful pregnancy action. Is it not the case that the harm in these actions is too corporeal, and that feminist strategies are required to broaden concepts of autonomy, responsibility and harm so as to integrate the relational and emotional aspects of unwanted pregnancy? Indeed, has it not been demonstrated that there is a real tension between the traditional personal injury framework and its application to harms that women suffer *as women*? And furthermore, given the analysis here, which has critiqued the traditional personal injury framework, have we not travelled light years away from a concept of personal injury describable under the terms of the Limitation Act 1980, of 'any disease or impairment of a person's physical or mental condition', by emphasising the harm as one that also holds a relational, emotional and affective dimension?

At the heart of these problems is that pregnancy ever came to be defined as a personal injury. We lose sight of what that 'injury' consists of through attempting the most inappropriate parallels between pregnancy and other physical injuries. It skews our focus so that we look for scars, biological evidence of injury, for traces of physical damage which no (rational) person would invite, wish for or consent to. From this perspective, it is quite easy to see that the very conceptual difficulties that commentators (and judges) in this field have continually confronted rest upon the fact that pregnancy *is* hard to describe in these terms – it is a natural biological function – and no doubt most women would be bewildered to hear that pregnancy, even unwanted, was in any way analogous to a fractured skull. Yet, law and medicine's engagement with our sexual and reproductive lives provides a history replete with similar examples. Intimate areas of our experience, those which lack a male counterpart, such as the natural processes of menstruation, pregnancy and menopause, have become increasingly medicalised; whether constructed and analogised in terms of malady, or defined and regulated, as in the case of abortion, through principally medical understandings. What is problematic about typifying pregnancy in such terms is not *only* that each model forces a particular view of the experience of pregnancy and draws such parallels with injuries and illnesses – my central concern is that these representations are *harmful*. Whether under the veil of 'equal treatment' or to justify the control and regulation of women, these ways of seeing act to exclude or misrepresent important aspects of women's experiences. Pregnancy should *not* be conceptualised as a disease, an injury, or a sickness,[19] but when it is an unwanted state, there is no doubt that it certainly *must* be recognised as a 'harm'. What forcibly emerges from this, is that defining pregnancy in these ways completely misses the point, or more emphatically, loses sight of 'the central political battle' (Purdy, 2001: 256) – notably, women gaining control over their moral, relational and social lives, of which this richer conception of reproductive autonomy is a key aspect.

But, this gives rise to a dilemma. If unwanted pregnancy brought about by negligence is *not* a physical harm, then does this automatically declassify the wrongful pregnancy suit as falling within the concept of 'damage'? As has been argued, however, 'damage' is not a self-evident and fixed notion: on this basis, then, might it be possible to claim that the broader conception of reproductive autonomy is a value capable of being set back, and therefore constituting 'damage' itself? In *McFarlane* there certainly seems to be an increasing willingness to typify unwanted pregnancy along such lines, albeit based on the much weaker notion of *bodily* autonomy. However, more recently, there have been strong indications of a fresh judicial approach to the question of 'what is the loss of unwanted pregnancy?'

Prior to her appointment to the House of Lords, Hale LJ (as she then was) in *Parkinson* adopted a critical stance of their Lordships' ruminations in *McFarlane* in relation to the child maintenance claim. Arguing that this was an inseparable consequence of the harm of unwanted pregnancy she commented that, 'it is not possible, therefore, to draw a clean line at the birth' (p 287). In the same judgment, and with equal force, Hale LJ expresses an utter lack of surprise at their Lordships' failure to detail what might be involved in conception, pregnancy and childbirth. Commenting on the 'profound physical changes' (p 285) that a woman experiences from the very point of conception, and the accompanying risks attendant upon pregnancy, Hale LJ emphasises that along with these go psychological changes. Noting that for some these changes may be seen as beneficial, while for others these might amount to a recognised psychiatric disorder, 'many are somewhere in between' (pp 285–6). By contrast to the marked 'foetal absence' in *McFarlane*, Hale LJ directly links these psychological changes to the existence of the child, where many women will develop, 'deep feelings for the new life as it grows within one, feelings which there is now evidence to suggest begin to be reciprocated by the growing child even before he is born' (p 286). And while there are physical and psychological consequences, these are accompanied by a 'severe curtailment of personal autonomy', where:

> Literally, one's life is no longer just one's own but also someone else's. One cannot simply rid oneself of that responsibility. The availability of

legal abortion depends upon the opinion of others. Even if favourable opinions can readily be found by those who know how, there is still a profound moral dilemma and potential psychological harm if that route is taken. Late abortion brings with it particular problems, and these are more likely to arise in failed sterilisation cases where the woman does not expect to become pregnant.

(p 286)

Many aspects of this judgment are notable. The framework adopted by Hale LJ is resonant of a broader conceptualisation of harm, in encompassing the physical, emotional and relational harms resulting from an unwanted pregnancy. Moreover, it constitutes a significant departure from previous accounts where the foetus is peculiarly absent – this framework, by contrast, emphasises that a pregnancy, whether wanted or not, cannot be understood without emphasising the very connectedness of the maternal/foetal bond. It is from this relationship that a woman's moral responsibilities and sense of connected identity emerge. As a result we are provided with an embodied and relational perspective of pregnancy, and it is one that is made all the more powerful by holding relevance not only to the experience of *wrongful* pregnancy, but in a non-legal context, to *any* pregnancy. It also provides an account of 'damage' firmly based on the loss of reproductive autonomy, rather than one based on a personal injury framework. Forwarding the view that the obligation to raise a child is part and parcel of this harm, rather than a separate head of loss, and disrupting the notion that these obligations are *purely economic*, Hale LJ explicitly rejects an account of 'harm', which emerges from a traditional personal injury approach:

> All of these consequences flow inexorably, albeit to different extents and in different ways according to the circumstances and characteristics of the people concerned, from the first: the invasion of bodily integrity and personal autonomy involved in every pregnancy. This is quite different from regarding them as consequential upon the pain, suffering and loss of amenity experienced in pregnancy and childbirth.
>
> (Hale, 2001: 763; see further, p 287 in *Parkinson*)

That this approach holds practical merits for the law is an understatement. This is not merely a conceptual metamorphosis, but arguably a 'paradigm shift' (Kuhn, 1996), not only in the way that an unwanted pregnancy is viewed, but also in the sense that it would seem to offer a stronger framework for (re)considering women's roles in reproduction generally. Therefore, while this may well be the case, there still remains the question as to whether such a perspective is likely to be embraced in the future: for there is one further notable (and unsurprising) aspect of this implicitly feminist framework – it is provided by a woman.

As Hale LJ questions extra-judicially, might *her* perspectives on conception, pregnancy and childbirth, be informed differently to that of a man (2001: 760)? This is a point hinted at by JK Mason (2002) who comments that Hale LJ's judgment in *Parkinson* is of:

> [S]pecial significance not only because it comes from *a woman who has had and has brought up a child* – even the latter experience being one that must be rare among men of more than middle age – but more so because it is the *only* woman's opinion on the subject.
> (Mason, 2002: 64; my emphasis)

It is at this point that we enter into murky waters. Few will have missed the fact that the most vitriolic attacks upon the wrongful pregnancy suit have been waged by *male* commentators and judges who have either expressed deep reservations in holding – or wholesale rejection – that wrongful pregnancy can be conceptualised as harm. When considering this, perhaps a more sceptical stance might hold that the awarding of damages for unwanted pregnancy is merely to avoid claimants being 'sent away empty handed' (*per* Lord Millett, p 114 in *McFarlane*). Indeed, as Conaghan ponders, 'because few judges ever envisage themselves as pregnant, let alone bring the actual experience to bear on their deliberations, their stance – in common perhaps with many tort commentators – is generally one of distance from perhaps even aversion to the whole messy business' (2003: 190). Maybe this goes too far, but the point of interest that arises here is whether the *experience* (or potential to) of conception and pregnancy could make a difference. As Hale LJ comments, it is this experiential facet of such processes that distinguishes men from women, and she concedes that her 'perception of these issues may differ' (2001: 761).

If experience, or even the *potential* to experience, makes a difference, then in the context of a predominantly male judiciary, the fact that some harms are unique to women will surely have a bearing on the delivery of judgments.[20] Some suggest that the integration of 'emotionally laden' personal experience might well prove an asset in judicial decision making (Nedelsky, 1997). If emotional and affective responses are generated through personal experience, and form an essential role in our ability to choose from an array of possible actions, then clearly experience must constitute an essential component. In this vein, Nedelsky queries, 'if past experience is crucial (if not conclusive) what happens to those who appear before a judge who has a very different background?' (1997: 107) Indeed, in the context of a wrongful pregnancy suit, should the judicial panel be composed primarily of those who have some experience to bear upon the dispute? And how significant is it that such a representative panel would be heavily composed of women? Or, if we pursue the notion of truly impartial judgment based upon 'a presumed unity of selves stripped of their affective, experiential and bodily differences'

(Nedelsky, 1997: 110), should we then automatically disqualify those *very* individuals on the pretext of bias? The latter option might, suggests Nedelsky, run the risk of selecting individuals who are 'blind to the problem' (1997: 110).

No easy answers are generated in relation to the wrongful conception suit. Some might offer the view that an increased representation of women with the experience of conception, pregnancy and birth, while desirable, might have little impact where 'certain forms of utterance are privileged by law in the construction of what is authoritative, and, by corollary, what (or who) lacks credibility' (Graycar, 1998: 10). But our problem here is perhaps less acute. It is not that the male component of the judiciary is denying that harm has occurred; that is clearly not the case. The possibility being explored here is to what extent a feminist conception of harm might be introduced and fully embraced into tort law, in the face of judges that 'just don't get it' (Nedelsky, 1997: 106). And perhaps this is where Hale LJ's enriched perspective might make a difference. If the dominant characterisation of harm in the wrongful pregnancy case is one typified by judges that are 'locked into one perspective, whether through fear, anger or ignorance' (Nedelsky, 1997: 106), then Hale LJ offers a broader perspective for the judiciary to take into account. Nedelsky has suggested that:

> What makes it possible for us to genuinely judge, to move beyond our idiosyncrasies and preferences, is our capacity to achieve an 'enlargement of mind'. We do this by taking different perspectives into account. This is the path out of the blindness of our subjective private conditions. The more views we are able to take into account, the less likely we are to be locked into one perspective, whether through fear, anger or ignorance. It is the capacity for 'enlargement of mind' that makes autonomous, impartial judgment possible.
>
> (Nedelsky, 1997: 107)

Therefore, on this view, Hale LJ's contribution is not important by virtue of it having been delivered *by a woman*, nor indeed because it might be the consequence of 'affective judgment'. Rather, the significance here must be that she has offered a different perspective for the judicial forum to take into account, a dialogue that embraces a diversity of experiential perspectives[21] – an opportunity to start to 'get it'. And consequently, for those who lack first-hand knowledge of the experiences of conception, pregnancy and childbirth, such an experiential deficit may not matter, *if* met by a willingness to integrate the voices of women.

Conclusion

The manner by which women's bodies have come to be regulated and objectified by virtue of biological difference is not a matter of historical interest; a notable feature of the wrongful pregnancy action is the extent to which Cartesian dualism still retains its influence in both law and medicine. The constructs that emerge define harm as a predominantly bodily experience, and present a disembodied view of (female) personhood and legal subjectivity thus serving to misrepresent women's experiences of conception, pregnancy and childbirth. The notion that a pregnancy can be divorced from its consequences, constitutive of a separate head of loss, not only masks how, for many women, pregnancy signifies the beginning of a seamless physical and emotional journey to the responsibilities which motherhood brings, but in the context of these cases, it conceals the fact that the journey is *enforced*, that those responsibilities are both unwanted and harmful.

This chapter therefore demonstrates that a wider jurisprudential view of harm that encompasses women's perspectives of reproduction is needed. No doubt, for some, this might be viewed as a further example of 'harm stretching', or an attempt to reinterpret misfortune in a way that 'diminishes the responsibility, indeed, the autonomy of individuals' (Weir, 2001: 6). However, in the context of wrongful pregnancy, this is far from the case. Not only does the foregoing analysis illustrate the inherent inadequacies of liberal conceptions of 'individual' autonomy within legal discourse, it also challenges the narrow conception of responsibility underpinning it. Pregnancy, whether wanted or not, is impossible to understand through an ideology that promotes individuation, discontinuity and separation. Indeed this process only becomes understandable by highlighting the *connected* nature of the relationship between a mother and her foetus. It is, however, essential that connectivity does not become a tool for paternalism, since as West observes this 'is not something to celebrate; it is that very connection that hurts us' (West, 1988: 30). Therefore, a more complex conceptualisation of female personhood illustrates that the unique moral and decisional burden that women carry through pregnancy must be viewed as imposing broader responsibilities that cannot be shifted, nor easily ended for many. Rather than constituting a separate head of loss, a particular and specific instance of harm, unwanted conception marks the point of a *continuing* source of personal responsibility and an *enduring* invasion of personal autonomy. Contrary to the view taken in *McFarlane*, the emotional, physical and relational harms do not stop at the point of childbirth.

As its primary objectives, this chapter sought to highlight some of the weaknesses of the traditional personal injury framework as a means of understanding harms specific to women, and to provide an alternative approach that challenged the narrow representations of how women are harmed through the processes of conception, pregnancy and childbirth. And this sets out the main argument from which the remainder of the book proceeds. Importantly, to gain a full appreciation of the author's framework, this chapter also sought to present the first seedlings of doubt surrounding the notion of 'autonomy'; as we have seen, this conceptual device can clearly justify a narrow reading of the injuries that women suffer in the reproductive realm. Therefore, it should be emphasised that while autonomy is a much celebrated concept, it is not the concept of autonomy *per se* that is celebrated here; rather the author seeks to forward a paradigm of autonomy, an approach that expresses *what it is about autonomy that is so valuable*. And just *why* this 'broader' conceptualisation of reproductive autonomy is so critical in rethinking the reproductive torts will be more fully explicated in the chapters that follow. However, it is important to first reflect on what the foregoing discussion tells us about the concept of harm.

No doubt, for some, the question as to whether wrongful pregnancy could constitute actionable damage might have seemed a rather rhetorical, pointless one. Yet, as this chapter demonstrates, the way that the courts and commentators have come to characterise that harm has been deeply problematic – some having even come to question whether a pregnancy brought about through negligence can be construed as harm at all. As I hope the reader has gained a strong sense of throughout, what constitutes 'harm', whether through the lens of 'personal injury', 'damage' or indeed for that matter 'autonomy', is far from self-evident, or based on a set of observable facts. An appreciation of the very slippery nature of the concept of harm, and a focus on those curious moments where injurious events do or do not translate into 'compensable harm', will allow a more critical reading of the cases that follow. What becomes clear, as we turn to look at cases involving *disability* rather than *health*, is that what constitutes compensable harm is a *judgement*, a *choice*, imbued with, and the product of, 'social, political and moral values' (Kennedy, 1981: 7).

Notes

1 In the context of trespass to the person, the US case of *Mohr v Williams* (1905) 104 NW 12 is illustrative. Here the plaintiff consented to an operation upon her right ear. During the operation, the surgeon discovered that the left ear, rather than the right, required surgery. Despite a successful operation on the plaintiff's left ear, the court held the surgeon liable for battery, having acted outside the ambit of consent provided.
2 With a number of recent exceptions (for example Witting, 2002; Conaghan, 2003), much of the literature in this field seeks to address the question of the recoverability of child maintenance costs as a head of damage flowing from wrongful conception claims. See for example, Milsteen (1983).
3 See in particular the case of *St. George's Healthcare NHS Trust v S* [1998] 3 WLR 936.
4 Damages for pain and suffering attendant upon pregnancy have been routinely accepted in both contract and tort: *Scuriaga v Powell* (1979) 123 SJ 406; *Udale v Bloomsbury Area Health Authority* [1983] 1 WLR 1098; *Thake v Maurice* [1986] QB 644; *Allen v Bloomsbury Health Authority* [1993] 1 All ER 651 (although Brooke J off-set the 'advantage' of not undergoing a termination of the pregnancy).
5 The Limitation Act 1980, s 14.
6 Note, however, that Mrs Walkin did not make a claim for the pain and suffering

attendant upon personal injury, but framed her (second) writ as a claim for the economic losses in raising a healthy unwanted child. Her reason for doing so was to avoid the three-year limitation period serving to statute-bar her claim. On this basis the Court of Appeal held that her claim for the economic losses could not be separated from that of the personal injury. Nevertheless, the absence of a personal injury claim under these circumstances cannot, in my view, lead to the conclusion that the loss she has suffered is *purely* financial.

7 See for example, *McFarlane*; *Thake v Maurice* [1986] QB 644.

8 Note that the point of injury here turns not on conception, but the continuation of pregnancy – a wrongful birth claim. Therefore the claimant argues that negligence deprived her of the opportunity to terminate under the Abortion Act 1967.

9 A hospital casualty department can be responsible for making an incorrect diagnosis and sending a patient away without treatment (*Barnett v Chelsea & Kensington Hospital Management Committee* [1969] 1 QB 428); or indeed failures to detect abnormalities in cervical screening (*Penney v East Kent HA* [2000] Lloyd's Rep Med 41).

10 An unwanted birth can result from negligent words (advice that contraception is not necessary following surgery; failure to advise of the possibility of spontaneous reversal of vasectomy; advice about a hereditary condition on the basis of which the claimants decide to have a child) or negligent actions (a failed sterilisation or abortion; failure to diagnose pregnancy, or failures in foetal screening).

11 This is reinforced by the *dicta* of May LJ where he states that: 'There may be a claim for what may be characterised as a personal injury, but that claim does not extend to the loss of earnings claim with which this court is concerned' (p 1291 in *Greenfield*).

12 For example, *Allen v Bloomsbury Health Authority* [1993]; *Scuriaga v Powell* (1979).

13 Note that numerous losses resulting from tort are describable as economic, however these are categorised into consequential and purely economic losses. The law of negligence takes a restrictive approach towards the latter, which, by contrast with *consequential* losses, constitute financial damage that neither results from personal injury or property damage.

14 See for example, *Phelps v London Borough of Hillingdon* [2001] 2 AC 619, where the House of Lords held that the failure to ameliorate the effects of dyslexia can be harm, albeit leaving open the question of whether this would constitute a personal injury or an economic loss claim. Nevertheless, see the later (and fascinating) case of *Adams v Bracknell Forest Borough Council* [2004] UKHL 29 in which Lord Hoffman stated that these claims of 'educational neglect' constituted claims (in a post-Cartesian world) for personal injury.

15 This is contentious for several reasons. First, *most* women is not *all* women. Certainly, it is true that the numbers of women who *choose* childlessness, or remain childless because of infertility, remain in the minority, but it is a growing one (see further: Belcher, 2000). Second, it should be questioned what 'readily avail' means; as Laura Purdy (1997) notes, pregnancy often results, not out of *desire* for motherhood, but rather through the non-use of contraception or because of the unavailability of abortion services. While the former tends to be conceptualised as careless or irresponsible, as Lee and Jackson (2002: 128) point out, the perception of 'the reliability of contraception is fundamentally flawed'.

16 As Quick (2002: 7) suggests, 'such references to reasonable public attitudes are a convenient but poor disguise for judicial policy-making'.

17 Eileen McDonagh (1996) argues that the injury of wrongful pregnancy is analogous to the law of rape, or indeed kidnapping, since these are wrongs based on the

absence of consent. Similarly, Alistair Mullis (1993: 325) places considerable emphasis on whether a pregnancy is desired or not, and suggests that as 'a consequence, pregnancy may be a personal injury in some cases but not in others'.
18 See further the Judicial Studies Board Guidelines (2004: 56, 25 respectively). The disparity of awards for injuries to the female reproductive system is particularly curious. General damages for infertility range from £3,500 to £93,000 (at the lower end, damages of between £3,500 and £7,000 may be recovered even where the injured person would not have had children in any event), while a failed sterilisation attracts an award 'in the region of £5,500'.
19 Betty Friedan (cited in Eisenstein, 1988: 105) puts forward a similar view in the context of maternity rights, commenting: 'I think the time has come to acknowledge that women are different from men, and that there has to be a concept of equality that takes into account that women are the ones who have the babies. We shouldn't be stuck with always using a male model, trying to twist pregnancy into something that's like a hernia.'
20 This enquiry is, however, slightly different to saying that men and women tend to approach and understand moral obligations differently, as theorists such as Carol Gilligan (1982) have claimed. Gilligan's research findings revealed that while women tend to privilege relationships and their connection to others, men, by contrast, value individual autonomy and separation. Here, however, the claim queried is whether *experience* rather than *gender* might valuably inform judicial decision making.
21 See further, Erika Rackley's (2006) excellent critique as to the significance, both in terms of understandings of the judge and judging, of Baroness Hale's appointment to the appellate committee of the House of Lords.

Chapter 3

Health, disability and harm

> The inspector took another sweet and pushed the bag to me.
> '... and each foot shall have five toes', he quoted. 'You remember that?'
> 'Yes', I admitted, unhappily.
> 'Well, every part of the definition is as important as any other; and if a child doesn't come within it, then it isn't human, and that means it doesn't have a soul. It is not in the image of God, it is an imitation, and in the imitations there is always some mistake. Only God produces perfection, so although deviations may look like us in many ways, they cannot be really human. They are something quite different.'
> (Wyndham, 1955: 55)

According to Barry Schwartz, everything suffers from comparison. Rather than measuring human experience as either 'good' or 'bad' in absolute terms, 'comparisons are the only meaningful benchmark' (2004: 181). In many contexts, this proves generally unproblematic, but, as history testifies, physiological, sexual, gender, ethnic or religious benchmarking has served to exclude and oppress those who fail to fit within the privileged, 'normal' blueprint that comparison so often gives rise to. Of course, these are not self-evident or objective norms: as Georges Canguilhem comments in the context of physiology, the concept of norm 'cannot be reduced to an objective concept determinable by scientific methods. Strictly speaking, then, there is no biological science of the normal' (Canguilhem, 1991: 228). Yet despite the apparent ease by which the 'normal' elides with the 'natural', such norms arise neither 'naturally' nor 'innocently':

> A norm is in effect the possibility of a reference only when it has been established or chosen as the expression of a preference and as the instrument of a will to substitute a satisfying state of affairs for a disappointing one. Every preference for a possible order is accompanied, most often *implicitly*, by the aversion for the opposite possible order. That which diverges from the preferable in a given area of evaluation is

not the indifferent but the repulsive or more exactly, the repulsed, the detestable.

(Canguilhem, 1991: 240)

Among the most susceptible to exclusion from the 'elusive' physiological model of 'normality' are people with disabilities. Portrayed as 'tragic victims of some unfortunate accident or disease, as people who do not function normally' (Watson, 1998: 147), as 'objects of pity, and burdens to society' (Phillips, 2001: 195), it is hard to disagree that disability 'seems to be all about real bodies that are physically, sensorily or intellectually different in *undesirable* ways' (Thomas, 2002: 64). And in the realm of reproduction, what may be viewed as 'undesirable' increasingly translates into a 'risk', a potentially avoidable consequence. As prenatal and pre-implantation genetic diagnostic techniques offer 'new alternatives for action in fields which up until now were beyond human influence' (Hildt, 2002: 69), prospective parenthood no longer turns upon quantitative questions alone ('How many children?'). Our increasing ability to detect an ever-greater range of 'harmful' genetic conditions means that parents frequently confront the question of qualitative choice ('What kind of child?'). But the question of what kind of child to have, as Buchanan *et al*, (2000: 210) comment, is 'one of the most controversial components of reproductive freedom'. Disagreements exist here as to the justification for, and interests implicated in, utilising reprogenetic and abortion practices to avoid the 'risk' of a disabled child. Seen by some as driven by cost-benefit analyses to avoid the state or individuals bearing the costs of disability (Bailey, 1996), or as confirming a general public hostility towards those with impairments (Barnes *et al*, 1999), reprogenetics are viewed as inherently discriminatory. An alternative perspective suggests that the avoidance of conception or termination of pregnancy might actually benefit the prospective child under circumstances where it would otherwise live with intolerable pain and suffering as a result of severe disability (Morgan, 1990). But, of the most widely cited justifications is the 'Parental Interests Argument', which holds that parents should be entitled to avoid the prospect of a disabled child since the hardship involved in its care may be substantially greater than caring for a non-disabled child.

Taken at face value, the 'Parental Interests Argument' seems quite convincing; since it is canvassed in terms of the 'harms' that parents might face in caring for a disabled child, it most certainly appears to centralise the *interests* of parents. Furthermore, it seems to hold some resonance with the idea that the desire to have a child healthy and free from disability is 'natural' – a position that is not regarded as being incompatible with the 'generally accepted notion that an individual already born with that condition should receive appropriate respect with full civil and human rights' (Deech, 1998: 713). However, a close attention as to *when* the 'Parental Interests Argument' comes into play reveals that it is far from a value-neutral or permissive concept. Rather than affording broad scope to parental interests in the reproductive realm, as the term might seem to imply, we find instead that it holds a quite qualified and contingent application. For example, in the context of English abortion legislation where this justification is commonly invoked, what it justifies is *differential* treatment between particular reproductive outcomes; and significantly, for abortions past 24 weeks, the 'Parental Interests Argument' critically depends on the prospective child being born *disabled*. While section 37 of the Human Fertilisation and Embryology Act 1990 ('1990 Act') created a general gestational upper limit of 24 weeks for lawful abortion, under section 1(1)(d) of the Abortion Act 1967 ('1967 Act'), a woman may lawfully terminate up to term where there is a substantial risk that if born, a child will be seriously handicapped.[1] As Sheldon and Wilkinson (2001: 88) comment, the impact of s 1(1)(d) is to create a strict dichotomy in 'explicitly distinguishing between the termination of (presumed) disabled foetuses and non-disabled foetuses in the sense of providing that the former is permissible while the latter, in the absence of other contraindications, is not'.[2] In other words, absent of other considerations such as a serious risk to the pregnant woman's life or health, a termination is only justified beyond 24 weeks on the grounds of foetal abnormality; all other abortions (including that of the presumed healthy foetus) must occur before that point. Given the large disparity in treatment between disabled and non-disabled foetuses, it is hardly surprising that disability rights activists regard existing abortion law as serving to discriminate against individuals with disabilities (see for example Morris, 1991). And, the same provision is also open to a further claim; since a woman's ability to terminate a pregnancy past 24 weeks is contingent upon which of the two classes of foetus *she* carries, it is arguable that English abortion law discriminates against 'particular' kinds of women (Priaulx, 2006).

As this chapter wishes to make apparent, the view that the 'Parental Interests Argument' actually advances parental interests is deeply flawed. While foregoing analysis has illustrated initial concerns with the concept of autonomy and its invocation in the wrongful pregnancy suit, this chapter adds greater force for that view in the context of claims for child maintenance. As will be argued, although often advanced in the name of reproductive autonomy, rather than justifying 'reproductive freedom', this theoretical perspective has not only served to *restrict* and limit reproductive choice, but has perpetuated harmful and invidious assumptions about individuals living with impairment. Yet, the Parental Interests Argument has proved pervasive, and it is precisely this theoretical perspective that has shaped the recent development of the wrongful conception and birth cases in English law. While the dramatic disparity in the treatment of different kinds of reproductive outcomes can be seen in relation to English abortion legislation, this has also become a central feature of the reproductive torts, where ultimately, success in these suits has pivoted upon whether the negligently born child is *healthy* or *disabled*; and it is this very dichotomy that lies at the heart of the 'Parental Interests Argument'.

Illustrating the limitations of the notion that caring for a disabled child is harmful and sufficiently distinctive from the (judicially viewed harm*less*) experience of caring for a non-disabled child, this chapter demonstrates the need for a contextual view of reproductive outcomes in the actions for wrongful conception and birth. Since caring for *any* child must be seen as bringing about a significant caring responsibility, if there is a difference in the burden and hardship that does result, this will be a matter of *extent*, not kind. Also, taking a critical view of the House of Lords' determination of *Rees v Darlington Memorial Hospital* [2003] UKHL 52, this chapter argues that nor can a 'common approach' to all claims of wrongful conception and birth offer an equitable alternative. Ignoring context and treating all reproductive outcomes equally for the purposes of compensation is certain to result in manifest unfairness. The thrust of the argument is that it is essential that the law embrace a more contemporary and contextual approach, one that arises from a broader and richer conceptualisation of reproductive autonomy. Such an approach, it is suggested, might better resonate with individuals' diverse experiences of reproduction and the lived reality of caring for *any* child, as well as offer a different perspective by which to challenge the problematic health/disability dichotomy so readily embraced within these reproductive torts.

Emerging dichotomies

As Chapter 1 illustrated, the House of Lords in the case of *McFarlane v Tayside Health Board* [2000] 2 AC 59 determined that in the case of a healthy child, if parents had suffered any loss, then this was 'pure economic loss', which was far *outweighed* by the considerable joys parents acquired as a result of the 'blessed' child they took deliberate measures to avoid. At the heart of their reasoning was a policy decision – one that has been subjected to a fair amount of criticism. Nor is it difficult to see why. First, *McFarlane* constitutes a departure from established English law; as their Lordships recognised, under the normal principles of tort law the claim for child maintenance would succeed. Yet the justifications for this departure are quite opaque. Take, for instance, Lord Steyn's appeal to the principles of distributive justice and the 'commuter on the Underground', in determining the 'just distribution of burdens and losses among members of a society', and what the 'ordinary citizen' would expect of the law of tort in the case of a healthy child. Not only does the lack of an empirical foundation suggest that the answers yielded are entirely a matter of (judicial) speculation, but the process of deliberation raises serious questions as to *which* distributive outcomes 'carry the most weight' or are 'determinative', or whether this is an instance of 'the judge . . . consciously applying an outcome or merely struggling to explain an intuition'

(Maclean, 2004: 37). Second, and related to this, while the 'health' of the child was central to all of their Lordships' rejection of maintenance damages, even this unifying strand was undermined. While their Lordships rejected the 'set-off' argument, assessing that the benefits of having a healthy child were *incalculable* in monetary terms, Lord Hope considered that it would not be 'fair, just or reasonable' to leave such benefits out of account, otherwise the parents would be unjustly enriched. Similarly, in declaring this exercise as capable of producing 'morally repugnant' results, Lord Millett also engaged in the same process, finding that *society* must take the blessing of a healthy baby to *outweigh* the disadvantages of parenthood. However, while *McFarlane* was clear in asserting that parents with an unplanned but healthy child have suffered no loss, the future application of the 'blessings' principle was most certainly not. As one might reasonably question, if it is assumed that a *healthy* child is a blessing, then how does one conceptualise a *disabled* child without articulating that it should be afforded less dignity and status than its healthy counterparts? As the case law reveals, in the case of the disabled child, the 'harm' that parents have suffered has been conceptualised very differently indeed. And although the point was not raised in *McFarlane*, even Lord Steyn commented that the matter might need to be adjudicated differently.

Following *McFarlane* this was no easy task. Defying legal principle, largely as a result of no clear *ratio* emanating from *McFarlane*, lower courts finding themselves confronted with precisely this scenario awarded the *additional* costs of child maintenance to parents of disabled children. Some, seeking to distinguish such cases in the light of the 'blessings' rhetoric in *McFarlane*, found themselves, perhaps understandably, saying that while a disabled child was still a 'blessing', and carried the 'advantages' of a healthy child, these would be more 'difficult to discern' in the case of a disabled child (*per* Newman J in *Rand v East Dorset* (2000) BMLR 39). And, while the House in *McFarlane* also sought to *deny* damages in cases of healthy children on the basis of the third element of the duty of care principle, notably, that it would not be 'fair, just and reasonable' to award such damages, lower courts have also utilised the flip-side of this somewhat vacuous device to *justify* compensation: in the case of a disabled child, 'an award of compensation which is limited to the special upbringing costs with rearing a child with a serious disability would be "fair, just and reasonable"'. But, as the following passage demonstrates, others were willing to go much further:

> I do not believe that it would be right for the law to deem the birth of a disabled child to be a blessing, in all circumstances and regardless of the extent of the child's disabilities; or to regard the responsibility for the care of such a child as so enriching in the ordinary nature of things that it would be unjust for a parent to recover.
> (*per* Toulson J in *Lee v Taunton* (October 2000, unreported))

Of course this discourse of parental 'tragedy' in caring for a disabled child emerges largely as a result of the *McFarlane* legacy and its celebration of health. If the 'commuter on the Underground' considers that a healthy child is a blessing and its birth an occasion for joy, would they say the same of the birth of a disabled child? By *comparison* with the stories of parents who are left *un*harmed by the birth of a healthy child, identifying relevant 'harm' might seem clearer in both wrongful conception and birth claims where, as a result of negligence, 'one or both parents reluctantly sacrifice their life to nurse their severely disabled child' (Savulescu, 2002: 66). Here, we might intuitively sense a difference; by contrast with those who care for a healthy child, the failure of these parents' reproductive choices seems to make them that much *worse off*. Not only do parents confront serious financial and emotional repercussions, but also a significant and enduring responsibility in providing the hands-on care for a disabled child.

Recognition that an unplanned child heralds more than *financial* repercussions in cases involving disability marks a clear point of departure from *McFarlane*. These cases do not conceive of the loss as *wholly financial*, nor accept that a woman's caring and emotional role is the 'price of parenthood'. Rather the jurisprudence reveals a dimension to these cases, which is so clearly masked in the case of the healthy child: that the allocation of the extensive burdens and costs of reproduction are typically gendered, and that in the case of a disabled child, 'parent' so often means *mother*. Quite strikingly, the acknowledgement of this dimension to the mother–child dyad is also met by a willingness to give value to the caring services of the mother and recognise her as *directly wronged* through the birth of an unwanted child. And one could speculate that by contrast with *McFarlane*, it is the very *recognition* by lower courts of the work that women do within the family home that has led to some measure of success in cases involving disabled children, insofar as 'additional' maintenance damages have been permitted by reference to the child's disability. These cases present a very different story, acknowledging that beyond the straightforward costs of child maintenance, other losses are also attendant upon the birth of an unplanned child. Not only will a child entail a significant and enduring caring burden, but a series of fairly intangible costs and sacrifices that flow from the significant disruption to one's life plan – these individuals now confront a future that must adjust to meet the fresh responsibilities entailed in parenting a child that they took active measures to avoid. Yet, the overall picture is quite troubling, since could one not say the same of *any* unplanned child? Is it not fair to conclude that all parents in such circumstances will suffer harmful consequences? Why are damages permitted in actions for wrongful birth and conception cases where the unwanted child is *disabled* – what is it that makes the difference?

Certainly, wrongful *birth* cases are different; here the parents' failed reproductive expectations can be clearly referenced to section 1(1)(d) of the 1967

Act, which legalises termination where there is a substantial risk that if born, the child would suffer from such physical or mental abnormalities as to be seriously handicapped. In such cases, the parents *wanted* a child, but a healthy one. Typically the negligence at issue includes failures in genetic counselling, whether actual diagnosis or information provision. The crux of such claims is that, but for the negligence, the female claimant would have elected to terminate the affected foetus under the Act. By contrast, however, wrongful *conception* claims involving the birth of a disabled child do not turn directly upon such provisions. In such cases, parents sought to avoid the birth of a child entirely, and the disablement of their unwanted offspring will have been a matter of coincidence, rather than intentional avoidance. Thus viewed, from a motivational stance alone, these parents are in no different a position to the claimants in *McFarlane*. But arguably, even where lost abortion rights are not at issue, alluding to the Act's underlying legal policy might nevertheless strengthen claims. Here, we might point to the singling out of the 'seriously handicapped' child, rather than *any* child, as a ground for termination. This distinction, coupled with the absence of a gestational time limit under s 1(1)(d), might well indicate that, unlike the potential birth of a healthy child, the law regards disability as a 'harmful' reproductive risk best avoided 'wherever possible' (Bailey, 1996: 159). Given these difficulties, just how can the law justify awarding damages to parents of wrongfully conceived disabled children, while at the same time denying such damages in the case of the healthy child?

The 'disability' exception

> It seems that *McFarlane* has spawned malformed progeny which the judges are now attempting to control and subdue. It is . . . arbitrary to award compensation to the parents of a disabled child but not to those of a healthy child. This problem arises, however, only because of the arbitrary nature of the decision in *McFarlane* itself. In other words, had the House of Lords in *McFarlane* awarded compensation referable to the loss, the arbitrariness would not arise.
>
> (Morris, 2004: 15)

Beyond the discourse of blessings and burdens and the concession in *McFarlane* that the disabled child might require a different response, as noted earlier, lower courts were presented with a difficult task in finding a convincing legal basis for distinguishing such cases from *McFarlane*. In the Court of Appeal judgment of *Parkinson v St James' & Seacroft University Hospital NHS Trust* [2002] QB 266 for instance, the first wrongful conception case following *McFarlane*, Brooke LJ justified the award of additional child maintenance damages to the parents of a disabled child born as a result of a failed sterilisation in the following terms: first, the disabled child was a foreseeable consequence of the negligent sterilisation; second, that there was no difficulty in accepting in principle that the surgeon should be deemed to have assumed responsibility for the foreseeable and disastrous economic consequences of his negligence; third, that since the purpose of the operation was to prevent the claimant from conceiving further children, including those with congenital abnormalities, the duty of care was strictly related to that purpose; fourth, that parents similarly situated had been able to recover damages prior to *McFarlane*, so this would not be a radical step into the unknown; fifth, and since foreseeability and proximity were satisfied, an award of compensation limited to the additional costs of raising the disabled child would be 'fair, just and reasonable'; or alternatively, one could call in aid the principles of distributive justice, of which Brooke LJ opined that:

> [O]rdinary people would consider it would be fair for the law to make an award in such a case, provided that it is limited to the extra expenses associated with bringing up a child with a significant disability.
>
> (p 283)

However, not just 'ordinary people', but also Sir Martin Nourse who felt content to simply state 'I agree', and Hale LJ, who though reaching the same conclusion did so on quite different principles. In distinguishing *McFarlane*, Hale LJ stressed that while the principles of distributive justice were concerned with fairness between different classes of claimant and defendant, so too were they concerned with different classes of claimant. In this respect, she emphasised that this could explain why Lord Steyn in *McFarlane* compared the parents of a healthy child with the unwillingly childless or the parents of a disabled child – they were so much better off (p 290). Utilising the 'solution of deemed equilibrium', Hale LJ noted that since *McFarlane* concerned healthy children, where the costs of raising a child are equal to the benefits it confers upon its parents, the same could not be said where a child was disabled. In this respect, she commented that there was no need to take the *McFarlane* limitation any further, and since a disabled child needs extra care and expenditure, the additional costs attributable to the disability should be recovered (p 293).

As has been noted by many, the judgments in *Parkinson* are extremely powerful – as Mason comments, the case, 'in its own way, is as important as *McFarlane*' (2002: 64). Not only does the Court illustrate a great sensitivity to the facts of the case, but the judgments express clear sympathy for the claimants. Who could not be moved by a story in which the narrator relays how the conception and birth of a child were 'catastrophic events', of a family living in 'cramped accommodation', a husband who must work extra overtime to make ends meet, a mother of four other children who, finding herself caring for an unwanted fifth, but severely disabled, child, must now give up all hope of returning to work, and the 'intolerable strain' placed on a marriage that eventually breaks down? Yet sympathy does not provide a *legal* justification – so how can the judgment be reconciled with *McFarlane*? Articulating this concern is Laura Hoyano, who comments:

> Surely it would be strained to assert that a surgeon in undertaking the procedure does not assume responsibility for the maintenance costs for a healthy child, but does assume responsibility for the statistically less likely possibility of an unhealthy child? *A fortiori* it is untenable to argue that extraordinary care costs are proportionate to the doctor's fault when ordinary ones are deemed to be disproportionate. So it appears that parents of a handicapped child might be rescued only by the application of the offset formula to conclude that the child was a burden rather than a blessing, or by some formulation of distributive justice.
> (Hoyano, 2002: 891)

In the context of the wrongful conception claim, Hoyano's observations are quite correct. It may be true that a disabled child 'costs more', but whether a doctor should be liable for that greater cost is another question entirely; surely the consequences would be more disproportionate? And while assumption of responsibility is unproblematic in the context of wrongful birth cases, where the very aim of the medical procedure is to avoid disability, the same cannot be said of wrongful conception where the whole purpose, akin to *McFarlane*, is to avoid the birth of *any* child. Indeed, by their Lordships' (highly questionable) account in *McFarlane*, while a surgeon is under a duty to prevent pregnancy, he does not assume responsibility for the costs of child maintenance. Why, then, should a surgeon assume responsibility for the maintenance costs of *any* negligently born child? Since, the child's disability in wrongful conception cases is not caused by the doctor, but the disability arises as a matter of chance, holding clinicians responsible for this less likely consequence seems entirely arbitrary. It would seem, then, that the only means of attempting to 'legally' justify the *Parkinson* decision is through the remaining devices of 'fair, just and reasonable' and 'distributive justice'. Of the former, it goes little further than finding a possible chink in the *McFarlane* armour: 'it would not be fair, just and reasonable to award compensation which went further than the extra expenses associated with bringing up a child with a significant disability' (per Brooke LJ p 283). So, in other words, because *McFarlane* applied to healthy children, an exception can be made?

But, legally speaking, this is less than satisfactory; as Hoyano notes, 'it is anomalous to fashion a duty of care by reference to the *degree* rather than the type of loss – particularly where the rule is not calibrated to the impact of the loss on the particular family unit and its capacity to absorb it' (2002: 897). And on this basis there is nothing to separate the claimants in *McFarlane* from those in *Parkinson*. If the duty of care cannot extend to child maintenance costs in the former, nor should it extend any further in the latter. Perhaps then, we can look to the principles of distributive justice where people in society 'would consider that it would be fair for the law to make an award in such a case, provided that it is limited to the extra expenses associated with the child's disability' ([50]). Or perhaps not, since it is here that we find Hoyano's most scathing attack:

> Distributive justice has become yet another label, without pretending to intellectual rigour.... Appeals to commuters on the Underground to decide duty of care issues allows the courts to avoid confronting the sharp edges of tort policy – deterrence, external scrutiny of professional standards of competence, cheapest cost avoidance of risk, insurability against loss, other modes of loss-spreading – and whether carving out *ad hoc* exceptions to well-established legal principles is a matter for parliamentary rather than judicial action.
>
> (Hoyano, 2002: 904)

Hoyano's criticisms do not stand alone – and the principal reason for this is that unless one articulates that a disabled child is *not* a blessing, it is simply impossible to find a convincing legal explanation for the exception created in *Parkinson*. However, given that *McFarlane* has proved a less than universally popular decision, could it be that the Court of Appeal's judgment in *Parkinson* is driven by a 'tug of sympathy' for the claimants in this case, coupled with not just a small measure of contempt for the House of Lords' decision in *McFarlane*? As Maclean has noted, the Court of Appeal (Hale LJ in particular) 'was keen to minimise the scope and the impact of the House of Lords' decision' (2004: 23–4). And, after all, it is worth bearing in mind that but for *McFarlane*, it would neither have been necessary, nor perhaps possible, to draw such lines between cases involving healthy and disabled children.

Yet, more recent developments have brought the reproductive torts to a nail-biting juncture. As if to provide a dramatic demonstration of the inherent problems of such line drawing, the courts were presented with a further challenge – another factual variant of the wrongful conception case. Shortly after the adjudication of *Parkinson*, the Court of Appeal was called upon to determine the case of *Rees v Darlington Memorial Hospital NHS Trust* [2002] QB 20. And while the case concerned disability, it contained a crucial twist: for it was the parent, and not the child, who suffered from a disability. Here, the claimant – Karina Rees – suffered from a severe and progressive visual disability, retinitis pigmentosa. Having already given up work because of her impaired vision, she requested a sterilisation because she considered that her eyesight would render her unable to care for a child, and was also anxious about the effect of labour and delivery upon her own health. The sterilisation operation was performed negligently, and the claimant later gave birth to a healthy son, Anthony.

Now one might imagine that since the child in *Rees* was healthy, the outcome must be clear. Since *McFarlane* ruled that parents of healthy children were not entitled to the costs of child maintenance, the same must be said of this case; no issue could arise around parental disability (a view held by the judge at first instance who ruled against the claimant). However, in closely following their judgment in *Parkinson*, the majority of the Court of Appeal (Waller LJ dissenting) decided differently and awarded Karina Rees the additional costs as related to her disability in raising her healthy child. As Hale LJ rationalised, where the extra costs involved in discharging parental responsibility towards a disabled child are recoverable, 'so too can the costs involved in a disabled parent discharging that responsibility towards a healthy child' (p 28) be recovered. In delivering the leading judgment in *Rees*, Hale LJ endeavoured to provide a distinction between the abilities of the actors in *McFarlane* and *Rees* to illustrate that the former were able to discharge their parental responsibility. By contrast, a disabled parent requires help to discharge the most basic responsibility. But, if ordinary parents are denied recovery for the costs of maintaining a healthy child, why should the law treat a disabled mother differently? The fact that here, like the cases of disabled children, it will 'cost more' for the disabled claimant mother to raise a healthy child is equally unsustainable on principles of law; this hardly provides a compelling legal reason to extend a doctor's liability to these additional costs.

Nevertheless, the underlying point is clear. In addressing the question of whether harm has been suffered and to what extent that harm impairs an individual's life can only be answered by reference to the interests the parent(s) sought to protect. But analytically this approach is impossible to reconcile with the judgment of *McFarlane*. Quite simply, *Rees* breaks with precedent, further illustrating the inherent flaws of the assumption that parents of a negligently born but healthy child suffer no harm. Perhaps Karina Rees will incur greater hardship in raising her healthy child and find greater difficulty in adapting her life to care for a child she believed herself unable to parent. These aspects of her case, coupled with a biological father playing no role in the child's upbringing, may certainly sway one's sympathies in favour of recovery. But *McFarlane* takes no prisoners: this is pure economic loss – the birth of a healthy child is an incalculable blessing and an occasion for joy, and outweighs all the costs of parenthood.

To a large degree what the cases of *Parkinson* and *Rees* demonstrate is a 'mess' (Lunney, 2004).[3] While the Court of Appeal was clearly attempting to carve out a series of exceptions in order to minimise the injustice that *McFarlane* could be causative of, it was perhaps sympathy rather than strict adherence to the law that formed the justificatory force of those exceptions. In this respect, beyond strict legal doctrine, we find that the judgments of *Parkinson* and *Rees* are simply overflowing with reasons as to why claims involving disability should form the exception to *McFarlane*. By comparison with the 'normal' and 'ordinary' experience of caring for a healthy child, the presence of disability is emphasised as 'costing more', requiring 'extra' care, involving 'more time', imposing greater levels of stress upon the family and so on. But the overall impression of these cases presents a further dimension; for what is expressed is not merely that disability raises an *additional* burden, but that the familial experience of disability is completely different in *nature* and *kind* from that in the (harm*less*) healthy parent–child dyad and therefore justifies differential treatment. And significantly for present purposes, all these reasons can be understood by reference to the 'Parental Interests Argument', which draws precisely this exclusive dichotomy where *only* 'disability' matters. So, in assessing the 'Parental Interests Argument', we should query at this stage why it is that disability should make *all* the difference, and what are those defining elements that construct the parental experience as being so serious, exceptional and *harmful* under those circumstances.

Parental autonomy

In one sense, the 'Parental Interests Argument' might be thought of as an alternative means of expressing the value of reproductive autonomy. This line of reasoning might suggest that the 'Parental Interests Argument' also embraces the notion that because reproduction is such an intimate area of our lives and the consequences can be far-reaching, we should respect an individual's rights to make choices and take actions based upon their personal values and beliefs. Arguably, the fact that the 'Parental Interests Argument' only applies where there is a risk of disability simply expresses the idea that it is *more* important under those circumstances to respect an individual's autonomy because the repercussions are much more *serious*. And as proponents of this interpretation might also suggest, in reality many of the 'choices' available to us in the medical realm also reflect this view. Individuals can exercise their 'autonomy' by seeking genetic counselling and screening, prenatal and preimplantation genetic testing, and where a foetal abnormality is detected, women may seek a lawful termination under the 1967 Act expressly for the purpose of avoiding the birth of a disabled child *up to term*; and of course, we should not forget the law of tort's particular recognition of the negligent failure to prevent the birth of a disabled child. All these instances might be said to reflect that some reproductive outcomes are more serious, and are therefore deserving of *particular* respect.

Indeed, in the context of abortion legislation, an example to which I referred in the introduction, such a reading seems fairly consistent with the interpretations of section 1(1)(d) of the 1967 Act. Mason, for example, notes that this provision is directed to the 'effects on the mother resulting from the birth of a defective child' (1990: 100), and as Douglas argues, considerations of the serious impact upon the parents 'seem[ed] to have qualified the compelling nature of the argument that a handicapped child's right to life is as valid as that of any other' (1991: 93). The impact in question, of course, is commonly related to the emotional, financial and caring burden that results from the birth of a disabled child, and is well elucidated by Barnes *et al.*:

> The justification offered is that a disabled child places an excessive burden on the woman/family/society – both in terms of additional time needed to support the child as well as the financial and emotional resources that must be devoted to its well-being – with a consequent deterioration in the quality of family life and relationships.
> (Barnes *et al.*, 1999: 222)

On these accounts, parental interests are central to justifying the differential results on the basis of foetal abnormality. The serious burden that every disabled child imposes justifies investing would-be parents with an ability to avoid that particular reproductive experience in law. But, accepting for the moment the assumption that disability raises such different considerations, if we think carefully about the *conditional* nature of parental interests, does this offer a complete or satisfactory explanation? Although fully appreciating that reproductive autonomy is not 'an absolute right admitting of no exceptions or qualifications' (Jackson, 2001: 320), does it not seem slightly odd that in the abortion context 'women are seen as having the "right" to "late" abortions only on a special-case basis, where the status of the foetus so allows' (Sheldon, 1997: 320)? Perhaps then, we should treat these so-called interests as fairly circumspect. As various analyses of the differential treatment under abortion legislation suggest, not only is it nigh impossible to find an *acceptable* justification for the foetal abnormality ground (Radcliffe-Richards, 1999), but more particularly, the important question it leaves begging is – 'If parental interests are *really* at issue here, then why should a woman with a normal foetus be subject to an earlier gestational time-limit?' Rather, if abortion legislation is based on parental (maternal) interests, then as Savulescu suggests, this would strongly imply that:

> [W]e should liberalise our approach to [late termination of pregnancy] and eschew considerations of foetal abnormality as a ground for [late termination of pregnancy]. If we are to give any weight to maternal interests, this should be the sole ground for justifying [termination of pregnancy], early or late.
> (Savulescu, 2001: 169)

The importance of these analyses cannot be emphasised enough, for the same question clearly arises in the context of the reproductive torts. If parental interests are the central concern in these cases, then why only respect the reproductive autonomy of parents when disability is at issue? Why doesn't reproductive autonomy matter in *all* cases where parents seek to avoid the birth of *any* child? Since parents' interests in the reproductive realm are only considered valuable and worthy of recognition when seeking to avoid a *disabled* child, we might be justified in wondering whether s 1(1)(d) or the outcomes of the reproductive torts are really about parental interests in reproductive autonomy at all.

However, if we assume for argument's sake that the driving force of these differential outcomes is to protect parents' interests so that they may avoid the significant burden of caring for a disabled child, then what good 'reasons' might justify recognising parental interests in those cases, but not in others? Of interest, Rosamund Scott (2003) has attempted to address this question in a detailed examination of the relationship between abortion and wrongful birth. Outlining her position, she notes that while accepting the value of reproductive autonomy ('broadly speaking'), 'the difficult question always concerns its limits' (2003: 300). In examining the limits presently drawn in both wrongful birth and abortion, she argues that:

> [E]ven if the fetus is arguably not a moral person, unless we hold that it has no moral value there should be some moral justification for aborting it. This means that *reasons* should be offered to justify fetal demise. This can only plausibly occur when the reasons are of a good, that is, serious nature. Arguably, the question of the moral justification for aborting in such cases should be related to the seriousness of the condition that the prospective child might have. This is because serious conditions will significantly impact on parents' lives and hence seriously invoke their reproductive interests. In this way our perception of the appropriate extent of reproductive autonomy in this context might be related to the severity of the child's condition and the impact of that condition on the parents.
>
> (Scott, 2003: 303)

Now these are truly intriguing claims and, at first sight, they appear fairly convincing. But the reason they appear initially convincing is that ultimately, these are largely restatements, not justifications of the current position in the reproductive torts, the law of abortion, and the 'Parental Interests Argument'. Unsurprisingly then, many questions are left begging by this analysis. Why, for example, are 'serious reasons' restricted to the 'serious' condition that the child might suffer from, if born? Furthermore, while it may well be true that caring for a seriously disabled child might significantly impact upon parents' lives, could this not be said of *any* unplanned child? And, in the context of abortion, even if committed to a 'gradualist view of foetal moral status', might not the exercise of reproductive autonomy itself, by a woman already invested with full moral personhood and legal rights, constitute a 'serious reason' for trumping the claim of a foetus who is, 'arguably not a [full] moral person'. Why then, morally speaking, should we be concerned about the presence of a serious foetal condition?

In truth, although undoubtedly well-meaning, there is little here to provide us with an analytical tool by which to critique *or* justify existing law and the disparities between outcomes in the reproductive torts or, for that matter, the law of abortion. Without a careful and perhaps 'objective' explanation of what each instance of 'serious' actually means, it looks rather like a 'seriousness' loop. But such analyses, which are used by others to justify the exceptional treatment of disability, demonstrate the dangers of using 'serious reasons'. For example, what does it mean to invoke reproductive autonomy seriously? Do not all 'choices' to avoid reproduction matter, or deserve being taken seriously? And more specifically, how do we adjudge which choices are more important or 'serious' than others? If this question is to be answered by the consequences, then it enters into very dangerous territory, since what it does not answer is: 'Who is the judge of "serious reasons"?'

At a more general level, however, arguably it is the failure to explicate such concepts, which has compromised women's reproductive autonomy, for all too quickly can the assumption of 'seriousness' become a mask so as to limit, override and control reproductive bodies. Beyond abortion and the reproductive torts, one can quickly point to alternative examples. The sterilisation of the intellectually disabled and enforced Caesarean section cases, both provide examples where coercive medical practices were judicially authorised on the basis of preventing some ulterior harm. Yet there is no doubt that at that time, judges considered that the risk of a viable foetus's death, or of the world being 'swamped with incompetents' (per Mr Justice Oliver Wendell Holmes in *Buck v Bell* 274 US (1927) 207) gave rise to 'serious' enough conditions so as to *override* autonomy interests. And similarly, we can point to the hierarchical treatment of those seeking fertility services under section 13(5) of the Human Fertilisation and Embryology 1990 Act; no doubt 'the need of that child for a father' also appeared to give rise to 'serious' enough concerns to render single and lesbian women's autonomy conditional.[4]

As has been argued, there is little to justify *why* the 'Parental Interests Argument' only applies to cases of disability. And in particular, it is the *qualified* nature of the 'Parental Interests Argument' that is at issue here. In the absence of a full explanation as to what 'seriousness' means in this context, the argument that the qualification is needed because it only applies to 'serious' exercises of reproductive autonomy, simply fails. Rather, if reproductive autonomy *matters*, then this provides no justification for the dichotomous treatment of health/disability. Instead, the only coherent approach to the reproductive torts is to recognise that negligence that results in the birth of *any* child (that is, irrespective of health or disability) will always bring about an additional burden, since parents underwent invasive medical procedures to avoid that very reproductive outcome. And such a view, I suggest,

The importance of context

> When considering the parenting of a child with a cognitive impairment, people seem to forget the fact that *every* child is more or less a burden to her parents. . . . Families of children with impairments do not necessarily experience any more difficulties than families with so-called normal children – their problems are just different.
>
> (Vehmas, 2002: 472)

Attempting to challenge notions of 'seriousness' is, perhaps, a thankless task; no doubt, some at this stage may dispute a few of my claims, in particular: 'Of course the birth of a disabled child is more serious than a healthy child's birth!' But to be clear at this stage, this chapter is not necessarily arguing otherwise. What *is* being argued is that the concept of 'seriousness', like 'harm', takes on an almost self-evident quality – we know what it is, or we'll know it when we see it. Yet, what I hope to have illustrated in part is that it is this very danger that should prompt us to ask a set of important questions: Who decides what counts as 'serious', and by reference to what values? But, it is not merely our tendency to rely on concepts that we think are 'intuitively' right that is the real problem – at the heart of the difficulty is the manner by which we measure notions of seriousness against what we think, by 'comparison', is non-serious and draw rigid lines between them. And the 'Parental Interests Argument' as it arises in the wrongful conception and birth case law provides a useful illustration of this.

As we saw earlier, the main justification for the differential treatment of health and disability in wrongful conception and birth suits rests upon the serious impact that a severely disabled child would have upon its parents – an assumption that by analogy also led the Court of Appeal to permit additional damages to a disabled parent with a healthy child. By comparison with the healthy children cases, the outcome certainly sounds more serious, since in many cases parents will have a greater (and longer) caring, financial and emotional burden. Indeed, as the facts of the cases involving disabled children demonstrate, distinctions can be drawn. Take, for example, the facts of *Hardman v Amin* [2000] Lloyd's Rep Med 498, where the mother's caring burden involved 'spending almost all her waking hours attending to [the disabled child's needs]', or those of *Rand v East Dorset* (2000) BMLR 39, where the mother 'assumed almost total responsibility for the care and upbringing' of her disabled child, to the exclusion of her husband 'from all but very limited support and participation'. Both provide female biographies that, as Janet Read suggests, are quite typical of the 'patterns of informal care provided by mothers and fathers of disabled children' (2000: 52). And, as

Hale LJ clearly recognised in her sensitive analysis in *Parkinson*, many of these cases do raise clear examples of where a disabled child raises a much more extensive burden, since s/he:

> [N]eeds extra care and extra expenditure. He is deemed, on this analysis, to bring as much pleasure and as many advantages as does a normal healthy child. Frankly, in many cases, of which this may be one, this is much less likely. The additional stresses and strains can have seriously adverse effects upon the whole family, and not infrequently lead, as here, to the break up of the parents' relationship and detriment to other children.
>
> (p 293)

If we now focus on the case of the healthy child, and assume the opposite, we will have made our first mistake, albeit a simple one – because our intuition leads us to assume that health is the necessary opposite of disability, and that it is the fact of disability that adds the additional burden, which is absent in 'other' cases. And, it is that very fact that tends to blind us to the real context of the reproductive torts: these individuals do not want *this* child at all. So, when these individuals' reproductive expectations fail, for whatever reason, quite simply, they all confront an additional financial, emotional and caring burden. A further dimension to these cases that we also tend to ignore – again possibly because we are so focused on finding the 'serious' case, and weeding out its direct opposite – is that the legal subjects of the wrongful conception and birth cases are individuals, with distinct biographies, different social circumstances, priorities and emotional make-ups. In the Court of Appeal adjudication of *Rees*, Waller LJ's dissenting judgment elucidates the danger of forgetting this contextual dimension:

> Assume the mother with four children who had no support from husband, mother or siblings, and then compare her with the person who is disabled but who has a husband, siblings and a mother all willing to help. I think ordinary people would feel uncomfortable about the thought that it was simply disability which made a difference.
>
> (p 35)

Parallels can be drawn. The hardship involved in caring for a child need not derive from the fact of 'disability' alone. Lone parenthood, coupled with a lack of social and familial support, typifies an analogous situation where individuals may honestly believe themselves to suffer exceptional hardship in caring for a healthy child, although to what extent will inevitably vary. So, in other words, if we can draw a distinction between the cases involving disability, and those involving health, the difference lies not in the 'kind' of harm and burden these individuals suffer, but rather a contextual approach suggests that it can only be one of degree.

And this point cannot be emphasised enough; although Hale LJ remarks in *Parkinson* that 'the difference between a normal and a disabled child is primarily in the extra care that they need, although this may bring with it extra expenditure' (p 295), as she also acknowledges, this is far from saying that caring for a healthy child is a harm*less* experience. In a compelling essay she details at length the severe loss of autonomy involved in pregnancy, childbirth and motherhood, recognising that the impact on individuals will be experienced 'to different extents and in different ways according to the circumstances and characteristics of the people concerned' (p 287). Clearly critical of *McFarlane*, she comments that 'parental responsibility is not simply or even primarily a financial responsibility' (p 287), but nor is it necessarily a shared responsibility. Illustrating that the burden of child care, 'in the great majority of cases' typically falls upon women (p 294), she emphasises that the burden of caring for *any* child is an extensive and enduring responsibility, since the 'obligation to provide or make acceptable and safe arrangements for the child's care and supervision lasts for 24 hours a day, 7 days a week, all year round, until the child becomes old enough to take care of himself' (p 287). So, while the foregoing emphasises the need for context, where does this take us in the debates over the reproductive torts?

As a consideration of the wrongful conception and birth cases demonstrates, the categories of disability and health as indicators of harmful (or harmless) reproductive outcomes, are deeply flawed; indeed, 'serious reasons', as we saw failed to provide any explanatory power for maintaining a distinction between different kinds of reproductive outcomes. Second, rather than assessing outcome by reference to the health or otherwise of the unplanned child, a closer attention to context and the actual differences between the individuals that care for that child serves to challenge the health/disability binary currently embraced within the law of tort. But, that is not to say that law has not been interested in context – it has. As Hensel (2005) has convincingly argued, while 'disability' is at least partly a societal construction, where social barriers rather than physical attributes, are largely causative of disability, the courts have nevertheless embraced a purely medical model of disability. And inevitable problems stem from this approach. The assumption that it is simply disability that makes the difference creates a tight nexus between disability and incapacity, and fails to appreciate that 'the disabled' are not a monolithic entity. Rather, as a social model emphasises, individuals' experiences of living with disability or caring for a disabled child are variable and will also depend on contextual factors. Conflating disability with incapacity only serves to perpetuate pathologising assumptions about the effects of parental disability on children and a child's disability on its parents. But perhaps one can go further than this – as Anthony Jackson has commented of the law's exceptional treatment of individuals with disabilities:

> It cannot represent anything other than a value-judgment on behalf of

society that the lives of the handicapped are worth considerably less than those of a 'normal' person. This is particularly true when giving birth to a handicapped child in itself merits legal compensation while the birth of a healthy child, in similar circumstances, does not.

(Jackson, A., 1995: 607)

What this suggests is that the judicial approach to disability in the reproductive torts is not merely problematic for overlooking the parenting burden that arises from the birth of *any* unplanned child, but that it is also arguable that the law is susceptible to the claim that it is sending out discriminatory messages about the value of individuals with impairments. And the culmination of these arguments, I suggest, provides a compelling case for rethinking the current approach of wrongful conception and birth cases. As has been argued here, the law should now look towards a contextual and broader social view that acknowledges that *any* unwanted child will bring about precisely the same *kind* of hardship: emotional, caring and financial. If any difference can be drawn between health and disability, in many cases (but not necessarily all) this will be one of *extent*. But, among the many questions that this might beg, the most significant must be: 'Is this an approach that the English courts might come to accept?'

Rees in the House of Lords

What this sequence of cases shows is that if the Law Lords . . . are to take their law-making function seriously . . . they must, at least, be prepared to contemplate the possibility that it may be dangerous to consider individual cases too much in isolation and on their precise facts. If the increasingly popular notion of 'distributive justice' is to earn its keep, it must force judges beyond the mantra of treating like cases alike to thinking hard about the criteria of likeness – which involves, at least, comparing and contrasting the case before the court with cases not before the court. Stumbling from one set of facts to the next is, as *Rees* shows, a formula for confusion and instability in the law.

(Cane, 2004: 190–1).

The amount of judicial energy expended over the issue of the 'unwanted' child *since* the House of Lords ruling in 1999, demonstrates the controversial and difficult, if not incoherent, nature of the *McFarlane* decision. By contrast with Lord Millett's reflection in *Rees* that 'experience has not shown there to be unforeseen difficulties in application; nor that the decision is productive of injustice' ([103]), as this chapter illustrates, the lower courts' difficulties in applying *McFarlane* have been incurred precisely in efforts to avoid the injustice it brings about. Yet, had their Lordships foreseen the numerous challenges to their own position on the 'unwanted child',[5] as well as the lower courts falling helplessly into invidious positions so as to carve out such exceptions wherever possible, perhaps *McFarlane* might have been resolved differently. In a broader context, however, *McFarlane* and subsequent cases illustrate a further concerning trend; some have come to regard the case law in this field as illustrating 'how far negligence law has come adrift of principle' (Hoyano, 2002: 900) while others consider the English position to provide 'a preview, and a warning, against following the same course' (*Cattanach v Melchior* [2003] HCA 38 (Australia) [128] *per* Kirby J).

And adrift of principle it is. In denying damages that would otherwise be recoverable under the conventional principles of corrective justice, their Lordships in *McFarlane* found the 'answer' in more nebulous concepts of benefits, blessings, and of course, our trusty commuter, the oracle of distributive justice. But where distributive justice has taken us presents a confused picture of the reproductive torts, where: a healthy child is declared a blessing, but the same cannot be said if the parent is disabled; however, if the parent is healthy and the child is disabled, then there too, an overtly blessings analysis should fail to apply – is this not a state of affairs that surely begged a return to the House of Lords for clarification, or perhaps a much hoped-for quiet U-turn with 'good grace and no loss of face' (Mason, 2002: 66)?

Expectations of either were soon to be disappointed. Following the Court of Appeal's adjudication of *Rees*, the defendant NHS Trust was granted an appeal to the House of Lords, although of interest, at the same time, the claimant invited the House to review their previous decision of *McFarlane* under the *Practice Statement (Judicial Precedent)* [1966] 1 WLR 1234. Yet despite the bad press to which *McFarlane* had been subject, the now seven-strong House of Lords refused to depart from this decision, holding that it would be 'wholly contrary to the practice of the House to disturb its unanimous decision in *McFarlane* given as recently as 4 years ago, even if a differently constituted committee were to conclude a different solution should have been adopted' ([7]). In other words, even if their Lordships considered the previous ruling incorrect, the *McFarlane* decision would remain?

Commentators in the field, such as Clare Dixon, have suggested that 'the main significance of *Rees* lies in the fact that the challenge to *McFarlane* failed; and the introduction of . . . conventional damages for the loss of autonomy suffered as a result of unintended conception and birth' (2004: 1733). It is certainly true that the split majority of 4:3 overturned the Court of Appeal's ruling in *Rees*, substituting the additional maintenance award for that of 'conventional' damages amounting to £15,000 – a fixed, if not meagre sum, which will now apply to all unsolicited parents in the reproductive torts. So, the *Rees* situation is now clarified – the birth of a healthy child, irrespective of the health status of the parents, is a joy that cannot resonate in damages for child maintenance (albeit a joy causative of £15,000 worth of loss of autonomy). However, it would be incorrect to say that the challenge to

McFarlane completely failed; in fact the 'creation' of this 'conventional award' is fairly *radical*. Although finding little favour with the minority, who regarded the creation of such an award as straying into the 'forbidden territory' of Parliament ([46] per Lord Steyn), or feared that what the majority considered a 'modest sum', might well be seen as 'derisory', the conventional award nevertheless illustrates a significant departure from *McFarlane*. After all, since the disabled claimant in *Rees* gave birth to a healthy child as a result of a failed sterilisation, the clear ratio of *McFarlane* covered precisely this occurrence in rejecting child maintenance damages. So was there any need to introduce a conventional award? If, as Lord Steyn considered, the decision in *McFarlane* to be such a 'sound one' ([33]), then why, in common with his two fellow dissenters, did his Lordship consider that a disabled parent should form the exception to this rule and receive additional damages? Does the creation of either a conventional award or an exception for disabled parents with healthy children indicate that their Lordships are truly abiding by *McFarlane*? It seems that the award might well be a grumbling – and most certainly derisory – concession that *McFarlane* might have been adjudicated differently.

In relation to the conventional award, it is far from conventional, spanning back only as far as Lord Millett's suggestion in *McFarlane* that parents should not be sent away empty-handed, but receive a modest sum (then of £5,000) 'to reflect the true nature of the wrong suffered', that wrong consisting of a loss of autonomy (p 114). Although falling flat in *McFarlane*, in *Rees* such a notion greatly attracted Lords Bingham, Nicholls and Scott. Lord Bingham, for example, considered the award to be consistent with the rationale of *McFarlane*, despite no other member of the *McFarlane* court having taken up such a suggestion. Furthermore, his Lordship considered that such an award would not be intended to be compensatory or the product of calculation. For Lord Bingham, this award, neither nominal nor derisory, of £15,000 would afford some measure of recognition of the wrong done, and such a gloss would provide a 'more ample measure of justice than the pure *McFarlane* rule' ([8]). While Lord Nicholls considered that the amount of the award should be made to recognise the far-reaching effect that the birth of a child will have upon its parents, his Lordship conceded that the amount would 'inevitably have an arbitrary character' ([17]). But it would be less arbitrary, according to Lord Millett, than drawing lines between the disabled parent and the healthy parent, the very exercise that their Lordships Steyn, Hope and Hutton indulged in. The creation of such boundaries, Lord Millett maintained, would be 'destructive of the conception of distributive justice' as well as rendering 'the law incoherent' if not leading to 'artificial and indefensible distinctions being drawn as the courts struggle to draw a principled line between costs which are recoverable and those which are not' ([121]. In such cases, his Lordship considered, drawing lines between able-bodied and disabled parents must equate the provision of damages in the latter as an award 'for the disability' ([118]). True it is that such distinctions are problematic, but should no distinction be drawn between the two on their factual merits? According to Lord Millett:

> It is, with respect, no answer to say that the disabled parent has no choice in the matter; and that if a mother's disability makes it impossible for her to look after the child, she must perforce employ someone else to do it for her. The normal, healthy parent may also have no real choice in the matter. A single mother with no disability allowance may have no choice but to go out to work ... By contrast, a disabled mother may have a husband, parents and other members of the family to give support and look after the child.
>
> ([115])

In Lord Millett's idealistic vision of reality and 'choice', all mothers, whether poverty-stricken like the 'old woman who lived in a shoe' ([115]: per Lord Millett) or those living off state benefits, can afford to 'employ' another to care for their child. On his analysis, there is no reason to distinguish between differentially situated individuals, since the commonality that links them is 'choice'. Any hardship incurred after birth can be freely transferred, whether through financial or familial means. And herein lies the problem with this so-called conventional award that embraces 'distributive justice'. Despite Lord Millett's protestation that the 'loss of this right is not an abstract or theoretical one' ([123]), in practice his vision of autonomy is restricted to the moment of the failure of the prospective parent's initial choice. The award applies:

> [N]ot for the birth of the child, but for the denial of an important aspect of their personal autonomy, viz, the right to limit their family. This is an important aspect of human dignity, which is increasingly being regarded as an important human right which should be protected by law. The parents have lost the opportunity to live their lives in the way that they wished and planned to do. The loss of this opportunity, whether characterised as a right or freedom, is a proper subject by way of damages.
>
> ([123])

But, while there are clear problems with the conventional award, and its complete failure to address the significant losses that parents suffer as a result of an unplanned child, what is particularly intriguing about *Rees* is the clear division in the House on nearly every point. Between the seven judges we find rifts over whether a conventional award should apply to all cases of wrongful conception and birth, a lack of consensus (and lack of resolution) as to whether the *Parkinson* decision was correct in creating an exception over the disabled child or whether there, too, the conventional award should apply, and a split as to whether additional damages or the conventional award should apply to the disabled claimant in *Rees* – but why? In essence, all the problems clearly emanate from *McFarlane* and the assumption there that one can locate a 'normal, healthy' parent–child dyad and a 'normal and proper upbringing' (Lunney, 2004: 148). Indeed, as Mark Lunney suggests, 'it is far from clear whether either of these ideals have any grounding in reality' (2004: 148). While all of their Lordships expressed an allegiance to the principles of *McFarlane*, which, if correct, must logically result in denying claims such as *Parkinson* and *Rees*, some of their Lordships were less than comfortable with treating those cases as being on a par with *McFarlane* – on the factual merits of those cases, they sensed that justice demanded a different approach. Speaking of the disabled child, Lord Hope commented:

> But the scene changes if, following upon a wrongful or unconvenanted pregnancy, the mother gives birth to a child who is seriously disabled and is likely to remain so throughout its childhood. Here too there is the inevitable mixture of costs and benefits, of blessings and detriments that cannot be separated. One cannot begin to disentangle the complex emotions of joy and sorrow and the intangible burdens and rewards that will result from having to assume responsibility for the child's upbringing. But there is no getting away from the fact that the parent of a seriously disabled child is likely to face extra costs in her endeavour to make the child's upbringing as normal as possible.
>
> ([56])

In line with my earlier criticisms, this conclusion (which also attracted Lords Steyn and Hutton) is incorrect as a matter of law. And as Lunney suggests, this approach cannot be reconciled with *McFarlane* since, 'it is hard to see how this avoids doing what *McFarlane* says is prohibited – weighing up the burdens and benefits of a child, albeit disabled, and deciding that the child is more trouble than it was worth' (2004: 148). Lord Scott, on the other hand, while not endorsing *Parkinson* took a different view of the wrongful *birth* suit, since in those cases, avoiding the birth of a disabled child was the whole purpose of the medical procedures; although it is a point still caught by Lunney's insight that this will surely offend *McFarlane*.

Yet, of the different approaches, the one that offends *McFarlane* least (although might offend Parliament, and future claimants in these circumstances) is that of the conventional award and its standard application to *all* cases, irrespective of disability, health, hardship and need. While sympathetic to the plight of the claimant in *Rees*, Lord Bingham clearly recognised that following *McFarlane*, holding a doctor liable for a disability that he did not cause, but not for the birth that s/he did, was 'arguably anomalous'. On that basis he suggested the application of the conventional award, 'without differentiation, to cases in which either the child or the parent is (or claims to be) disabled' ([9]). And, Lord Millett, while wishing to keep the point open on *Parkinson*, nevertheless considered that the 'proper outcome in all these cases is to award the parents a modest conventional sum by way of damages, not for the birth of the child, but for the denial of an important aspect of their autonomy, viz, the right to limit the size of their family' ([122]). At the same time, he also recognised that 'the award of a modest sum would not, of course, go far towards the costs of bringing up a child. It would not reflect the financial consequences of the birth of a normal, healthy child; but it would not be meant to' ([125]).

While some consider that 'there is much to be said for the introduction of such a conventional award' (Lunney, 2004: 153), the present author begs to differ. Although undoubtedly true that the award will be simple to administer, it is highly questionable what the award is for, and more particularly whether it is *fair*. An award for the loss of autonomy, but not for the birth of the child – how else, one must ask, is the loss of autonomy to be properly measured other than relating it to the impact upon the individual situations of those caring for their unwanted child? If the 'harm' resulting from unsolicited parenthood is based upon the creation of a relationship between parent and child, and the enduring dependency that this entails, how can autonomy hold any meaning without reference to that relationship? Does this pay any respect for the value of reproductive autonomy? Not only is the award *derisory* in a financial sense, certain to leave parents for the greater part reliant upon their own resources in caring for the products of negligence, but so too must their Lordships' respect for autonomy be seen in a similar light.

It may be true that the award 'makes no unjustly arbitrary distinction between the claimants' (Maclean, 2004: 41). However, this still begs the question as to how does the assumption that *all* parents are *identically* situated (with the same impact on their lives through the birth of an unplanned child) illustrate respect for the notion of individual autonomy? Undoubtedly, the health/disability dichotomy has been problematic, but that is not to say that on the factual merits of these cases there are no differences at all. As this chapter has argued, many of the cases involving disability *do* display a much greater caring, financial and emotional burden, but one of the manifest problems with the *McFarlane* decision has been to assume that those who fall within the category of 'health/normality' are not harmed at all. A close attention to context illustrates that the birth of an unplanned child is a serious issue for all parents, a parental harm that is suffered, irrespective of health and disability. As has been stressed, if there is a difference in the burden that parents will suffer, this will never be one of kind, but one of extent, dependent upon individual circumstances. So, while the conventional award seems initially attractive, its flattening approach is, as Lunney comments, a risky strategy:

> It is risky because it may end up pleasing no one, except perhaps the

NHS. Given the potential costs involved in raising a child, the parents of a healthy child may still feel hard done by. Disabled parents may feel aggrieved because the comparatively small award is unlikely to meet the additional costs incurred because of their disability. Those in favour of a full award in line with corrective justice principles may feel that the solution fails to do justice and those who believe *McFarlane* was a wholly just decision may feel that the judgment has been undermined.

(Lunney, 2004: 41–2)

The conventional autonomy award may well find merit with some in drawing *no* distinctions between (differently situated) individuals, but it remains nevertheless unjust and arbitrary. And, for all these reasons, English law should deeply resist the temptation to shift towards a common approach. Given that the House of Lords is yet to resolve the *Parkinson* dilemma of the disabled child, and determine whether additional damages or the conventional award should apply, there is still time for their Lordships to completely rethink their past approaches to the reproductive torts. And there are yet more reasons for their Lordships to do so, for *McFarlane* and *Rees* illustrate much broader problems within the law of negligence.

While their Lordships in *Rees* were more open about their reasons for denying compensation for child maintenance, notably the concern of providing large sums of damages to parents of healthy children against a publicly funded National Health Service (NHS) 'always in need of funds to meet pressing demands' ([6] per Lord Bingham), as Morris comments, 'the law of negligence has not previously applied different rules as to levels of compensation according to whether defendants are part of the public as opposed to the private sector. If the laws of tort were to be reformed in this regard, it would be better not to do it by a sideswipe, albeit by the House of Lords' (2004: 12). And, in the context of claims for clinical negligence, the various 'solutions' adopted in both *McFarlane* and *Rees* are undoubtedly anomalous; creating a partial immunity to the NHS against liability for wrongful conception and birth suits must now raise difficult questions of *all* clinical negligence claims, as to which are the most deserving of compensation and those that are not. And judgments of this nature are not ones that the judiciary should be tackling. But once again, we can go much further than this. As Kirby J's recent ruminations in the Australian wrongful conception case of *Cattanach* indicate, the *McFarlane* decision goes well beyond the merely unconventional: 'it is arbitrary and unjust' ([162]). In his opinion, not only is the 'commuter' a mask for 'unreliable personal opinions' and the language of blessings and benefits illustrative of legal analysis overwhelmed with emotion, but significantly, Kirby J comments that the distinction between the immediate and long-term costs of medical error 'could be said to be discriminatory':

> [G]iven that it involves a denial of the application of ordinary

compensatory principles in the particular given circumstances of childbirth and child-rearing, circumstances that biologically and socially pertain to the female experience and traditionally fall within the domain of women. If such a distinction is to be drawn, it is the responsibility of the legislature to provide it, not of the courts, obliged as they are to adhere to established legal principle.

([162])

The current 'solution' in English law, however, overlooks this *critical* aspect of the cases; the prevailing judicial wisdom determines that beyond the initial failure of choice, negligence resulting in the birth of any child is a harmless and inevitable part of life, for which individuals, in particular women, must now be prepared to bear the costs. In a society that promotes the benefits of family planning, such a message communicates dangerous signals and serves to demean the importance of choice and control within women's reproductive lives. Having stressed earlier that the law should now acclimatise its treatment of such individuals and place a greater emphasis on care, dignity and respect, providing a force that promotes a more expressive characterisation of autonomy, what is being advocated here clearly extends beyond either of the approaches suggested in the House of Lords' adjudication of *McFarlane* or *Rees* – both of these cases pay mere lip service to the value of autonomy in the field of reproduction. What is meant by autonomy in this context is a commitment to recognising the *diverse* situations of individuals, the varying degrees that individuals may be harmed through the negligent frustration of their reproductive choices. Such an approach entails responding to what the harm of unsolicited parenthood consists of in 'individual' circumstances by reference to the relationship of dependency created through negligence. If the law is to provide a convincing account of the loss in these cases, then clearly it must encompass an understanding inclusive of women's perspectives of pregnancy and childbirth and of men and women's experiences of parenthood; this requires a framework that assesses the specific interests individuals sought to protect and the impact on their lives as parents. If the law is truly to respect individual autonomy, then it must be recognised that a 'self' is always implicated in that concept – whether the harm is founded in disability, or indeed located in isolation, poverty and hardship – the experience of unsolicited parenthood will be different in each situation, based on differential experience, lives and aspirations. If 'autonomy' is ever to play a meaningful role in the reproductive torts, then the law must display a commitment to recognising and embracing the diversity of individuals.

Conclusion: What kind of autonomy?

> Terms like autonomy ... have no independent meaning or definition and can be understood in conflicting and incompatible ways. These concepts

often become battle cries for diverse political movements. Their amorphous, overarching and imprecise nature means that they can be used simultaneously by those holding disparate positions in regard to any proposal.

(Fineman, 2004: 25–6)

At this point, one might sensibly enquire as to how the English law of tort can possibly respond to these arguments. As this chapter has highlighted, the differential outcomes of the reproductive torts leaves the law susceptible to claims that it discriminates against women and expresses dangerous signals about individuals with impairments in society. If one is to say that an unplanned but healthy child is a joy, while its disabled counterpart is not, it is extremely difficult to avoid this conclusion. Moreover, if the concept of reproductive autonomy is as valuable as their Lordships suggest, then this too demands that the law must recognise that irrespective of disability or health, *all* individuals whose reproductive plans fail through negligence are harmed and suffer a series of losses that impact upon their lives in differential ways. In this respect, the 'Parental Interests Argument', which deploys the notion of 'seriousness' to claim that reproductive autonomy only *matters* or matters *more* in cases of disability, must fail. It is less than apparent that parental interests are really at stake in this argument; if reproductive autonomy really matters, in the sense that we respect that individuals have the right to construct their own reproductive plans, then the particular reproductive outcome that materialises is irrelevant. Notions of 'seriousness', without further explanation, provide no convincing basis for differentiating between those choices. Instead, what the 'Parental Interests Argument' does convey is the message that disability is an outcome best avoided; and this, I suggest, is a conclusion that we should feel less than comfortable about. On the other hand, I have also argued that a 'common approach' to the reproductive torts is equally problematic and is certain to result in manifest unfairness. Such an approach ignores the very real differences between individuals, which are not differences in the *kind* of harm that results from an unplanned child, but in *extent*. And this is an important point – while I have demonstrated that experiencing hardship in parenting a child is quite contingent upon context, there is no doubt that in many of the cases involving disability, individuals do experience a much greater caring, emotional and financial burden. So, where does the answer lie?

In one sense, the solution is astonishingly simple. Recognising that all individuals are harmed as a result of clinical negligence in family planning does not require an overhauling of the law. Nor indeed does the recognition that individuals may suffer more extensive losses that require greater compensation introduce a difficult or even unique approach to such claims. Indeed, prior to *McFarlane*, when the law was content to apply the orthodox rules of tort law, rather than relying upon nebulous concepts of distributive justice and 'fair, just and reasonable' (and of course, the 'commuter on the Underground'), this is precisely how such claims were adjudicated. And, against the current tide in the reproductive torts, for the author, here lies the solution: if enriched by a firm commitment to this broader conceptualisation of reproductive autonomy, the principles of 'corrective' justice must surely provide the way forward in adjudicating these disputes. For some this may seem like a distinctly retrogressive step, but progress is not always to be found in creating 'new' solutions.

And, perhaps that is the most important message that this chapter wishes to convey – for what often seems like a sensational progression in law, can in fact constitute a radical setback. While the concept of 'autonomy' has become a fundamental principle in medical law, the usage of this concept in the reproductive torts is a fairly new addition to judicial vocabulary. At a time when individuals are able to exert even greater control over their sexual and reproductive lives, one might imagine that this language offers the potential to provide an even more expressive characterisation of the losses that individuals suffer when reproductive plans are set back through negligence. Undoubtedly, Baroness Hale's judgments in *Parkinson* and *Rees* provide us with a strong insight into the potential of an autonomy-based perspective. As we saw from Baroness Hale's careful analysis of these cases, her commitment to the value of autonomy not only entailed an exploration of the various ways that an unwanted child might impact on the claimants' lives, disrupt their choices and life plans, but in cases such as *Rees*, it demanded an evaluation as to whether, in the context of a life plan already subject to challenges and disruptions, these events might serve to exacerbate matters. Significantly, such an approach arrives at a very different 'solution' to the cases of wrongful conception and birth; it shifts the focus from the rhetoric of the 'child as a blessing' to the real cause of the injury and directly challenges the view that those repercussions are natural, inevitable and *purely* financial in nature. Nor does such an exploration canvass a merely abstract and gender-free account of harm; as arises powerfully from Baroness Hale's judgments, it is critical to regard these injuries not only as ones that are *individually* suffered, but as injuries and assaults upon autonomy, which can only be fully understood in the context of *women's* lives. And the importance of this characterisation of autonomy is its full commitment to the *equal* worth of individuals' choices within the reproductive realm. Significantly, what this strongly suggests is that English law can no longer justify differential outcomes based on concepts of health and disability, nor continue to displace the context of individuals' sexual and reproductive lives; indeed, what it illustrates, and quite powerfully, is the real need for the law to embrace a fuller, richer and contextualised expression of autonomy.

However, this richer engagement with the value of autonomy is unquestionably in the minority. As the House of Lords' adjudication of *McFarlane* and *Rees* illustrates, where judgments are simply *replete* with references to the concept of autonomy and its importance in matters of reproduction, their Lordships appear keener to attach a financial value to 'autonomy' than to assess what it is about autonomy that is so *valuable*. And this, I suggest, presents us with a dilemma; how is it that the value of autonomy can come to be read in such differential ways? How is it that an autonomy-based solution can render the same events both harm*ful* and harm*less*? To gain an insight into this paradox we can turn to JK Mason and his discussion of an 'approach' to the wrongful conception action which he observes, 'was scarcely discussed in *McFarlane*' (2004: 15). Reflecting on the New South Wales Court of Appeal's decision in the case of *CES v Superclinics (Australia) Pty Ltd* (1995) 38 NSWLR 47, Mason comments:

> Here, it was accepted 'as the highest common denominator of the majority' that expenses for the upkeep of an unconvenanted child were recoverable up to the time when the parents could have opted for its adoption. Justice Kirby dissented from this view ... Although, perhaps, taking a minority stance, this writer feels that the option should not be foreclosed – legal principle as to limitation of damage notwithstanding. The importance of a woman's autonomy is, of course, agreed. Nonetheless, *it is at least arguable that the exercise of that autonomy involves acceptance of the consequences of the exercise.*
> (Mason, 2004: 15; my emphasis)

What the importance of a woman's autonomy might consist of here needs some serious scrutiny – it would not appear that this claim is necessarily advanced in the name of reproductive freedom. Although Mason concedes that women's autonomy is important, the approach he advocates is that *whatever* they choose, *they* should expect to be responsible for consequences. Given the context of his discussion, which consists of the 'choice' to keep a child born as a result of negligence or place it up for adoption, this most certainly looks like a suspicious reading of autonomous choice. But this, I suggest, does provide us with a valuable insight into the nature of the autonomy ideal and, in particular, how it might be invoked in the reproductive torts. Just how pernicious this reading of autonomy is, alongside the critical question as to whether Mason's stance is really a 'minority' one, forms the context for discussion in the next chapter. However, before we turn to consider this claim, it is worth questioning at a more general level – why should it be problematic to think of autonomy in this way? After all, most would accept that reproductive autonomy is not simply about making choices – it is *also* about taking *responsibility* for those *choices*. And importantly, this is a conceptual marriage that carries the language that the law knows best: that of the celebrated and venerated notion of individual autonomy. Under this liberal vision of autonomy, the concept of 'choice' is inextricably tied to questions of responsibility for, in making a decision, the 'self becomes an agent, an autonomous and responsible subject' (Douzinas and McVeigh, 1992: 3). This ideal legal actor, as Ngaire Naffine comments, is 'the rational and therefore responsible human legal agent or subject: the classic contractor, the individual who is held personally accountable for his civil and criminal actions' (Naffine, 2003: 362).

While the notion of responsibility has certainly not escaped feminist scrutiny, a notable feature of discussions of the autonomy ideal in the clinical domain is the extent to which questions surrounding 'choice' so often seem to dominate centre stage. And, of course, this attention on 'choice' is well merited; this concept is critically central to our consideration as to who counts as an autonomous agent, since by making a choice, 'one controls the shape of one's life, and thereby realizes autonomy' (McCall Smith, 1997: 24). But a focus on to what extent this has been realised for *women* illustrates the limitations of this somewhat optimistic account; while women confront many choices that serve to differentiate them from men (Williams, 1988: 831), as we have seen, it is precisely that *difference* that has served to exclude women from the realm of legal personhood as responsible and choosing agents. While women's choices to avoid continuing a pregnancy should matter, in the context of abortion, the decisional authority of medical personnel matters *more*, and *choices* to terminate 'handicapped foetuses' are taken that much more *seriously* than other kinds of abortion. And looking more broadly in the field of reproduction, although technological advance may be seen as increasing choice in reproduction, a careful scrutiny here reveals that in so many situations women are in fact presented with remarkably *few* choices. Not only should we be left with serious concerns as to what extent legal and societal perceptions of women's reproductive choice 'remains an aspiration rather than a reality' (Sheldon, 2003: 183), but we should be feeling distinctly uneasy about the concept of 'choice' more generally. However, as a deeper examination of the reproductive torts illustrates, there is perhaps another contributing factor for our disquiet – one that is impossible to divorce from concerns about the double-edged nature of 'choice' under the autonomy ideal: the increasing *responsibility* of women for reproductive choices.

Notes

1 Section 1(1) of the 1967 Act states, 'subject to the provisions of this section a person shall not be guilty of an offence under the law relating to abortion when a pregnancy is terminated by a registered medical practitioner if two registered medical practitioners are of the opinion, formed in good faith:

  (a) that the pregnancy has not exceeded its twenty-fourth week and that the continuation of the pregnancy would involve risk, greater than if the pregnancy were terminated, of injury to the physical or mental health of the pregnant woman or any existing children of her family; or
  (b) that the termination is necessary to prevent grave permanent injury to the physical or mental health of the pregnant woman; or

(c) that the continuance of the pregnancy would involve risk to the life of the pregnant woman, greater than if the pregnancy were terminated; or
(d) that there is a substantial risk that if the child were born it would suffer from physical or mental abnormalities as to be seriously handicapped.'

2. While Sheldon and Wilkinson suggest that the parental interests argument provides the strongest justification for this differential treatment, they nevertheless suggest caution in invoking because of the danger of colluding with social discrimination against people with disabilities. Their work also explores a number of other justifications, including the 'Foetal Interest Argument'. This holds that abortion on the grounds of foetal abnormality prevents suffering. However, as Sheldon and Wilkinson conclude, this argument fails. First, this would constitute a restrictive reading of s 1(1)(d), which requires merely a 'substantial risk' of 'serious handicap'. Second, it would only apply to a narrow range of cases where it would be possible to say that if born, the child would be better off dead, or never having been born. Such a reading is wholly out of line with UK abortion practice where one of the most common grounds for termination is Down's syndrome, which does not necessarily involve any suffering.
3. See also *Groom v Selby* [2001] EWCA Civ 1522 and *AD v East Kent Community NHS Trust* [2002] EWCA Civ 1872.
4. See Jackson, E (2002).
5. Beyond those cases already mentioned, see further *Rand v East Dorset Health Authority* (2000) 56 BMLR 39; *Hardman v Amin* [2000] Lloyd's Rep Med 498; *N v Warrington Health Authority* (unreported, 9 March 2000); *Lee v Taunton & Somerset NHS Trust* [2001] 1 FLR 419; *Greenfield v Irwin* [2001] 1 WLR 1279.

Chapter 4

The harm paradox

> There was only one catch and that was Catch-22, which specified that a concern for one's own safety in the face of dangers that were real and immediate was the process of a rational mind. Orr was crazy and could be grounded. All he had to do was ask; and as soon as he did, he would no longer be crazy and would have to fly more missions. Orr would be crazy to fly more missions and sane if he didn't, but if he was sane he had to fly them. If he flew them he was crazy and didn't have to; but if he didn't want to he was sane and had to. Yossarian was moved very deeply by the absolute simplicity of this clause of Catch-22 and let out a respectful whistle.
> 'That's some catch, that Catch-22', he observed.
> 'It's the best there is', Doc Daneeka agreed.
>
> (Heller, 1961: 54)

Childbirth is no longer the inevitable consequence of pregnancy. Natural miscarriage aside, the availability of legal abortion means that for many women, the 'natural' consequences of sexual intercourse can be avoided. While women's 'self-identity and social role have been defined historically by their procreative capacities' (Ryan, 1999: 97), it is difficult to overstate the significance of this development. Gaining the freedom to decide whether or not to bear and nurture children through the wider availability of contraception and access to legal abortion has been, and remains, high on the feminist political agenda. The supply of abortion services, as Leslie Bender comments, is 'one part of women gaining control of their reproductive lives, an essential prerequisite to women freeing themselves from male dominance' (1993: 1263). Not only is this central in securing a *right* to reproductive autonomy, but ultimately, an identity untied to reproduction. Of course, on its face, the Abortion Act 1967 falls far short of granting such a 'right'; as we noted earlier it is a restrictive piece of legislation more concerned with granting decision-making responsibility to the medical profession, than to women. While this remains the case, the 'reality' of abortion provision presents a different picture. As Ellie Lee comments, there is a disparity between 'law and practice', where the availability of abortion 'has outpaced that which the law might appear to allow' (2003a: 533). So despite a lack of entitlement to abortion services, given that around 180,000 terminations are performed each year in England and Wales, this suggests that *in practice*, medical practitioners are taking a less restrictive view as to when the terms of the 1967 Act are met. And certainly the Act does afford a more liberal reading. Considering that pregnancy and childbirth are *always* more dangerous to a woman's health than an abortion procedure, then s 1(1)(a) will be easily satisfied providing the woman's pregnancy sits within the gestational time limits.[1] Furthermore, it may be argued that this provision of the Act, coupled with the social ground under s 1(2), which permits account to be taken of the 'woman's actual or reasonably foreseeable environment', is capable of rendering lawful the termination of *every* pregnancy within the prescribed time limits. As JK Mason suggests of abortion: 'it is difficult to see how one could be refused in the circumstances' (2002: 49). Therefore it is perhaps unsurprising that in practice, 'there is a widespread assumption that the 1967 Act seems to have provided reasonable access to abortion services performed in safe conditions for most women' (Sheldon, 1998: 46). But some would go much further than this; as Lord Denning MR remarked of the Abortion Act 1967 in *Royal College of Nursing of the United Kingdom v Department of Health and Social Security* [1981] AC 800:

> It legalised abortion if it was done so as to avoid risk to the mother's health, physical or mental. This has been interpreted by some medical practitioners so loosely that abortion has become obtainable virtually on demand. Whenever a woman has an unplanned pregnancy, there are doctors who will say it involves a risk to her mental health.
>
> (p 803)

Taken at face value, the ability of women to access abortion services certainly raises serious questions in the context of the wrongful conception suit. For those seeking compensation for the consequences of negligence, notably the pain and suffering attendant upon pregnancy *and* the maintenance costs relating to the birth of an 'unwanted' child, we confront an apparent paradox. While pregnancy was an unavoidable consequence of negligence, arguably any further 'unwanted' repercussions were *avoidable*. So, is it not worth questioning, as Mason does, 'why, in fact, do failed sterilisations ever come to a live birth when there are often multiple reasons for a legal termination of pregnancy which are accepted in the Abortion Act 1967?' (1998: 100). Or for those unable to access a lawful abortion, is it not reasonable to suggest that parents who complain of the burden of an unwanted child could have been spared 'considerable "distress", legal expenses, and anxiety if they placed their child in a more loving home' (Jackson, A., 1995: 602)? Given that claimants in these cases had options to avoid these so-called unwanted consequences, perhaps we should not take at face value that the birth of a child *really* left the parents in a worse position. Can a child *ever* be conceptualised as 'unwanted' when the overwhelming majority of parents in these suits not only keep their child, but declare it to be 'loved, loving and fully integrated into the family'? As Anthony Jackson considers, if we strip these claims down to their 'bare essentials', we see that 'these parents are doing nothing more than appearing in court and proclaiming that the birth of their child was worse than not having it at all' (1995: 602).

A 'bare essentials' approach generates some fairly convincing arguments. How can parents be harmed by an outcome they took no steps to avoid? Does it not seem contradictory to complain that one has been *harmed* by the birth of an 'unwanted' child and the responsibilities that child brings, when in fact, it would appear that those very consequences were wanted? By powerfully illustrating the contradictory nature of parents' claims in wrongful conception suits, such arguments not only raise *general* questions as to the credibility and conduct of claimants, they also raise particular questions in law.

In negligence, such arguments translate into the mitigation doctrine. Placing a *positive* 'duty' on the claimant to act *reasonably* to minimise their losses following the defendant's breach, the doctrine entails that a failure to act will result in a denial of recovery of damages in respect of any 'unmitigated' losses. Therefore, the mitigation doctrine relates to *quantum* of damages, rather than ultimate *liability* of the defendant.[2] This distinction is important; although mitigation speaks the language of 'duty', this is misleading since the claimant commits no wrong by failing to minimise their losses. The underlying theory of mitigation is that following a breach, the claimant 'is not entitled to sit back, do nothing, and sue for damages' (Cooke and Oughton, 2000: 305) or 'indulge in his own whims or fancies at the expense of the defendant' (Rogers, 2002: 762). While the mitigation doctrine has ease of application in contractual contexts, it also applies to personal injury cases and medical treatment. Thus a claimant who has been injured through negligence should seek medical treatment that will *improve* his or her condition. However, since the court must keep in mind that the defendant's breach *forced* the claimant to mitigate, the claimant would not generally be expected to submit themselves to procedures that hold substantial risk of further injury or uncertain outcomes. Therefore, the question asked is whether 'the plaintiff acted reasonably in refusing surgery'; although what is deemed 'reasonable' depends on the circumstances, including the medical advice received (*Selvanayagam v University of the West Indies* [1983] 1 All ER 824, 827). However, as Geoffrey Samuel comments, what may amount to 'unreasonable behaviour is not always an easy or uncontroversial matter' (2001: 236). And in the context of wrongful conception this is undoubtedly true, for mitigation raises highly controversial questions. Can we truly speak of an 'improvement' in the claimant's condition when contemplating a duty to mitigate by terminating a pregnancy, or conclude that claimants realise a 'positive benefit' (Cooke and Oughton, 2000: 306) when surrendering a child for adoption? Do these constitute 'reasonable' steps? And might we feel uncomfortable in describing the claimant as indulging in 'whims or fancies' by virtue of their 'choice' to keep their child?

While mitigation clearly raises difficult questions in the wrongful conception action,[3] some will view the author's interest in this doctrine as a purely theoretical one. After all, there is widespread agreement that the courts in the UK have now firmly rejected the mitigation doctrine in the wrongful conception action. And to the author's knowledge, no commentator has suggested to the contrary. Even in *McFarlane* itself, the House of Lords emphatically rejected that they would ever indulge such arguments had the defendants advanced them. So on this account, the rejection of child maintenance damages must necessarily be explicable through alternative legal routes. Nor does one find much assistance from looking further afield. In the United States, commentary reflects a similar trend. In many jurisdictions the mitigation doctrine for the greater part is inoperative in these actions (Seymour, 2000; Milsteen, 1983); as Fred Norton comments of the US, 'in wrongful pregnancy actions, no court has ever required mitigation of damages' (1999: 836).

The present author challenges these views. Rather than revealing a hypothetical problem, an exploration of the development of the mitigation doctrine and a closer analysis of the reasoning deployed by the House of Lords in both *McFarlane v Tayside Health Board* [2000] 2 AC 59 and *Rees v Darlington Memorial Hospital* [2003] UKHL 52, contradicts the notion that no court 'would indulge such arguments'. As shall be argued, the assumptions carried by the mitigation doctrine directly underpin the courts' reasoning that parents are left unharmed by the birth of a healthy child and should therefore be denied child maintenance damages. And there are two reasons why this analysis should be seen as critical. The first is how the reasoning of the courts is constructed upon the notion of 'autonomous choice', a view that firmly resonates with JK Mason's claim that 'it is at least arguable that the exercise of that autonomy involves acceptance of the consequences of the exercise' (2004: 15). As becomes evident, although members of the judiciary are uncomfortable with the notion that individuals *choose* to keep their unwanted children, many are entirely satisfied with the Catch–22 it justifies: whatever 'choice' a woman *makes or fails to make*, she will be left carrying full responsibility for the harm*less* repercussions.

And it is the broader significance of this Catch–22 that forms the second reason for exploring mitigation; although clearly invoking a pernicious reading of the value of autonomy, it does nevertheless provide much *explanatory power*. As we saw in the last chapter, the 'Parental Interests Argument' deployed to justify how parents of disabled children are harmed provided no sensible legal basis for articulating that parents of healthy children are not.

On the latter, although we are presented with unanimity that such claims should be excluded, the justifications for that conclusion are diverse. The question therefore remains as to what 'unifying strand' justifies the legal response that parents are left unharmed by virtue of the birth of a healthy child and why, in these cases, the line should be drawn at birth. And an analysis of the doctrinal and policy concerns of the mitigation argument I suggest, unifies the divergent legal responses that have culminated in the retraction of liability in cases of wrongful conception. However, by no means does this analysis divorce the operation of other policy concerns. Alternative factors that have plausibly contributed to this development include deference to the medical profession (Sheldon, 1997), fears of defensive medicine, floodgates, or that this is merely part of a general trend in retracting 'non-traditional' claims in negligence law (Stapleton, 2001: 942). But no longer need we second-guess; while *McFarlane* left us in some doubt as to where the House of Lords' concerns lay, in the case of *Rees,* their Lordships were more candid:

> [T]o award potentially very large sums of damages to the parents of a normal and healthy child against a National Health Service always in need of funds to meet pressing demands would rightly offend the community's sense of how public resources should be allocated.
> ([6] per Lord Bingham)

Such factors may well culminate so as to provide a *compelling* explanation, but do they yield a convincing or complete one? Some scholars, in the light of broader developments in tort law, have argued that such an explanation is indeed plausible. As Emily Jackson comments:

> It could be argued that the majority in *Rees* was attempting to find a judicial solution to some of the problems clinical negligence poses for the NHS. Patients who are treated negligently do deserve some recognition that they received inadequate care . . . But at the same time, giving them full compensation for all of their losses undermines the capacity of the NHS to provide adequate healthcare to the rest of the population. . . . In these circumstances, it could be argued that it would be more sensible for patients who are the victims of inadequate treatment to receive a standard notional award, which recognizes that a wrong has been done to them, but does not attempt to provide full compensation.
> (Jackson, E., 2005: 681)

As I argued in the last chapter, in the absence of a complete NHS immunity against *all* clinical negligence claims (or indeed standardised awards in other areas of clinical negligence), or a practice of shielding impecunious defendants like the NHS from large damages awards, this is not a convincing explanation. While certainly outside the courts moves are afoot to create an alternative (though non-obligatory) scheme of redress for victims of clinical negligence via the NHS Redress Act 2006,[4] this does not explain why the *judiciary* has taken on the role of limiting damages *only* in cases of wrongful conception and birth.[5]

On this view, only the 'healthy child' (alongside the flawed belief that it constitutes a universal blessing) remains as a plausible concern. But tort law is generally unaccustomed elsewhere to pointing out the alternative emotional fortunes cast upon claimants as a result of negligently caused economic losses, and, as we have seen, notions of 'health' and 'normality' similarly fail to provide answers that, by themselves, withstand logical analysis. This chapter therefore constitutes the search for a coherent explanation. As it shall be seen, the ethic of mitigation and its conception of reproductive autonomy yields the very conclusion that the courts have arrived at: a no-win situation for parents with an 'unwanted' healthy child – and this, I suggest, is the harm paradox.

The mitigation ethic

Under the tort of negligence, our central actor is the tortfeasor. Through the claimant's attempts to establish liability, via the doctrines of duty, breach and causation of damage, our focus is drawn to the defendant: his/her situation, alleged wrongdoing and conduct. But rarely does our focus remain there – it shifts. In many such actions, questions will arise in relation to the claimant's conduct and responsibility for the damage they suffer. And in negligence, such questions straightforwardly translate into two established doctrines: mitigation and causation.[6] Although the doctrinal scope of causation is broader than that of mitigation,[7] the latter sometimes referred to as a type of 'claimant's negligence' (Pomeroy, 1992: 1116), both doctrines are capable of subjecting a claimant's behaviour to scrutiny.[8] Applicable to both claims in both contract and tort, these doctrines govern 'aspects of the relations between the plaintiff's actions, the defendant's breach and the damage caused and suffered' (FitzPatrick, 2001). The central thrust of both mitigation and causation in this context is that claimants should not gain 'a windfall where they have been in some way responsible (in part or in whole) for the loss they have suffered' (FitzPatrick, 2001). However, in terms of their general application, there are important differences between the two.

By contrast with causation, which scrutinises the course of events leading to the injurious event and therefore deals with ultimate liability, the mitigation doctrine retains its focus upon the claimant's behaviour subsequent to the injurious event and relates only to issues of quantum. Nevertheless, where the two doctrines arise together in examining the same conduct, it is arguable that there are few relevant differences between the two doctrines, other than the precise justification of the outcome. And this is certainly the case in wrongful conception. Here, the defendant might claim that the claimant's unreasonable conduct (through a failure to terminate, or place the child for adoption), constitutes a *novus actus interveniens*, an intervening act that breaks the causal chain between the defendant's breach and the damage. Because of the claimant's failure to act, the damage is not seen as a reasonably foreseeable result (that is, 'naturally flowing') of the initial breach, since the 'background assumption' is that claimants will act reasonably (Smith, 2004: 24). Should a court be inclined to agree, the defendant will escape liability in damages – the child maintenance damages – since the claimant's unreasonable behaviour would be seen as the effective cause of that loss. Alternatively, the defendant could argue that since the claimant is under a duty to act reasonably so as to minimise his or her loss, the same unreasonable conduct constituted a failure to mitigate loss. Since the allegedly avoidable loss here is child maintenance costs, the success of such an argument would act to deny the claimant recovery of those damages also.

In the context of wrongful conception then, the doctrinal approaches of both intervening cause and mitigation articulate the same notion: that it would be unfair to make a defendant liable for losses that are in some way attributable to the claimant's conduct. And importantly, these are *responsibility shifting* exercises: both express the claimant's responsibility for losses resulting from the claimant's reactions to the tort, whether acts or omissions. This latter point is significant. While tort law is hesitant to impose liability on defendants for nonfeasance, rather than misfeasance, as Peter Cane comments, 'no such wariness seems to apply to the attribution of responsibility to plaintiffs' (1997: 179). The difference in treatment, Cane suggests, 'seems grounded on a widely held ethical principle of self-reliance to the effect that people who do not take care of themselves cannot expect others to bear the costs of their lack of care' (1997: 179). So what we are dealing with is a type of 'claimant's law', which expresses an ethic of *self*-care, responsibility and efficiency. Therefore, while the legal doctrines of intervening cause and mitigation involve separate enquiries, our central concern here is upon what they both express: the mitigation ethic. Although in linguistic terms causation invokes metaphors of 'chains and links', and mitigation talks of 'reasonable steps' and loss avoidance, from a theoretical perspective, the doctrines are virtually indistinguishable in the context of the wrongful conception suit; one doctrine invokes the theoretical concerns of the other.

Mitigation is dead...

[I]n a few years' time, when abortion perhaps has become a less controversial and more acceptable form of birth control, the imposition of a duty to seek an abortion ... may not appear as unreasonable as it does today.

(Robertson, 1978: 155)

The law does not entertain charlatans or malingerers too readily. A hint of unreliable evidence may well cast doubt on the rest; or so Park J considered of the claimant's evidence in the case of *Emeh v Kensington and Chelsea and Westminster AHA* (*The Times*, 3 January 1983). Here, the claimant, a mother of three healthy children, underwent a sterilisation operation. Later discovering that she was about 20 weeks pregnant, the claimant refused to have an abortion and subsequently gave birth to a child with congenital abnormalities. In response to her claim for child maintenance damages, the defendants argued that the claimant's refusal to have an abortion was so unreasonable as to constitute an intervening cause that broke the chain of causation, or alternatively a failure to mitigate loss. Considering the claimant to be 'unreliable', and on many matters an 'untruthful witness', Park J disregarded the claimant's evidence that she was 'afraid of having an abortion', and stated that:

> Despite her evidence to the contrary . . . I am sure that, within a few days of realising that she was pregnant, she made a firm decision to have the baby and abandoned any thought of obtaining an abortion, if ever she had entertained such an idea.
> (*Emeh v Kensington and Chelsea and Westminster AHA* [1983] *The Times*, 3 January 1983)

Deeming her decision to continue the pregnancy as a 'commercial' one rather than motivated by fear, coupled with her prior experience of abortion, Park J at first instance dismissed her action on the basis that her conduct in failing to take steps by having an abortion was such as to constitute an intervening cause.[9] Nevertheless, such suggestions of fraud and commercial gain were swiftly and unanimously rejected by the Court of Appeal (*Emeh v Kensington and Chelsea and Westminster Area Health Authority and Others* [1985] QB 1012), which found Park J's view both unjustified and hard.

Accepting that certain aspects of the evidence were unreliable, Waller LJ considered that had greater consideration been given to the claimant's fear of abortion, as well as the advanced nature of her pregnancy, the judge might not have taken such a hard view of Mrs Emeh's conduct. Furthermore, Waller LJ noted that the degree of unreasonable conduct required by law was very high (*McKew v Holland & Hannen & Cubbitts (Scotland) Ltd* [1969] 3 All ER 1621), and for these reasons, the judge's finding that the claimant's conduct constituted either a *novus actus interveniens* or a failure to mitigate was incorrect, and such pleas must fail (p 1019). And similar criticisms were provided by Purchas LJ who, noting that the claimant's motivation was irrelevant to causation (although relevant to mitigation), also considered that it would be 'intolerable' if a defendant, having placed the claimant into a position where a decision had to be made, through his own admitted negligence, should then be able to closely analyse that decision 'so as to show that it might not have been the right choice and thereby escape his liability' (p 1027).

Nor was Slade LJ greatly impressed by Park J's holding. Expressing 'profound disagreement' with the trial judge's finding (p 1024), Slade LJ considered the question as to whether or not the claimant had contemplated an abortion as being irrelevant; nor did he consider that defendants in such a situation had any right to expect that a woman should or could procure an abortion at such an advanced stage – rather 'she had the right to expect that she would not be faced with this very difficult choice' (p 1024). Continuing a pregnancy to term following its late discovery, he suggested, was a reasonably foreseeable consequence of the negligently performed operation. Whether such arguments might operate in the future, Slade LJ commented:

> Save in the most exceptional circumstances, I cannot think it right that the court should ever declare it unreasonable for a woman to decline to have an abortion in a case where there is no evidence that there were any medical or psychiatric grounds for terminating the particular pregnancy.
> (p 1024)

Taken as a whole, Slade LJ's passage poses quite an intriguing riddle, which has already formed the subject matter of some speculation (for example Norrie, 1988; Brazier, 2003; Davies, 2001): just what might those 'exceptional circumstances' consist of? One possibility is that the 'exception' might apply in circumstances where grounds exist for an abortion under the Abortion Act 1967.[10] Might this elucidate the circumstances under which Slade LJ conceives his general rule operating? This seems highly unlikely; as previously noted, most, if not all women who find themselves unexpectedly pregnant within the gestational time limits would easily satisfy the criteria,[11] thus rendering the rule quite *un*exceptional. Nevertheless, considering the small number of abortions performed for reason of foetal disability, might the substantial risk of a child being born disabled constitute the 'exception'? This, too, seems unlikely; the judgment never once refers to Mrs Emeh's disabled child in any such context. Alternatively, might the *early* discovery of pregnancy form the exception? Such a possibility is envisaged by Andrew Grubb (1985: 31), and is *advocated* by others (Milsteen, 1983) as a relevant consideration.[12] Plausibly, timing might constitute one such factor, given that in *Emeh* some emphasis was placed on the *lateness* of the plaintiff's discovery of pregnancy.

Slade LJ stressed that abortion at that stage was not without risk, and furthermore, that it was highly foreseeable that she might well decide to keep the child, 'particularly after some months of pregnancy' (p 1024). Nevertheless, it would seem that other factors were taken into consideration. Waller LJ, for example, suggested that the plaintiff's decision was 'all the more understandable' when considering the claimant's arguments with her husband over abortion (p 1019), while Slade LJ thought the prospect of undergoing yet another operation in such a short expanse of time highly disagreeable. But peculiarly, he also thought it significant that 'the child in this instance was that of her husband' (p 1024). Might a refusal by a single mother constitute the exception?

In the unlikely event that this is what Slade LJ meant, the preferred view is that the court had not sought to advance any specific exception, but merely leave the question open for future courts. On this basis, what constitutes an 'unreasonable refusal' is likely to turn on *all* the circumstances. As Anna Reichman suggests, 'the stage at which the pregnancy is discovered will obviously be a relevant – although not a determinative – factor, as will the plaintiff's past history regarding abortions, as well of course as any suggestions of fraud' (1985: 586). This latter point is significant, since there are fairly uncontentious applications of intervening cause. While an act of sexual intercourse by itself would generally never constitute an intervening cause, the doctrine might well apply so as to defeat the presence of fraud where the claimant *knows* that they remain fertile. Such an issue arose in the Scots case of *Sabri-Tabrizi v Lothian Health Board* (1997) 43 BMLR 190 (Court of Session, Outer House). The claimant in this case became pregnant following a failed sterilisation, but chose to terminate the pregnancy. Shortly thereafter, she became pregnant once again and gave birth to a stillborn child. In response to the claim for damages for both pregnancies, the defenders pleaded that in respect of the second pregnancy, the claimant's decision to have sexual intercourse after the first pregnancy constituted an intervening cause. Such knowledge of fertility, held Lord Nimmo Smith, rendered her conduct unreasonable in exposing herself to the risk of further pregnancy. Accordingly, the causal chain was broken, relieving the defenders of liability for the second pregnancy. Could there be a better example of a claimant 'on the make'? Perhaps then, on differentially situated facts, Andrew Grubb's suggestion that 'if the plaintiff resolved the dilemma in favour of keeping the baby because of the prospect of obtaining damages, the court might be disposed to deny her expectations!' (1985: 31), might well apply.

While fraud, past history of abortions, risk of foetal disability, the risks entailed with abortion and timing might well constitute factors to which the *Emeh* court was alert, are these the only relevant considerations when scrutinising a refusal to terminate a pregnancy? As John Seymour explains, 'The suggestion that the unwanted birth is the result of the woman's choice to allow the pregnancy to continue need be taken seriously only when there is *nothing* to prevent a woman who would otherwise have an abortion from doing so' (2000: 80). It is not easy to discern quite what Seymour means here. Arguably this is hinting at the type of case to which Grubb alluded; albeit how precisely one determines whether a woman would 'otherwise' have had an abortion is fairly questionable. Even in cases where women have undergone abortion procedures in the past, this should not in itself evidence the unreasonableness of a later refusal. The other possibility, and one which may be in line with Slade LJ's dicta in *Emeh* ('where there is no evidence that there were any medical or psychiatric grounds for terminating the particular pregnancy'), is that such refusals might be evaluated where *objective* medical grounds exist to justify lawful termination.

Certainly in other personal injury contexts where mitigation and intervening cause arise, deference to medical opinion is quite typical. So the question in such cases would be: 'Would a reasonable man, in all the circumstances, receiving the advice which the plaintiff did receive, have refused the operation?' As Hudson suggests, succumbing to one's own fear of operations or dislike of doctors, rather than deference to doctors, would be regarded as unreasonable bases for refusing medical treatment (1983: 51). But does this exclude the operation of other factors – subjective factors – such as sincerely held religious beliefs? In the Australian case of *Flynn v Princeton Motors* [1960] 60 SR (NSW) 488, the claimant suffered serious injuries in a car crash, which necessitated the delivery of any future children by Caesarean birth – and at great risk to her life and health. In response to the suggestion that contraceptives might prevent such dangers, the claimant, a devout Roman Catholic, claimed that her faith precluded such a course of action. The Supreme Court of New South Wales held that in assessing damages, the jury should consider the sincerity of her religious belief, and assess whether this was conscientiously held.

Having regard to the religious and moral acrimony over abortion, this would surely suggest that *some* individuals, at least, might well object to abortion on similar grounds to *Flynn*. So could religions or moral beliefs constitute important caveats to the exceptional circumstances rule articulated by Slade LJ? Or are abortion procedures to be treated no differently to any other medical procedure, such as sterilisation? While in objective *clinical* terms, there is little difference in terms of seriousness between an early stage abortion and that of an initial tubal ligation, as Rogers argues:

> [I]t would be foolish to ignore the fact that many people who see no ethical objection whatever to sterilization (which is, after all, no more than a form of contraception) might have the strongest possible objections to abortion of a healthy foetus.
>
> (Rogers, 1985: 302)

Although overshadowed by arguments with the father-to-be, the 'disagreeable' nature of undergoing a further operation so late into pregnancy, the notion that other factors, such as moral convictions, might complicate a decision to terminate, arises more implicitly in *Emeh*. Accepting that the plaintiff made a conscious decision not to have the pregnancy terminated, Slade LJ considered that in arriving at that decision 'a large number of mixed motives would have influenced her'. But more emphatically, he commented that 'she had the right to expect that she would not be faced with this very difficult choice'. Given that these comments have application to most, if not all, wrongful conception cases, does this not suggest that 'exceptional circumstances' will arise in only the *rarest* occasions?

Of course, *Emeh* judgment was delivered in 1983 and, arguably, the perceived need to keep the matter open was to take account of possible future changes in reproductive norms. As the reproductive torts undoubtedly testify, much time has elapsed since courts viewed sterilisation as injurious;[13] and undoubtedly abortion procedures have gained *greater* acceptance in an increasingly secular society. The shifting nature of reproductive norms is a factor pointed to by Milsteen (1983: 1187), who concludes that it would be unjust if *all* refusals of abortion were beyond the scrutiny of the courts, *given* how such procedures have become relatively 'commonplace' in society. And more recently, such a possibility was furnished by Callaghan J in the Australian case of *Cattanach v Melchior* [2003] HCA 38, in which he considered that: 'It may be that because of the possibility of changed views in society about reproductivity, the Court may be forced to confront an argument that a decision not to abort, or not to offer for adoption, should be regarded as a failure on the part of the parents to act reasonably' ([294]).

There are, however, serious problems with these accounts; in the context of such arguments being raised in court, even if abortion procedures have become *more* acceptable, this falls far short of what is required for the purposes of the doctrines of mitigation and intervening cause:

> The real question is whether the *refusal* is unreasonable, not whether an *acceptance* of abortion is reasonable. Just because an act is reasonable, does not make the refusal to undertake the act unreasonable, for both decisions may be reasonable: otherwise the law would be compulsory rather than permissive.
>
> (Norrie, 1988: 259)

While the *acceptability* of a procedure might well point to the unreasonableness of its refusal in other medical contexts, in relation to strictly regulated abortion procedures, the same cannot be said. As Mason (2000: 199) notes in the context of English abortion legislation, while abortion may be available on demand in a *de facto* sense, 'it certainly cannot be seen as that *de jure*'. Linked to this, although unclear *which* refusals Milsteen considers should be open to legal scrutiny, arguably he converts a procedure, which is accessed by *some* women, into a procedure that women in wrongful conception cases should be duty-bound to access. Is there room for such a duty under the Abortion Act 1967? Confronted with the argument that a *doctor* should owe a child a duty of care to prevent its disabled existence, Stephenson LJ in the wrongful life case of *McKay v Essex Area Health Authority* [1982] QB 1166 questioned:

> [H]ow can there be a duty to take away life? How indeed can it be lawful? It is still the law that it is unlawful to take away the life of a born child or of any living person after birth . . . Another notable feature of the Act is that it does not directly impose any duty on a medical practitioner *or anyone else* to terminate a pregnancy . . .
>
> (p 1179)

Rejecting that a doctor could ever be under such a duty in the absence of specific legislation to achieve this end, Ackner LJ stated that such a proposition ran 'wholly contrary to the concept of the sanctity of human life' (p 1188). And these comments must be seen as holding considerable force here; the 1967 Act would certainly not support the creation of the duty that Milsteen suggests. Imposing such an obligation upon a woman, Margaret Brazier argues, 'is more repugnant to the concept of sanctity of human life than to impose an obligation to abort on a doctor' (2003: 383). And significantly, unless the woman's life is threatened by continued pregnancy, *no* doctor is under a duty to perform an abortion by virtue of a conscientious objection clause under section 4 of the 1967 Act.[14] Therefore, while a doctor's objection may derive from Hippocratic or religious origins, what of those who, in accordance with *Emeh*, would be required to submit their bodies to such treatment? Indeed, it is the *moral dimension* of abortion that s 4 of the Abortion Act explicitly protects, which is all too quickly forgotten by proponents of mitigation and intervening cause. In this regard, Lord Denning MR's comments in *Royal College of Nursing* provide a suitably cautionary note:

> Abortion is a subject on which many people feel strongly. In both directions. Many are for it. Many are against it. Some object to it as the destruction of life. Others favour it as the right of the woman. Emotions run so high on both sides that I feel that we as judges must go by the very words of the statute – without stretching it one way or the other – and writing nothing in which is not there.
>
> (p 805)

There are some, however, who would argue that neither intervening cause nor mitigation create such a 'duty' – rather, the duty is a 'hypothetical' one (Block, 1984; Jackson, A., 1995). Of course, this is true to the extent that both doctrines effectively result in the denial of damages from the point at which the 'reasonable' claimant *could have* acted to avoid greater damage. Therefore, a woman's failure to act simply means that she foregoes damages that could have been prevented. Yet in the context of wrongful conception, it is behind this 'hypothetical' veil that proponents of mitigation and intervening cause so frequently hide; rather than being seen to advocate abortion, it neatly avoids the argument that these doctrines convert an 'entitlement' into an 'obligation', and thereby diffuses all the messy moral implications that flow from this. And it neatly sidesteps the most pressing question that these doctrines give rise to: Why is a refusal to terminate a pregnancy, or place a child for adoption so 'very unreasonable'? If, as the courts suggest, parents' decisions to *keep* their children are 'reasonable, praiseworthy and socially valuable' (per Lord Steyn in *Rees* at [136]), might not logic dictate that, hypothetical duty or not, compelling parents against their will to dispose of their children in this way is *far* from reasonable? And finally, how could it ever be considered reasonable to transfer complete responsibility to a woman, when negligence has given rise to the very dilemma she had the right to avoid? Arguably, such a conclusion ignores the fact of a prior breach by the defendant. It would seem that it is not only the concept of 'duty' that is hypothetical here, but the very notion of *reasonableness* itself.

Despite these criticisms, however, perhaps we can take refuge in the fact that the 'exceptional' approach advocated by Slade LJ in *Emeh* has been 'followed almost universally' (Mason, 2000: 199). And this is a sentiment that is widely shared; as others have commented, no matter how the matter was put, 'a doctor who seeks to defeat an unwanted birth by asserting that parents are under an obligation to minimize the harm caused by the birth of a child [was] likely to fail' (Seymour, 2000: 81); 'In reality, and quite correctly, there seems little prospect of the plaintiff in such a case being "punished" by a reduction of damages for not having an abortion' (Davies, 2001: 186); 'It is clear that a woman has no obligation to mitigate her loss by having an abortion' (Petersen, 1996: 521). Or perhaps we could go much further than this – as Hale LJ commented in *Parkinson* following the House of Lords decision in *McFarlane*:

> Their Lordships unanimously took the view that it was not reasonable to expect any woman to mitigate her loss by having an abortion. Realistically, some may think, the result of their Lordships' decision could well be that some will have no other sensible option.
>
> (p 286)

Hale LJ's pessimistic view, of course, relates to the fact that their Lordships were *also* unanimous in rejecting child maintenance costs on *alternative* grounds. Therefore, unless a woman takes active steps to avoid parenthood following negligence, she *will* be lumbered with the costs of raising an unwanted child. Thus viewed, the rejection of the mitigation requirement unquestionably constitutes a hollow victory. Nevertheless, while *McFarlane* closes the issue of child maintenance costs, so too does it appear to put an end to the post-*Emeh* speculation, for here each of their Lordships took the opportunity to reject the operation of mitigation (despite the absence of such a claim in the defenders' pleadings); but of the most passionate and emphatic, we can turn to Lord Steyn:

> I *cannot conceive* of any circumstances in which the autonomous decision of the parents not to resort to even a lawful abortion could be questioned. For similar reasons the parents' decision not to have the child adopted was plainly natural and commendable. It is *difficult to envisage* any circumstances in which it would be right to challenge such a decision of the parents. The starting point is the right of parents to make decisions on family planning and, if those plans fail, their right to care for an initially unwanted child. The law does and must respect these decisions of parents which are so closely tied to their basic freedoms and rights of personal autonomy.
>
> (p 81; my emphasis)

In a passage that illustrates a judge struggling to imagine *any* circumstances that might lead a court to entertain the mitigation requirement, particularly in view of parental autonomy, surely there can be little doubt that the message here must be, by contrast with *Emeh*, absolutely *never*? Although criticised for having given 'little reason for their unanimity on the question', which, according to Mason, has left us 'to fend for ourselves in establishing why it is unacceptable' (2000: 199), their Lordships present clear opposition to such an argument being presented before any court. If it were suggested, whether on the basis of remoteness or intervening cause, Lord Slynn remarked that he would reject such contentions (p 74); echoing this, Lord Clyde remarked that this would constitute his view, even if the courses of abortion or adoption 'were available or practicable' (p 105). Lord Hope, by contrast, fully accepted the pursuers' claim that they had no other choice but to accept the child, it being 'unthinkable for them to have put her out for adoption once she had been born' (p 90). Lord Millett, by contrast, stood alone in conceding that the mitigation requirement might operate, albeit in 'hard to imagine' circumstances:

> I regard the proposition that it is unreasonable for parents not to have an abortion or place a child for adoption as far more repugnant than the characterisation of the birth of a healthy and normal child as a detriment. I agree with Slade LJ in *Emeh* that save in the most exceptional circumstances (which it is very hard to imagine) it can never be unreasonable for parents or prospective parents to decline to terminate a pregnancy or to place the child for adoption.
>
> (p 113)

Despite Lord Millett's sympathy with *Emeh*, the majority line seems quite clear. Whether described as repugnant, inconceivable, unthinkable, a breach of autonomy or unreasonable, is it not beyond question that *McFarlane* heralds the end of the mitigation requirement in the action of wrongful conception? Does it not appear that, 'the language of the speeches is so strong that the contrary would seem unarguable in any imaginable circumstance' (Whitfield, 2002: 243)? Certainly, for most, *McFarlane* constitutes the end of the matter. No longer will the courts ever construe a refusal to terminate a pregnancy or surrender a child for adoption as so unreasonable as to constitute either a failure to mitigate or a break in the chain of causation. And significantly, no UK court since has attempted to invoke either doctrine.

But what if for one moment, we remove this talk of chains, intervening cause, duty to take reasonable steps and loss minimisation? What arguments can be advanced so as to enable the courts to *deny* child maintenance damages? Reflecting on comparative law on the subject, Lord Steyn remarked that the grounds for such decisions are diverse:

> Sometimes it is said that there was no personal injury, a lack of foreseeability of the costs of bringing up the child, no causative link between the breach of duty and the birth of a healthy child, or no loss since the joys of having a child always outweigh the financial costs. Sometimes the idea that the couple could have avoided the financial costs of bringing up the unwanted child by abortion or adoption has influenced decisions. Policy considerations undoubtedly played a role in decisions denying a remedy for the cost of bringing up an unwanted child.
>
> (p 81)

The diversity of responses demonstrates more than a judicial eagerness to reject these claims; it also illustrates the highly interchangeable nature of legal doctrine. Having reflected on the close relationship between the doctrines of intervening cause and mitigation, this must beg some questions: What differentiates these from concepts of duty or damage? Do all these concepts play their own distinct roles in the action for wrongful conception? As previous chapters have sought to illustrate, these concepts are not merely 'self-evident, objective and gender-neutral categories' that guide the judge in his 'fact-finding' mission towards an *objective* resolution. Rather, these concepts overlap and intersect; they are variable, interchangeable, policy-laden smokescreens, 'open to judicial manipulation' (Conaghan and Mansell, 1999: 52). In the context of wrongful conception, the notion of judges speaking in 'five different voices' (per Brooke LJ p 277 in *Parkinson*), or concessions like those of Lord Hope that 'there may indeed be other ways of expressing the point' (at [52] in *Rees*), do little to disguise the policy-driven and interchangeable nature of legal doctrine – they fully expose that something else is at play.

Therefore, removing these doctrinal distinctions might well enable us to hear what judges are *really* saying. For once we do so, what we are left with is a highly emotive language that speaks of benefits, love, joy, acceptance, and *much wanted* children. But this picture of familial bliss is far from innocuous – it is a policy decision, one that still entails the shifting of responsibility to *women* for failing to *choose* to exercise their reproductive autonomy. As the next section argues, although *McFarlane* rejected the mitigation doctrine, the arguments generated in its stead are surprisingly familiar.

... Long live choice!

Our daily existence confronts us with a series of choices; many of them fairly trivial and others quite critical with quite serious repercussions. We choose to get out of bed in the morning, to go to work, to purchase a television set, to have a family, to care for a sick relative, to move country and so on. Undoubtedly some of us have a greater range of choices available to us than others, and the wealth of choices we experience will depend upon a series of factors, including socio-economic ones – but the fact remains, all of us make a staggering number of choices throughout our lives. However, what constitutes a 'choice' isn't quite this straightforward; going to work, for example, might not feel like much of a choice if one considers that the bills do not pay themselves, and stomachs do not get filled on nothing. And it is precisely this view that complicates how we feel about choice. Whatever our personal sentiments, we do still have to make a decision to work – and if we think that a 'decision' can be equated with a choice, then deciding, not deciding, or even letting things happen by themselves, also constitute choices. But what if for some reason one's decision occurs under less than perfect conditions, does this still count as a choice? Arguably, decisions made under harsh conditions, perhaps where the consequences of any decision are too horrible or because vital information is lacking, still constitute choices, but just not nice ones, or informed ones. Given this, we can choose to choose, choose not to choose, and we still choose even when those choices don't feel like choices at all. If one feels slightly bamboozled by whether these instances of choosing *should* really constitute a choice or not, the reader can take some refuge in the fact that judges aren't really sure either.

The mitigation doctrine, of course, concerns claimants' choices; and the view of the *McFarlane* court was that to conceptualise the failure to choose an abortion or place a child up for adoption *as unreasonable* was quite repugnant – more repugnant than declaring a healthy child to be a detriment. On the other hand, that is *not* to say it isn't a choice – there is still the issue that the parents had nevertheless *kept* the child. So was that a choice, even if not an unreasonable one? Not wishing to place 'undue emphasis' on the fact that the pursuers 'chose to keep the child', it is much easier, decided Lord Hope, to discard all this talk of choice – even accept that 'they had no other choice' (p 97). But, his Lordship concluded, the fact remains 'they are now bringing the child up within the family' (p 97). So perhaps they did make a choice? Also clearly baffled by the question of whether parents might *choose* to keep a child or not was Lord Millett. Accepting that if it was a choice, 'it is one they should never have been called upon to make'; or he considered, perhaps it might not be a choice at all, 'if there is no realistic alternative'. A better substitute must surely be the word 'decision' – but he conceded, 'even this is not necessarily appropriate' (p 113). Continuing these painful deliberations his Lordship stated:

> It is doubtful whether Mr and Mrs McFarlane made any conscious decision to keep Catherine. It is more likely that they never even contemplated an alternative. The critical fact is that they have kept her, not that they deliberately chose or decided to do so. It is, of course, that act which has inevitably involved them in the responsibility and expense of bringing her up.
>
> (p 113)

So, not really a choice, or a realistic alternative, and nor is it appropriate to call it a decision; or if it *is* a choice then by no means a conscious one, and certainly not one they should have had to make – but it is a choice, or perhaps an act, and one for which they should inevitably be responsible. But if that fails to convince, then perhaps one could place emphasis on the fact that the pursuers 'accepted the addition to their family' (per Lord Clyde p 105); should that sound too much like a decision, then we might just say that they simply 'end up with an addition to their family' (per Lord Clyde p 105). Or perhaps, like Lords Steyn and Slynn, it is just better all round to avoid the word 'choice' and reject child maintenance damages via notions of distributive justice or duty. Indeed, their Lordships' utter lack of unanimity here perhaps serves to illustrate the propensity of their concerns with the concept of choice – but why?

Well, conceding that the pursuers have *no choice* makes their Lordships' conclusion that child maintenance damages should be denied that much trickier to arrive at; after all, it hardly seems reasonable to hold pursuers responsible for negligence, which has placed them in the position of having no choice. Making individuals fully responsible for the torts of others, where all the ingredients of negligence are made out *and* when the claimants' own conduct is beyond question, is clearly problematic. However, if their Lordships were more candid in expressing that the pursuers *do* have a choice and did exercise a choice thereby evidencing that the outcome was wanted, rather than harmful – an entirely desirable route in justifying these claimants' responsibility for the consequences – then that necessarily entails a discussion as to what the choice precisely consists of. And herein rests their Lordships' dilemma. Choosing to keep the child logically implies that pursuers could have chosen *otherwise*; and the only legal means of exercising such a 'choice' would be via abortion or adoption. The problem for the *McFarlane* court is that holding the pursuers responsible *for not* exercising this choice sounds rather like saying that they have acted 'very unreasonably'. In other words, this analytical route would require the court to invoke the very doctrine that they unanimously rejected – mitigation – hence their Lordships' prevarication over choice.

In an attempt to avoid these difficulties, slightly different strategies were employed. Lord Hope, clearly uncomfortable with the concept of choice, instead placed great emphasis on the 'benefits' arising out of (unwanted) parenthood and considered it unreasonable to leave such benefits 'out of account'. Invoking a slightly different line of analysis was Lord Clyde, who suggested that:

> A stronger argument can be presented to the effect that the obligation to maintain the child is an obligation imposed upon the parents of the child and that they will not be held to have sustained any loss caused by the defenders' negligence if, *despite the negligence*, they are able to meet those obligations.
>
> (p 103)

At first glance, it is not quite clear what his Lordship is saying here; does he mean that because the (uninsured) claimants can *afford* to pay for the child's upbringing, the defendants should escape liability? A curious kind of reasoning that if applied generally would leave wealthy claimants, who are better able to absorb losses than poorer ones, uncompensated. Or is the central emphasis upon the parents' *choice* to keep the child? Rejecting that the decision to keep the child could constitute an intervening cause, Lord Clyde considered the situation a peculiar one:

> Without surrendering the child the pursuers cannot realistically be returned to the same position as they would have been in had they not sustained the alleged wrong. But it cannot reasonably be claimed that they should have surrendered the child, as by adoption or, far less, by abortion, so as to achieve some kind of approximation to the previous situation . . . There is no issue here of mitigation of damages. But while it is perfectly reasonable for the pursuers to have accepted the addition to their family, it does not seem to me reasonable that they should in effect be relieved of the financial obligations of caring for their child.
>
> (p 105)

Unreasonable to expect parents to surrender the child, reasonable for them to keep the child, but unreasonable for them to receive compensation – does this make *any* sense? It does if we insert the words his Lordship conveniently avoided – what he is really saying is that the parents *benefit* from keeping the child. On this view, his approach is no different to that of Lord Hope. Although many of their Lordships rejected the 'benefits' approach, arguably this strategy is employed by all; the judgments are simply littered with judicial pronouncements as to how the child, though originally unwanted, is now very clearly wanted, having been accepted willingly and lovingly into the family (Lord Slynn, p 75; Lord Hope, pp 89, 97; Lord Steyn, pp 77, 82; Lord Clyde, pp 104–5; Lord Millett, p 106). But by no means are these judicial commendations; rather, these literary tools are designed to illustrate how the apparently injurious situation is really a positive and wanted one:

> In situations in which parents are pleased to keep their children, it is suggested that it is straining the concept of an 'injury' to state that one has been suffered by them. It appears contradictory to state on the one hand that a child is so unwanted that damages should be available for its very existence and upbringing, while on the other confirming that it is so wanted by these parents that they have chosen to keep the child.
> (Jackson, A., 1996)

Choice emerges here, but more implicitly. This approach not only stresses parental expressions of joy, but takes the view that keeping the child provides *objective* evidence that no actionable damage arises in such cases. Indeed, failing to surrender the child illustrates how parents have now come to regard their once unwanted child as very much wanted, for is it not true that 'by and large, a person who is deeply injured will go to considerable lengths to avoid the consequences of that injury' (Mason, 1998: 101)? In other words, this approach *assumes* that parents *did have a choice*, but it is not one that they chose to exercise. Why then, the argument runs, should a tortfeasor be responsible for the financial costs of raising such a loved and *chosen* child? Despite their protestations to the contrary, the logic underpinning *McFarlane* is that parents who fail to avoid the consequences are not just left unharmed, but benefited. A conclusion made all the more remarkable considering Lord Millett's concession that the presumption had little, if any, factual evidential basis:

> [I]n truth the failure to have an abortion or to place the child for adoption *is no evidence* that the parents themselves regard the child as being, on balance, beneficial . . . But I am persuaded of the truth of the general proposition.
> (p 111)

Nor indeed, does it hold any legal basis. As Arthur Ripstein comments, if one person's negligence injures another, 'but also confers a benefit, the tortfeasor cannot appeal to the benefit in order to reduce the damages she must pay . . . since conferring a benefit is irrelevant, a mistaken belief about benefits conferred cannot excuse' (1999: 205).

So what conclusions might we reach at this stage? Conceding that claimants have *no choice* but to keep the child confronts the court with a dilemma;

this would absolve the *claimant* of all responsibility. Nor does an objective presumption of 'benefits' or 'no injury' provide a suitable means of avoiding the difficulties of choice, since it holds no factual or legal foundation. Perhaps then, the simpler route is to sustain that claimants *do* have a 'real choice' to keep the child? Such an argument was advanced by Priestly JA in the Australian case of *CES v Superclinics (Australia) Pty Ltd* (1995) 38 NSWLR 47. Rejecting that the defendants should be liable for the costs of child maintenance, the judge commented:

> The point in the present case is that the plaintiff chose to keep her child. The anguish of having to make the choice is part of the damage caused by the negligent breach of duty, but the fact remains, however compelling the psychological pressure on the plaintiff may have been to keep the child, the opportunity of choice was in my opinion real and the choice was made voluntarily. It was this choice which was the cause, in my opinion, of the subsequent cost of rearing a child.
>
> (pp 84–5)

In reaching this conclusion, Priestly JA found as 'a matter of ordinary commonsense' (p 85), that the plaintiff's choice, though a difficult one, should be seen as the true cause of the damage, and not the defendant's negligence. Though many might take exception with Priestly JA's 'commonsense' view of the matter, some of their Lordships in the House of Lords have nevertheless found the route most persuasive, including Lord Millett in *McFarlane*. Though rejecting the operation of intervening cause, his Lordship was greatly attracted by its conclusion. Offering a 'grudging support for this view' (Mason, 2000: 199), his Lordship used the 'thrust' of both the 'real choice' and 'benefits' arguments to deny child maintenance damages – albeit, following deliberations on both, his Lordship seemed less than certain that parents had made either a 'real choice' *or* derived a benefit (p 113). So perhaps better described as *unconvincing* support than a grudging one? However, while Lord Millett's application of this argument was somewhat closeted, a more enthusiastic endorsement was yet to follow – and here we must turn to consider the extraordinary judgment of His Right Honourable Lord Scott in the House of Lords' adjudication of *Rees*.

My family and other animals

> It's particularly shocking that someone in the position of a Law Lord should make that kind of comment ... Whatever the rights of the case that he is commenting on, the way in which the life of a child has been referred to as completely disposable is shocking and sickening ... There are a lot of people who don't want to have an abortion.
>
> (Strangeways, *This is The North East*, 17 October 2003)

Undoubtedly the wrongful conception case gives rise to some exceptionally sensitive issues; given the value we place on human existence, it is no wonder that the courts have struggled to answer the question of whether the costs associated with the birth of a human being should constitute actionable damage. Indeed, even the most apparently straightforward matter can get muddied when human life enters into the equation – and, for Lord Scott, this fact pointed towards a different starting point. A simpler version of the wrongful conception claim, his Lordship considered, would involve the negligent performance of a gelding operation on a two-year-old colt, resulting in a mare giving birth to a healthy foal. The mare, quite fortunately in this scenario, 'is not damaged by the experience, but the owner sues the vet for damages' ([134]). Noting that an account of detriment and benefit would need to be drawn up in ascertaining the potential liability of the veterinary surgeon, Lord Scott considered the situation quite 'absurd':

> It is absurd in my opinion, because the owner of the foal does not have to keep it. Its unexpected and originally unwanted arrival would present him with a number of choices. He could have the foal destroyed as soon as it was born. But this would be an unlikely choice for the foal would be likely to have some value and it would cost very little to leave it with its dam until it could be weaned. Or the owner could decide to keep the foal until it could be weaned and then to sell it ... Or he could keep it for his own use. Each of these choices, bar the first, would have involved the owner in some expense in rearing the foal. But the expenses would be the result of his choice to keep the foal.
>
> ([134])

Quite perceptively, Lord Scott acknowledges that the difficulty produced by cases like *McFarlane*, by contrast with the dilemma of the healthy foal, is that the originally unwanted progeny 'is a human being, not an animal', and for very deeply ingrained cultural and religious reasons, all human life is regarded by law as both precious and incapable of valuation in monetary terms ([135]). Despite these differences, however, Lord Scott embarked upon examining what he considered to form strong parallels. The expense of raising the 'originally unwanted but, once born, loved and cherished baby' must, according to his Lordship, be seen as resulting from the decision of the parents to keep the child. Indeed, we might reflect, the decisional situation of parents could be construed in remarkably similar ways to the owner of the unwanted foal, since:

> If the parents decided ... to place the child with an adoption society ... they would not incur those costs ... Nor would they incur them if,

for whatever reason, the mother had had her unwanted pregnancy terminated.

([136])

But Lord Scott, unlike his predecessors in *McFarlane*, is less ambivalent on the question of 'choice', 'if that is the right word' ([136]); realising that while the owner of the unwanted foal might well have a 'true choice', parents might not regard their decision to keep the child as 'representing a choice'. And of course, *their* perception of the matter might well be influenced by cultural, moral, religious and legal expectations under which parents are expected to accept responsibility for a child that holds 'no parallel in the case of the unwanted foal' ([136]). Accepting that parents may quite reasonably *regard themselves* as having no choice, his Lordship considered that this still did not answer the question as to why the defendant, albeit the *causa sine qua non* of the costs in question, should be liable 'for the economic consequences of the parents' decision to keep and rear the child, reasonable, praiseworthy and socially valuable ... that decision was' ([137]). So even where these parents do not have 'true choices' these still count as 'choices'? Does this mean that the law *should* always refuse to acknowledge situations where no 'true' choice appears to exist? *Whose* perspective *should* matter here? If one accepts that it is both reasonable and praiseworthy for parents to feel that they have no choice but to keep the child, then this line of reasoning leaves an important question unanswered: why should *claimants* be responsible when that *very* dilemma of choice arose as a direct result of negligence?

Perhaps recognising these difficulties, Lord Scott sought out 'determinative' arguments, and these rested firmly in the human world. Placing a monetary value on a child's head, his Lordship considered, would not only be inconsistent with the status of being a valued and loved member of the family, but with the fact that parents in wrongful conception actions never once suggested that the 'price was not worth paying' ([138]). Was it ever suggested by claimants that it *was* a price worth paying? These arguments, found Lord Scott, inevitably led to a departure from the normal application of tortious damages, since it was an exception based on 'the unique nature of human life, a uniqueness that our culture and society recognise and that the law, too, should recognise' ([139]). Indeed, so *unique* and *precious* is human life that his Lordship found it:

> [An] acceptable irony that the conclusion is the same conclusion as that which would have been reached in the case of the unwanted foal, but reached by an entirely different route.
>
> ([139])

And his Lordship's conclusion is one that will leave us wondering whether the mother of the wrongfully conceived child is intended to be the equivalent of the unharmed mare or the choice-bearing and therefore unharmed owner. However, if we consider Lord Scott's judgment overall, it is notable that on no occasion does he utter the word 'mitigation'. Nor indeed had Priestly JA in *CES Superclinics* conceptualised the issue as one of mitigation (although others in the *CES* court had interpreted Priestly JA's dicta in precisely such terms, including Meagher JA). And of course, in explicitly rejecting the mitigation requirement in *McFarlane* and constructing the issue instead as one of parental 'benefit' and 'no damage' (which, according to Lord Millet at p 115 raised quite different arguments to those in mitigation), is it reasonable to conclude on the whole that the mitigation doctrine no longer operates in these actions? Might it be a matter of confusion on the part of those who have quietly noted that these *alternative* routes appear to utilise the 'avoidance of consequences language' in holding that parental failures to surrender their children demonstrates that the benefits outweigh the costs (Block, 1984: 1115), or provides evidence of no injury (Mark, 1976: 89n)? For if such tentative conclusions are the product of confusion, then understandably so, given that 'it is not always clear which theory courts have in mind when they speak of a plaintiff's failure to abort the fetus or place the child for adoption' (Robertson, 1978: 154]). Yet, as Robertson asserts, these arguments are not, 'as some commentators have suggested, authority for the proposition that the plaintiff in a wrongful birth action must mitigate damages', but rather they relate to the 'somewhat tenuous implication [that] parents have suffered no loss or damage' (1978: 154). As a matter of 'strict' law, Robertson is absolutely right; it is simply incorrect to suggest that 'by limiting damage to pre-birth expenses, courts in effect have imposed the mitigation rule which they themselves admit is unreasonable' (Strasser, 1999: 200); but there is still a great deal of truth in such an 'incorrect' assertion. As we have seen, the very 'thrust' of intervening cause has been used by Lord Millett in *McFarlane* to support the finding of no damage and parental benefit, which might well suggest a less than apparent separation between these doctrines. And it would also appear that there is little to separate the notions of duty and distributive justice in this context, given Lords Steyn and Hope's emphases on the acceptance by parents of the 'much loved' and 'loving' child. Therefore, despite the differential nature of these doctrines, all scrutinise and question the claimant's conduct, and are capable of justifying the transfer of responsibility for reproductive risks onto the parents as constituting 'wanted' and 'chosen' outcomes.

Whether expressed through formal notions of causation, mitigation or not, all regard the claimant's conduct as the *prime mover* in generating the damage. *All* of these doctrinal approaches emphasise that claimants could have chosen otherwise. Consequently there must be room for suspicion of a court that declares that it cannot 'conceive of any circumstances' (per Lord Steyn, p 81 in *McFarlane*) by which parents' 'reasonable', autonomous decisions to refuse abortion or adoption could be questioned, when each of these approaches clearly so central to all of their Lordships' judgments, *do exactly this*. Doctrinal distinctions there may be, but both abortion and adoption continue to be used as sociolegal tools in wrongful conception – even if the mitigation doctrine as furnished in *Emeh* is dead, its ethic lives on.

Conclusion: A harm paradox?

Is there, as I claim, a paradox that emerges from the courts' construction of choice? If we set aside for one moment the obvious problems that judges have encountered with the question of whether parents *really* confront a choice or not, and accept at face value that the parents did have straightforward post-conception choices available to them, the paradox is very much there:

> According to the law, if the consequences of conception were really viewed as harmful, claimants would have chosen to avoid those consequences (by either terminating the pregnancy or placing the child up for adoption); their failure to do so evidences that they have not suffered compensable harm. However for who do regard the consequences as harmful, they will have avoided those consequences, thereby ridding themselves of any compensable harm.

On this view, the consequences that result from the birth of an unwanted child can *never* form the subject matter of damages, no matter what way the claim is put. However, not all paradoxes are beyond resolution; indeed their solution may well lie in questioning the unstated assumptions upon which they are premised. Insofar as the most obvious questions surround the construction of 'choice' and, in particular, the construction of the 'chooser', exploring what these assumptions consist of constitutes the subject matter of the chapter that follows. But for the moment, it is relevant to pose one pressing question in light of my claim that the courts have deployed the mitigation doctrine through the back door: If willing to use the *thrust* of the mitigation doctrine, why did the courts feel it necessary to reject the doctrine in the first place? Could this shift be explained by the courts' 'distaste for abortion' (Mason, 1998: 101), or, more likely, a reluctance to be explicitly *advocating* abortion or adoption? While the mitigation doctrine directly brings such issues into play, a conceptual focus on 'damage', 'duty' and 'benefits' only raises them inferentially, and allows judges to duck the whole messy business of determining under what circumstances individuals *should* be expected to access an abortion or adoption. But, as the next chapter illustrates, a formal application of the mitigation doctrine would arguably disrupt the very conclusions the courts have reached. Might it be significant that mitigation requires the court to take account of the fact that the only reason a claimant is placed in the position of having to choose is because of a prior breach?

Indeed, what has been sidestepped by the courts is a question that is central to evaluations of loss-avoidance behaviour *elsewhere* – one of 'reasonableness'. By contrast to assessments of breach of duty, which impose an objective standard of care on defendants, in mitigation the standard of reasonableness is not only *lower*, but holds a strong *subjective* element; in other words, whether an individual *really* experiences the decision to mitigate as a 'choice', *matters* on a strict application of the law. Given the importance of that enquiry in an area as intimate as reproduction, and the fact that women are being held to a much higher standard than is typical in a formal application of mitigation, not only does this suggest that lip service is being paid to the value of women's reproductive autonomy, but that women are being treated *unequally* in law.

There are, I think, good reasons for treating the courts' rejection of the mitigation doctrine as highly circumspect. In its wake the courts have favoured more ambiguous and ill-defined concepts such as 'damage' to find a 'solution' to these cases, approaches which we should regard as far *more* dangerous and objectionable than its predecessor. Courts have room to exercise discretion, construct new boundaries and rules, while at the same time fully embracing the 'thrust' of the mitigation doctrine. It is a pernicious strategy, one that extricates our attention from the fact of prior breach – and by emphasising the claimant's ability to avoid harmful consequences through exercising choice, we not only come to question whether negligence occurred at all, but ultimately such attempts to recover damages begin to look contradictory and suspicious, if not fraudulent. For under the new ideology of mitigation, no matter how the claim is put, every outcome is *objectively* a wanted one through the power of reproductive choice: after all, how can one be harmed by the very consequences that one has chosen?

Notes

1 Section 1(1)(a) of the 1967 Act provides one of the grounds under which a lawful termination may be performed. This applies where two doctors have formed the opinion, in good faith, that, 'the pregnancy has not exceeded its 24th week and that the continuance of the pregnancy would involve risk, greater than if the pregnancy were terminated, of injury to the physical or mental health of the pregnant woman or any existing children of her family'.
2 As this chapter later examines, the claimant's unreasonable conduct may also be construed under legal causation as constituting an intervening cause of his or her losses. Therefore the same issue can affect ultimate liability.
3 Arguably mitigation cannot operate in the wrongful birth case; certainly the 'option' of abortion is ruled out given that these claims turn on the 'lost' opportunity to terminate a pregnancy under the 1967 Act.
4 The NHS Redress Act 2006 is an enabling Act and provides for the Secretary of State for Health by secondary legislation to set up an NHS Redress Scheme. The purpose of the Scheme is to reform the manner by which lower value clinical negligence cases are currently dealt with in the NHS, and provide victims of negligence with an alternative to pursuing such claims in court. Alternative redress

under the scheme would include investigations, explanations, apologies and, where appropriate, financial remedies. Details as to how the scheme would operate in practice are to be detailed in secondary legislation.

5 However, Jackson concedes that while such standardised awards for victims of NHS care have many merits, 'it is at least arguable that the introduction of such a radical departure from the existing tort system should be a matter for parliament' (2005: 681).

6 In tort law, causation is separated into 'factual' and 'legal' causation. A claimant must illustrate that the defendant's breach was a *factual* cause (a 'but for' cause) of the damage: 'but for' the defendant's negligence would the claimant have suffered the damage he or she did? Once factual causation has been established the claimant must go on to show that the defendant was the legal cause of the damage.

7 Legal causation may involve an examination of the effect of intervening acts of *third parties* or those of the claimant, which occurred between the defendant's negligence and the claimant's injury. However, the question of legal causation also holds a strong policy role allowing the court to determine the 'appropriate limit to place on the defendant's liability as a matter of policy'. It should be noted that while the related approach of 'remoteness of damage' also holds a significant role in placing fair limits on liability for wrongful conduct, this doctrinal approach concerns questions as to whether a defendant should be responsible for outcome harm that occurred in some unusual or more extensive manner. In examining legal causation as it arises alongside mitigation doctrine in this chapter, the focus is upon an 'intervening cause' by the claimant.

8 Note that the doctrines of *volenti non fit injuria* and contributory negligence also scrutinise the claimant's conduct and there are significant overlaps between these and causation and mitigation. All express the claimant's individual responsibility for damage. *Volenti* is a voluntary agreement by the claimant to absolve the defendant from the legal consequences of an unreasonable risk of harm, under circumstances where the claimant has full knowledge of both the nature and extent of risk. Contributory negligence applies where it can be established that the claimant 'did not take reasonable care of himself and contributed, by this want of care, to his own injury' (*Nance v British Columbia Electric Railway Co Ltd* [1951] AC 601). Under the Law Reform (Contributory Negligence) Act 1945, s 1(1) damages will be reduced to the extent that a court thinks 'just and equitable having regard to the claimant's share in the responsibility for the damage'.

9 It is also notable that Park J did not feel himself bound by previous authority bearing similar facts. In *Scuriaga v Powell* (1979) 123 SJ 406, a case brought in contract, the court rejected the operation of intervening cause. However, Park J distinguished *Scuriaga* on the basis that the instant case presented very different evidence.

10 In cases where the claimant would be too late to obtain a legal abortion, defendants will be precluded from raising the failure to terminate in their defence (e.g. *Thake v Maurice* [1986] QB 644).

11 Even at the time of the *Emeh* judgment when the original provisions of the 1967 Act applied (later amended by s 37 of the Human Fertilisation and Embryology Act 1990) the statistics suggest that in practice abortions were performed fairly liberally at that time; by 1978 a total of 141,558 abortions were performed in England and Wales, rising to 183,798 in 1988.

12 The cases of *McKay v Essex AHA* [1982] QB 1166, *Scuriaga v Powell* (1979) 123 SJ 406 and *Richardson v LRC Products* (2000) 59 BMLR 1985 are also instructive on this point. In *Scuriaga* – a wrongful birth case brought in contract law – the defendant gynaecologist conceded that it would have been unreasonable to expect

the plaintiff to undergo a repeat abortion at the late stage of 18 weeks. In *McKay*, a wrongful life claim that arose from a failed abortion procedure, the defendant argued that the plaintiff's refusal to have a repeat operation in the 22nd week constituted an intervening cause. The trial judge dismissed this argument, indicating that it would not be unreasonable for the plaintiff to refuse an abortion at such a late stage since this presented far greater risks to a woman's health. In *Richardson*, Kennedy J was willing to construe as unreasonable a failure to obtain emergency post-coital contraception (which the claimant, perhaps *unreasonably*, failed to realise was efficacious for as long as 72 hours following intercourse).

13 As Lord Denning MR in *Bravery v Bravery* [1954] 1 WLR 1169 commented: 'Take a case where a sterilization operation is done so as to enable a man to have the pleasure of sexual intercourse without shouldering the responsibilities attached to it. The operation is plainly injurious to the public interest. It is degrading to the man himself. It is injurious to his wife and any woman who he may marry . . . It is illegal, even though the man consents to it . . .' (p 1180).

14 The Abortion Act 1967, s 4(1) provides that, except where treatment is necessary to save the life or prevent grave permanent injury to the physical or mental health of a pregnant woman, 'no person shall be under any duty, whether by contract or by any statutory or other legal requirement, to participate in any treatment authorised by this Act to which he has a conscientious objection'.

Chapter 5

Constructions of the reasonable woman

> Then the king said, 'The one says, "This is my son that is alive, and your son is dead" and the other says, "No; but your son is dead, and my son is the living one."' And the king said, 'Bring me a sword.' So a sword was brought before the king. And the king said, 'Divide the living child in two, and give half to the one, and half to the other.' Then the woman whose son was alive said to the king, because her heart yearned for her son, 'Oh, my lord, give her the living child, and by no means slay it.' But the other said, 'It shall be neither mine nor yours; divide it.' Then the king answered and said, 'Give the living child to the first woman, and by no means slay it; she is the mother.' And all Israel heard of the judgment which the king had rendered; and they stood in awe of the king, because they perceived that the wisdom of God was in him, to render justice.
>
> (1 Kings 3, vv 23–8)

Of the most criticised figures within feminist legal jurisprudence is English law's ubiquitous 'Reasonable Person'. He is a prominent, though 'classless' individual, impressively conversant with many disciplines of law; a chameleonic character whose age, gender, physical ability, skill, religion, ethnicity and foresight will surely vary when called upon to do so; he is the true mark of prudence, taking risks only when the burden of their avoidance is too great; he is utterly 'free from both over-apprehension and from over-confidence' (*Glasgow Corporation v Muir* [1943] AC 448, 457); and as Sir Alan Herbert once comically commented of this most remarkable person, he is 'an ever-present help in time of trouble, and his apparitions mark the road to equity and right' (1936: 2). However, despite his perfect virtue, the reasonable person is quite ordinary indeed, and is to be found sitting on the Clapham Omnibus, the Bondi Tram, the London Underground, or in the evening pushing a lawn mower in his shirtsleeves. Nor is he free of all shortcomings, but since these are few and far between he continues to occupy his quite privileged place in English law as 'an ideal, a standard, the embodiment of all those qualities which we demand of the good citizen' (Herbert, 1936: 2). So who or what, is this 'reasonable person'?

In the law of negligence, the 'Reasonable Person' exemplifies the standard of reasonableness itself; though still legally virtuous, this 'person' is a fictional character against whom others are compared. In the course of establishing tortious liability, the standard plays a critical role in determining whether or not an individual's behaviour amounts to a breach of duty, an enquiry central to establishing fault; thus, actions of litigants are evaluated in light of what this so-called reasonable person would have done in their circumstances, but it is only 'those who emulate the reasonable person who will be considered "faultless" and hence relieved of the consequences of their actions' (Moran, 2003: 18). Therefore, rather than constituting a person as such, what the reasonable person provides is an abstract and universal benchmark invoked by the common law to 'represent an objective standard of care against which all are measured' (Conaghan and Mansell, 1999: 52).

This legal personification of virtuous conduct, however, has been called into question; and as an illuminating and voluminous body of feminist legal scholarship illustrates, the judiciary's claim as to the 'objectivity' and 'universality' of this standard has long been doubted.[1] Once one considers the narrow set of questions that inform the evaluation of reasonableness as well as the morally perverse results that it is capable of generating ('Why should we accept that it is "reasonable" to let an accident happen when it is more expensive to avoid it when such a calculated approach to human suffering so affronts us' (Conaghan, 1996: 49)?), it *is* questionable whether there is anything objective or 'reasonable' about this standard at all. So, too, is there deep suspicion surrounding the identity of the 'reasonable *person*'; for although the reasonable man's clothes have changed, in favour of the androgynous uniform well suited to a reasonable person, as Reg Graycar tritely remarks, 'the reasonable man is what he remains . . . he is still wearing his Y-fronts underneath' (1997: 33–4). And while this character may be found on public transportation, he is very probably travelling to the courtroom since, 'despite his distinguished pedigree, the reasonable man represents little more than the subjective viewpoint of a particular judge' (Conaghan and Mansell, 1999: 53). Therefore, given the limited field from which the judiciary is generally employed (public school and Oxbridge), and its overwhelmingly male composition, it is unsurprising that so many come to doubt the standard's ability to apply to *women*, or others who similarly fail to share the same physical or cultural space (Macklem and Gardner, 2001: 816). As Conaghan and Mansell comment, 'far from being a neutral or even average standard, the standard of care reflects the views of a very narrow and select class in our society' (1999: 57).

Whether or not the reasonable person standard is still wearing his 'Y-fronts' is *not* the concern here; as Chapter 2 (albeit cautiously) concluded in the context of wrongful pregnancy, an experiential deficit does not necessarily preclude a proper assessment of injuries and harms particular to *women*; as I argued there, such deficits can be overcome if met by a judicial willingness to integrate women's perspectives. So, while there is an irresistible urge to correlate (in)sensitivity to gender-specific injuries and the identity of the judge, this may well lead us in the wrong direction; the gender of the judiciary is not *the* problem, but the gendering of judgment most certainly is. Therefore, continuing from my analysis in the previous chapter, my aim here is to illustrate *how* law constructs women's experience in the reproductive realm and to reveal its gendered content. To do so, I take up two interrelated queries. The first section of the chapter considers the mitigation doctrine and the assessment of reasonableness; although operating differently to determinations of the 'standard of care', the 'reasonable person' also plays a role here (as it does in assessments of contributory negligence). My specific concerns are focused upon the rejection of this doctrine, what has emerged in its wake and how these developments have served to *disadvantage* women vis-à-vis other parties before the law. Given the judicial recognition that claimants may not have confronted a 'true choice', the conclusion that claimants should nevertheless be held responsible appears anomalous. In the light of these concerns, the second part of the analysis questions why women are being held to a higher standard in the context of reproduction and parenthood, and why the law thinks this 'reasonable'. An investigation into what the law sees as reasonable not only illustrates what the law 'expects' of women, but significantly, what it does *not* expect – and it is precisely that point of the enquiry that is the most telling. Though a fictional character, the reasonable person nevertheless constitutes a 'personification' of legally virtuous behaviour and from this emerges powerful images of ideal/non-ideal people. As this chapter illustrates, it is through unravelling the make-up and attributes of these images, the 'Reasonable Person's' varying attitudes towards 'choice' following enforced reproduction and parenthood, that we gain a better insight into what law *thinks* about women in matters of reproduction, and how that thinking informs the drawing of the line between the 'reasonable/deserving' Woman and the *un*reasonable/*un*deserving Woman in the reproductive torts.

On being responsible

As the last chapter concluded, even if mitigation doctrine is dead, judges have been highly influenced by the conclusions it reaches. The notion of choice, although clearly confounding those in judicial quarters, was assessed from a purely *objective* rather than *subjective* stance. The rejection of the mitigation doctrine permitted the court to transform choices that claimants did not experience as 'true choices' into valid choices nevertheless, rendering parental failures to surrender a child as objectively 'wanted' outcomes. Nevertheless, as Jeremy Pomeroy (1992) explains, in theory an objective standard *is* open to the courts in determining the reasonableness of failure to take steps to avoid losses:

The range of ways in which a court could, at least in theory, define the 'reasonable mitigator' may be conceptualized as lying along an objective-subjective spectrum. At the objective extreme, a court could characterize this reasonable person as a rational agent stripped of all individualized characteristics or as the essence of humankind, devoid of all cultural or historical specificity. Moving closer to the subjective pole, a court might abstract the reasonable mitigator from the general community of the injured party. Further along the spectrum, the standard of reasonableness would be derived from the standards of the victim's immediate circle of associates. At the [furthest] extreme, reasonableness would be defined solely in terms of the standards of the party whose efforts to avoid tort consequences are at issue.

(Pomeroy, 1992: 1116)

Yet, as far as English law is concerned, this *is* theoretical.[2] As the most casual glance of decided cases on mitigation illustrates, this is imposing a *much* higher standard of 'reasonableness' upon claimants than would normally be the case. For example, if we look to the application of mitigation in *commercial* contexts this reveals a heavy leaning towards the subjective end of the spectrum. The law has not required claimants to accept goods of inferior quality (*Finlay v NV Kwik Hoo Tong* [1929] 1 KB 400), or to risk their commercial reputation (*London & South of England Building Society v Stone* [1983] 1 WLR 1242), or embark upon complex litigation (*Pilkinton v Wood* [1953] Ch 770), and nor can an employee be 'compelled to accept re-employment if it involves lower status, if relations are irretrievably affected by circumstances of dismissal ... or if it is likely to be less permanent than alternatives' (Beatson, 2002: 615). Presumably in each of these contexts the claimants considered that mitigation was not a choice, akin to the quite reasonable assessment that an impecunious claimant also has no choice (Cooke and Oughton, 2000: 306). How do we even begin to draw comparisons between a refusal to terminate pregnancy, or place a child up for adoption, against the clearly more *trivial* refusal of a Rolls-Royce driver to opt for a less prestigious vehicle (*HL Motorworks v Alwahbi* [1977] RTR 276; Harris *et al*, 2002: 110)? Might we not regard it as slightly suspicious that the former is judicially conceptualised as having a valid choice to mitigate, while the latter is assessed on *subjective* grounds as having no 'true choice'?

So, since concessions are permitted elsewhere under the doctrine of mitigation, what response can our claimant in the wrongful conception case offer as a means of demonstrating the 'reasonableness' of her failure to avoid such losses? How can she justify her 'failure' to terminate her pregnancy, or indeed, place a child up for adoption? As was noted in the previous chapter, abortion is not freely available in a *de jure* sense, and nor is it a procedure completely without risk.[3] Nevertheless, even if one points to the legal face of the 1967 Act, or the risks involved, this does not rule out the option of adoption. Here our claimant might forward that since adoption rates have significantly declined, the statistical likelihood of this choice is 'minimal' (Graycar and Morgan, 1996).[4] Or perhaps, we could point to the 'spirit' of the Children Act 1989, which expresses the value of children living with their genetic parents where possible (Talbot and Williams, 2003)? However, this is a *general* principle, and appealing to the law in this case does not establish that the claimant could not place the child up for adoption; rather it demonstrates a statistical unlikelihood of its finding adoptive parents elsewhere. Alternatively we might flesh out a possibility raised in the last chapter, and question whether it would be unreasonable to decline either of these options once we take account of the claimant's religious or moral scruples? And in law, this can be analysed in two ways. First, the claimant's religious or moral sentiments could be utilised to sustain that a refusal to mitigate was not unreasonable; or the issue of mitigation could be entirely avoided by applying the 'eggshell-skull rule',[5] the latter of which has been adopted in the US wrongful conception case of *Troppi v Scarf* 31 Mich App 240, 187 NW 2d 511 (1971). Here the court stated that:

> Most women confronted with an unwanted pregnancy will abort the fetus, legally or illegally. Some will bear the child and place him up for adoption. Many will bear the child, keep and rear him. The defendant does not have the right to insist that the victim of his negligence have the emotional and mental make-up of a woman who is willing to abort or place the child for adoption. If the negligence of a tortfeasor results in conception of a child by a woman whose emotional and mental make-up is inconsistent with abortion or placing the child up for adoption, then, under the principle that the tortfeasor takes the injured party as he finds him, the tortfeasor cannot complain that damages that will be assessed against him are greater than those that would be determined if he had negligently caused the conception of a child by a woman who is willing to abort or place the child for adoption.
>
> (p 240/519)

Indeed, according to *R v Blaue* [1975] 3 All ER 446, the eggshell-skull rule applies to both the victim's body and mind, including religious convictions held by the victim.[6] Since this principle applies to both criminal and civil law, the *Troppi* court's civil law application of the eggshell-skull rule would appear legally justifiable. However, some commentators have nevertheless expressed doubt as to whether it is really appropriate to analogise 'religious beliefs' with pre-existing conditions such as physical frailty or psychological incapacity; as Pomeroy contends, the answer 'hinges on whether we treat religious beliefs like the colour of one's skin, an immutable characteristic from which an actor cannot escape, or as a kind of "clothing" ' (1992: 1152). Such issues need not concern us here, for in law the reason for permitting religious convictions to count within the eggshell-skull rule or mitigation, according to Arthur Ripstein, 'is not that the belief is deeply held, nor that it is widely held ... rather that the law supposes that that particular category of belief is so important that it is reasonable to act on it' (1999: 129). While the increasing secularisation of society might lead to a lesser emphasis upon religion, it is nevertheless apparent that even those holding no particular religious sentiments can still hold strong views as to the morality of abortion. Therefore, insofar as the law currently accepts the eggshell-skull rule as embracing the physical *and* psychological make-up of the individual, it would also seem likely that in relation to both abortion and adoption, no differentiation between moral and religious objections could be sensibly drawn.

But while the foregoing has considered the more subjective determination of 'reasonableness' as it applies in mitigation, what of an 'objective' determination that would apply in establishing breach of duty? Although clearly unfair to hold claimants to this higher standard given that it is normally reserved for scrutinising a defendant's conduct, it is still questionable whether such an evaluation would yield the conclusion that the claimant's actions were 'unreasonable'. As William Prosser observes of the determination of reasonableness pertaining to the standard of care:

> [It] must be an external and objective one, rather than the individual judgment, good or bad, or the particular actor; and it must be, so far as possible, the same for all persons, since the law can have no favourites.
> (Prosser, 1971)

If, as is becoming typical of the law of negligence, we were to approach the question by asking commuters on the underground whether they considered a refusal to terminate a pregnancy or place a child up for adoption as unreasonable, what answers would we receive? It is doubtful that one could locate a clear consensus on adoption, and as Jeff Milsteen comments, the courts have focused less on adoption, and more on abortion since its decriminalisation (1983: 1185). So to the judicial eye at least, adoption would appear to be an 'option' in decline. And, perhaps it would be worth reminding our commuter that they are not being asked to determine whether placing a child up for adoption is reasonable; as we have seen, the question is whether it would be *unreasonable* for a woman to decline to do so. Yet, even if we cannot be certain as to the responses that the issue of adoption might give rise to, one might well anticipate a polarisation of views over abortion. As the US Court commented in the case of *Planned Parenthood of Southeastern Pennsylvania v Casey*, 120 L Ed 2d 674 (1992):

> Men and women of good conscience can disagree, and we suppose some shall always disagree, about the profound moral and spiritual implications of terminating a pregnancy, even in its earliest stage. Some of us

individuals find abortion offensive to our most basic principles of morality, but that cannot control our decision.

(p 697)

Fully embracing this view, Kenneth Norrie (1988) remarks that since individuals in society hold such radically opposing views, the law must provide recognition that such differing views can be 'reasonably held'. The law is in no position to prefer one view over another, but rather it must 'recognise that both views may be acceptable for particular individuals to hold, just as it recognises that two – often opposing – schools of thought in medical practice can each be reasonable and acceptable' (Norrie, 1988: 265–6). While slightly different considerations apply as to the judicial acceptance of opposing medical opinion,[7] Norrie's argument is forceful. But if we are looking for a potential trump card as to the question of reasonableness in the context of the failure to terminate a pregnancy, we can turn to Margaret Brazier who questions:

> Is it what the hypothetical reasonable woman in 2003 would do? ... Given that the Court of Appeal has finally confirmed that no woman can be forced to undergo a Caesarian section to protect the life or health of the foetus, to 'force' a woman to 'kill' her foetus would be illogical. Maternal autonomy demands that pregnant women's choices in this delicate arena of moral controversy should be respected.
> (Brazier, 2003: 384)

Although no woman is 'forced' to terminate as such, there is little doubt that Brazier's emphasis on maternal autonomy is absolutely central to our deliberations here. Bearing in mind that the *McFarlane* court emphatically declared that the law 'does and must respect these decisions of parents which are so closely tied to their basic freedoms and rights of personal autonomy' (per Lord Steyn p 81), could any court possibly argue that failures to terminate or place a child up for adoption were *so unreasonable* as to constitute a failure to mitigate?

Whether these refusals to mitigate can be considered unreasonable or not is really quite irrelevant at this stage; this is not the approach that the courts are now inclined to follow. But what this discussion does highlight is the differential application of rules to the domain of reproduction than in other contexts; and this is particularly striking. That women are so clearly disadvantaged vis-à-vis the application of the mitigation doctrine elsewhere becomes even clearer considering the much higher standard of care imposed upon the pregnant woman in these cases; and it is one of strict liability at the furthest end of the 'reasonableness' spectrum which permits no subjective assessment whatsoever. And significantly, it is extremely rare for English law to impose 'strict liability' upon *defendants* (let alone claimants) without compelling reasons, for example the existence of insurance. In determining the standard of care to be expected of a learner driver, Lord Denning in *Nettleship v Weston* [1971] 2 QB 691 stated:

> Thus we are, in this branch of the law, moving away from the concept: 'No liability without fault.' We are beginning to apply the test: 'On whom should the risk fall?' Morally the learner driver is not at fault; but legally she is liable to be because she is insured and the risk should fall on her.
>
> (p 700)

Although the relationship between liability and insurance is disputed (see Stapleton, 1995), Jonathan Morgan observes that there *is* a clear judicial 'approbation for loss-spreading, via insurance as a positive reason for imposing liability in negligence' (2004: 386; see *Vowles v Evans* [2003] 1 WLR 1607 and *Gwilliam v West Hertfordshire NHS Trust* [2003] QB 443). However, as a means of justifying the higher standard of care expected of wrongful conception claimants, this lacks explanatory power. Arguing that the loss should fall on the health authority, Alistair Mullis points out that the parents in these cases, 'will not only be unlikely to insure against the risk of pregnancy but they may well be unable to do so' (1993: 333–4). While insuring against such a risk may have been viewed in the past as 'unethical', as Janice Richardson comments, it now constitutes 'a bad risk for insurers, such that the premiums would be too high' (2004: 108). Therefore, the lack of social insurance coupled with the law's response to claims of wrongful conception, will leave many women, for the greater part, dependent upon their own resources, or those of the state to meet the costs of reproductive risks materialising even when brought about by negligence.

What, then, does the foregoing tell us? The most obvious point is that an analysis as to how mitigation would ordinarily apply to these cases renders the rejection of the doctrine in the context of wrongful conception most suspicious. An application of mitigation arguably makes it difficult to justify as a matter of law the transfer of financial responsibility for reproductive risks upon the claimant on the basis that they 'kept the child'. The heightened standard of care invoked in these cases is not only inapplicable to claimants, but in all but the most exceptional circumstances, would be unlikely to even apply to a tortfeasor. But the more significant point is this: if tort law aspires to conceptions of distributive and corrective justice, then the action for wrongful conception reveals that this is not merely a half-hearted aspiration, but one that has altogether collapsed. Given that notions of 'formal equality' and 'treating like cases alike' are suddenly suspended when the law enters into the reproductive domain, just why is it that claimants who are clearly less well positioned to bear the loss are held responsible for the negligence of others? What is it that informs the law's view that assigning responsibility to these women is reasonable?

Responsible women

> Aspects of law that connect women to their children or their childbearing capacities are the areas that are most readily identified with women, whereas areas of doctrine seen as 'gender-neutral', such as tort and contract, are rarely perceived as being relevant to women.
>
> (Graycar and Morgan, 2002: 172)

Of course, not all claimants bringing their claims for wrongfully conceived or born children have been denied damages; the courts have been fairly receptive to cases involving disabled children. However, in the case of the healthy child (excepting *perhaps* Karina Rees), the analysis takes a distinctive turn. While the *McFarlane* and *Rees* courts formed the view that mitigation should never operate in these actions, this did not preclude the House from nevertheless closely scrutinising the claimants' choices to keep their healthy products of negligence. Through a variety of doctrinal techniques, it was this fact that led to the conclusion that parents were left either unharmed or benefited, and that the defendant should not be held liable for *losses* that were the result of the claimant's choice. Yet, judges invoking the concept of choice were deeply uncomfortable with the idea that parents had 'truly chosen' to keep the child, some entirely unconvinced that this evidenced either 'no damage' or 'benefits'. So how does one explain the disparity between these cases? What assumptions have served to shape the law's view that *some* injuries constitute compensable harm/no harm, are deserving/*less* deserving and demand a response/no response? Upon what constructions of variously (un)harmed, (un)choosing and (un)reasonable claimant are the different approaches to the cases of wrongful conception and birth predicated?

As a starting point, it is instructive to first turn to the work of Sally Sheldon (1997) in her analysis of the parliamentary debates leading up to the enactment of the Abortion Act 1967, for the ideations that I suggest are invoked in the reproductive torts are ones with which the law is already quite familiar. In the context of these debates, Sheldon's analysis uncovers specific images of aborting women, 'the woman as minor, as victim and as mother' (1997: 35). Used variously to support reforming/opposing sides of the abortion debate, these images of women were based 'partially on stereotypes, and partially on real and concrete examples which continually recur within the debates as leitmotifs to become generalised as representing the reality of the woman who seeks abortion' (1997: 35). Revealing that these images were strategic and oppositional devices, Sheldon explains that while those seeking reform presented a type of woman deserving of an abortion as a marginal figure, emotionally weak and desperate, 'even suicidal' (1997: 35), opponents instead constructed this 'Woman' as selfish, irrational, immature and – unsurprisingly – undeserving. The third 'type' of woman that Sheldon identifies is one that is 'appropriated for the cause of both reformists and conservatives alike'

(1997: 40) – the 'Woman as mother'. Construed as a 'woman who rejects maternity', 'the very essence of motherhood' (1997: 40) therefore standing 'against a wider norm of women who neither need nor desire abortion' (1997: 35), she is simultaneously represented as a Woman whose maternal instinct, though intact, is deserving of access to an abortion, given that this would permit her to best fulfil her maternal duties towards an existing family (1997: 41). While resulting legislation reconciles these competing accounts, according to Sheldon, the 1967 Act nevertheless affirms the marginal/deviant nature of the Woman who seeks an abortion, as well as reinforcing 'the image of the good woman who does not seek to terminate her pregnancy and who provides the norm against which such deviance is to be measured' (1997: 42).

Although arising in the context of debates held some 40 years ago, these 'marginal' figures of deserving and undeserving women seeking abortion are far from exceptional stereotypes. These characters are constant, and have endured through deeply ingrained legal ideations of 'Reasonable Women' in the realm of reproduction; the deserving/undeserving women seeking abortion will still find their counterparts in the representations of women seeking damages for their unwanted children in the law of tort. Embedded in these various legal responses surrounding the 'choice' to keep a healthy child, we can locate two shifting but prominent characters: the woman who 'had a choice'; and the woman who 'had no other choice' and who 'never contemplated an alternative' but to 'accept the loved and loving addition into the family'. While the latter construction is undoubtedly the dominant narrative, the image of the 'natural woman' being one that the judiciary finds more convincing and seductive in portraying ideal womanhood, both representations are nevertheless premised upon very particular kinds of decision makers, stereotypes of 'Responsible Women' who have chosen these reproductive outcomes, whether through a careful economic rationalisation of the likely costs of (in)action and/or through the bonds of natural maternal love for their healthy child. But, juxtaposed against these choosing Women is another kind of woman: one who is deserving of our sympathy and pity. She is a tragic character, whose 'choice to keep the child' has gone virtually unquestioned, for the outcome is so obviously an unwanted one. Her claim is, by contrast, that much more deserving, her circumstances that much more serious. Akin to the *more* deserving figures of abortion, she too is a victim of her catastrophic circumstances, one who needs help to fulfil her maternal duties as she struggles to care for a child by virtue of her own, or her child's, disability. She is a 'Woman in Need', one who is both deserving and reasonable, and she demands, unlike the 'Self-regarding woman', or the 'Natural Woman', a legal response.

Self-regarding woman: 'Still a choice'

According to Phillip Levine and Douglas Staiger, although the abortion debate typically pivots around issues of philosophy, religion, ethics and feminism, 'rarely, if ever, does the debate regarding abortion policy focus on the results of economic analysis. Yet standard economic models of decision making under uncertainty when applied to this issue yield interesting predictions regarding women's behaviour' (2001: 1). Approaching abortion decisions as 'the result of a rational decision-making process in which a woman's actions are influenced by the expected costs and benefits of the choices she makes' (2001: 2), they suggest that a 'simple model of decision-making under uncertainty' yields the following results:

> The decision between abortion and birth is made after becoming pregnant and after learning whether the birth will be wanted or unwanted. A woman for whom a birth will be wanted will always give birth ... and receive a payoff of 1. A woman for whom a birth will be unwanted will abort if the cost of abortion is less than the cost of giving birth ... and will give birth otherwise. In this case the payoff represents the least costly option ...
>
> (Levine and Staiger, 2001: 4)

Is it *really* useful, as the authors suggest, to regard 'abortion as [a form of] pregnancy insurance'? Will it always be the case that a woman 'for whom a birth will be wanted' will *always* give birth? And what costs create incentives or disincentives for the exercise of such 'choice'? Despite recognising that costs might include both a financial and *psychic* dimension, it still leaves little, if any, room for ambiguity in decision making. Rather, the Solomite wisdom emerging from this economic model is that of the standard individuated, self-interested, rational decision maker. And it is the same decision maker that has made her appearance in the action for wrongful conception – she is the woman who 'still has a choice' and it is against her that others are judged. Akin to the 'Woman as victim' invoked in debates around abortion reform, she too is a woman who will abort 'according to her wishes or whims' (Sheldon, 1997: 36). She is, however, a more mature figure, one who objectively assesses her choices, calculating the costs and benefits of pursuing a course of action, resulting in a 'voluntary choice' that is *always* 'welfare-maximising'. But how well does this serve as a means of explaining reproductive decision making, or indeed for that matter, any 'choices' exercised within the family domain?

As scholarly criticism of 'family economics' illustrates, many aspects of the rational choice model are deeply problematic. The translation of human activity into economic terms, Ann Estin argues, overlooks the construction of the family, and fails to address the division of labour and power dynamics occurring within it (1994: 1019). Since children are productive of significant financial and caring costs, particularly for *women*, an economic perspective also fails to explain decisions *to have* children (Friedman *et al*, 1994; Himmelweit, 2002). Therefore, only decisions to *avoid* parenting are explicable as valid 'choices', thus rendering a contrary choice as irrational and inefficient. Further illustrating the limited application of economic theory is the impoverished view of personhood that emerges: the rational chooser is both selfish and self-interested, separate from society, and dependent 'only on the decision maker's assessment of her own well-being' (Himmelweit, 2002: 233). As Himmelweit remarks, the autonomous characteristic is that of 'a shopper who takes her given preferences to the market and makes the best bargain she can at the prices she finds there' (2002: 232). Although this can explain decisions *within* the market, the centrality of 'wealth-maximization' as a guiding value for exercising choice clearly provides a pernicious typification of parent-to-child relations. Not only does the language of market rhetoric fail to distinguish 'children from stereo equipment' (Estin, 1994: 1018), but more significantly, it objectifies the child *as a commodity* to be bought and sold on the market according to personal preference. As Margaret Radin comments, 'reasoning in market rhetoric, with its characterization of everything that people value as monetizable and fungible, tends to make it easy to ignore . . . other "costs" ' (1987: 1878). And so must the economic view be regarded as an extremely costly enterprise, for it 'erases important values and distinctions, such as the difference between selfishness and generosity or the personal characteristics of individuals' (Estin, 1994: 1016).

Yet, while the flaws of family economics might seem apparent, its language and reasoning have proved highly pervasive in law. And this is particularly true of tort law, which as Leslie Bender comments, has been 'weighted down by a language and value system that privileges economics and costs' (1989: 767). Injuries, remedies and justice are measured by goals of efficiency, cost-benefit analyses, and the costs and statistical probability of their prevention (Bender, 1989: 760). Therefore, assessments of 'reasonableness' under the standard of care in negligence can be economically guided to the 'right' answer in determining the difference between 'what the allegedly negligent party actually did and some particular undone thing it allegedly *should* have done' (Galligan, 1999: 159). But the would/should distinction has moral limits which are fully exposed in the infamous Learned Hand formula's guide to human 'other-regarding' behaviour: 'economically speaking, treat your neighbor as you would treat yourself. Only impose those costs on someone else that you would impose upon yourself' (Galligan, 1999: 159). So, if the burden of taking precautions to avoid the risk is less than the product of the probability of that risk occurring and the anticipated gravity of the risk should it arise, only then will one be negligent. But if the burden is deemed too great, and 'unreasonable' for the defendant to bear, then the claimant will bear the burden of their injury alone. And that remains the case, no matter how severe, or devastating the impact of an injury upon the claimant's life or those who care for them – the losses, financial, emotional and physical, will lie exactly where they fell.

But if we unwrap this language of economics as it underpins the standard of care in negligence (the likelihood of the risk materialising, the seriousness of the risk should it materialise, the social utility of the defendant's activity, and the practicability of taking precautions), does it really provide an 'objective' determination as to what is or is not 'reasonable'?[8] And what of economists' claims to 'neutrality'? As Thomas Galligan argues, the Hand formula is far from objective or neutral. Rather it encourages *efficiency*, which assumes that 'almost everything can be valued in some economic sense. Additionally, almost anything can be viewed as a cost or benefit of something else' (1999: 159). Therefore, 'risk', 'gravity', 'practicability of taking precautions' and 'harm' can all be understood more or less in financial terms. But, is it reasonable to measure human life in terms of efficiency? Is harm always commensurable with the language of money? What of pain, emotion, and suffering – how can we capture these 'harms' in financial terms? Since the standard of care holds a strong prescriptive/proscriptive dimension, is it reasonable to expect individuals' choices to be guided by economic goals of efficiency in their day-to-day lives and dealings with others?

Disillusionment with the coalition of law and economics has led some to call for the 'decommodification' of the law of tort (Abel, 2006; Radin, 1987). Such a perspective holds that compensating for intangible injuries, such as pain and suffering, contributes to 'a cultural view of experience and love as commodities' (Abel, 1981; cited in Radin, 1987: 1876), and violates 'our essential humanity by pricing bodily integrity, emotional well-being, existence and non-existence and relationships' (Abel, 2006: 291). If bodily integrity is an integral personal attribute and not 'a detachable object', Margaret Radin argues that 'hypothetically valuing my bodily integrity in money is not far removed from valuing *me* in money. For all but the universal commodifier, that is inappropriate treatment of a person' (1987: 1881). For Radin, the answer lies in denying recovery of these types of 'injuries' to articulate the notion that human life activity, 'or at least certain aspects of it, ought not to be traded, nor to be conceived of in market rhetoric or evaluated in market methodology' (1987: 1887). In attempting to overcome the flaws of the economic model, this thesis leaves quite significant questions unanswered. For example, if 'certain aspects' of human life should not be hypothetically traded like goods on the market, then what aspects of human life can be? And, is it inevitable that awarding damages for pain, suffering and loss of amenity that accompany injury result in the commodification of human life? If we conceptualise physical loss to the body as a loss of bodily integrity, does this not on their account also involve the commodification of human life? There is a vast difference between treating the individual *as* an injury, and compensating for the inevitable repercussions that flow from that injury. Whether or not it seems sensible to award damages for such intangible losses is of course one question, but whether that necessarily involves commodifying human life is quite another. Certainly financial damages are a crude substitute for loss, but the law of tort implicitly recognises commensurability problems, given that the purpose of damages is to provide the claimant with full compensation, *as far as money can do it*.

There are, I think, significant problems with commodification theory – too innumerable to mention here,[9] but at the same time, that is not to say that I would dismiss *all* of the concerns it expresses. One of the main issues in the context of tortious damages concerns the logical limits of the commodification theory; such an argument would seem to more sensibly articulate that only financial harms are commensurable with financial remedies for there is no aspect of our bodily materiality that can truly be priced to reflect its importance and meaning in our lives. But, more significantly, such a thesis proves itself to be quite dangerous once we consider the broader repercussions that might emerge from such a 'revolutionary' overhaul of the scope of tortious remedies. As we saw in Chapter 2, the 'harms' that tort law has traditionally excluded are precisely those that authors like Abel and Radin would also deny: the non-physical, non-pecuniary, intimate and relational – all of which have clear resonance in the lives of women, for whom the 'emotional work of maintaining human relationships has commonly been assigned' (Chamallas and Kerber, 1989: 814). The so-called decommodification of tort may well involve the systematic devaluation, privatisation and normalisation of harms, though sustained by many, more often than not are suffered by women.

Nevertheless, both Radin and Abel have a point; there is little doubt that the economic–legal alliance is problematic. Perhaps the most obvious question is that forwarded by Conaghan and Mansell who ask, 'Is our vision of human existence really so wretched that we feel comfortable about reducing everything to questions of efficiency and cost?' (1999: 61). While sympathetic to this point, it should be noted, however, that the law does not reduce *everything* down to questions of efficiency and cost. A woman's work in the family home, though imposing significantly more costs to her life than purely economic ones, nevertheless still expresses economic value – yet in law this is more likely than not to be construed as a gratuitous (rather than economic) activity that exists outside the market. Indeed, the problems emerging from economic thought lie not necessarily in what the law 'prices up' – but rather, in what it doesn't. If market rhetoric dominating legal thinking serves to devalue human life, it does so because of the narrow view as to what values guide human decision making, which in turn informs the law's assessment as to which elements of human life are valuable, and in their setback *should* be recognised as harmful. In other words, an economic approach severely limits what the law *sees* and therefore *counts* as harm.

It is exactly this narrow cost–benefit approach that has impacted hard on the wrongful conception cases. The policy decision that the economic losses suffered by parents were *pure* rather than *consequential* upon the breach is, I suggest, because of the courts' view that parents made a rational and welfare-maximising decision to take on those consequences, by keeping the child. On this view, allowing recovery of clearly avoidable consequences would serve to overcompensate; for although the parents' bank accounts will be affected, this was the result of a decision. And even on those rare occasions where courts are alerted to the 'economic costs' entailed in a woman's burden in caring for an unwanted child, as in *Greenfield v Irwin* [2001] 1 WLR 1279, such as her giving up paid employment to remain at home to look after that child, this too is constructed as a welfare-maximising decision – 'She has taken the decision to give up her employment to care for that child' (per Buxton LJ p 1281) – and not costs that inevitably flow from pregnancy. Rather, the costs are caused by:

> [T]he existence of the child, just as the family's expenditure on its other children is caused by their existence. That again is a short point, but it seems to me that it demonstrates again that this case cannot be solved in the plaintiff's favour by characterising it as a case of physical damage with contingent loss.
>
> (per Buxton LJ p 1287)

The stereotype of the rational welfare-maximising individual always benefiting through the exercise of choice, simply squeezes out any other perspective. It excludes and renders invisible the relational, caretaking and psychic losses flowing from parental (maternal) responsibility. And in assessing what harm a woman might suffer from wrongful pregnancy, here too, the courts' view of injury was narrowed to a physical assessment of loss, or one based upon a woman's 'rational' attitude towards her bodily state. While this Cartesian perspective could account for the involuntary invasion of her bodily integrity and the material limits pregnancy might impose, what it denied was the moral, relational and embodied dimension entailed in all pregnancies, quite irrespective of their relative (un)wantedness or physical repercussions. Indeed, one might come to question, 'but for' the unwantedness of, and physical aspects to pregnancy, was the foetus ever really there? As has already been argued, it is simply not possible to understand what the harm of wrongful conception and pregnancy consists of without reference to precisely these aspects. The stripping away of this moral dimension has not only resulted in a narrow and superficial view as to a woman's perception of pregnancy, her foetus and potential future child, but quite critically there is no notion as to how these aspects might relate to reproductive decision making and in particular the 'decision' to keep children born as a result of negligence. The rational mind quantifies the relative 'costs' and 'benefits' of continuing or terminating a pregnancy, and objectifies the passive and governed body in which an invading entity resides. Since the exercise of rational choice is the sole criterion for welfare maximisation, if a pregnancy is continued rather than avoided, the resulting 'unwanted' child will transform into a wanted one. After all, why would a woman rationally choose to give birth to a costly and unwanted child?

For all the flaws of the economic think-tank in the family domain, it is worth noting at this stage that none of the foregoing tells us *why* the law has constructed choice in this way, or why the law adopts a more contextual enquiry in seemingly more trivial matters than the choices confronting women in reproduction. Why *is* the choice in cases of wrongful conception constructed without reference to moral concerns where concessions are made to human frailty elsewhere? Why is this part of the enquiry, so clearly part of the mitigation doctrine, excluded? If the law, as Ripstein maintains, relieves individuals of responsibility not on the basis that the agent lacked control, but 'rather because the choice is too much to ask of a person' (1999: 292), then why does it seem so reasonable to impose responsibility onto women in reproduction, given judicial doubts that they had a 'true choice'? Just *why* are these women constructed as having 'voluntarily assumed' the risks of reproduction when those risks have been brought about by negligence?

Natural woman: 'She had no other choice'

> Society has not ... responded to the caretaker by counting, valuing, compensating, or accommodating her caretaking. Instead of a societal response, inevitable dependency has been assigned to the quintessentially private institution – the traditional marital family. ... It is conceptualised as placed beyond and protected from intervention by the state. Dependency, through its assignment to the private, marital family, is hidden – privatized within that family, its public and inevitable nature concealed.
>
> (Fineman, 2004: 38)

As a matter of legal tradition, the ideological institution of 'the family' has been characterised as 'a private realm not generally subject to regulation' (Conaghan, 1998: 136). Variously expressed as 'sacred', 'a sanctuary', 'private' and 'natural' (Fineman, 1995: 161), the domestic realm is seen as embodying values and norms that serve to differentiate it 'from the institutions occupying the public sphere, particularly those of the market' (Fineman, 1999: 15). The family is the jurisdiction of emotion, love, care, joy, sacrifice, mutual affection, gratuity and, significantly, it is so often the private province of women. But, as feminist critical appraisals illustrate, the idea of the family as a private sphere, 'supposedly untouched by law', is a complete fiction (Naffine, 2002: 80). As Ngaire Naffine argues, the family is 'itself a small society embedded in a larger society and so it is never really private' (2002: 80). Nor is this sacred institution one truly lying outside the law's jurisdiction; the law itself defines what the family is, its constitution and constituency: what it is to be a man, woman (mother, wife) and child (Naffine, 2002: 83). However, it is the perpetuation of this very dichotomy of public and private that leaves, as Lucinda Finley contends, 'law largely ignorant of and unresponsive to what happens to women within the private realm. Thus the "public" language of law contributes to the silencing of women' (1989: 899).

The exemption of the 'private' realm from the law's gaze, however, not only renders all that happens within the family home as non-legal but significantly, as non-economic. Therefore, women's work within the family home, whether caring for children or undertaking housework, is systematically devalued, and becomes merely 'what women just do' (Graycar, 2002) – forms of gratuitous labour, explicable through concepts of love and affection. As Anna Lawson (1996) comments, the devaluing of labour stereotypically associated with women is particularly apparent in the (non)acquisition of beneficial interests in the family home:

> Most women, and indeed most of their partners, would probably be surprised to learn that if they designed, painted and decorated the home in which they lived with their *de facto* husband, they would be deemed to be acting out of love and affection or a desire to live in comfortable, pleasant surroundings, whereas if they used a 14 lb sledgehammer to break up concrete in the garden, or even contributed regularly to household bills, so as to enable their partner to pay the mortgage, they would be deemed to be motivated by a belief that they owned or that by so doing, would own an interest in the property.
> (Lawson, 1996: 229)

By focusing on direct financial contributions, and labour that goes over and above 'what women just do', Simone Wong argues that such equitable principles 'ignore the effects of sexual division of labour in such relationships, which place women at a disadvantage' (1998: 388). In a similar vein, Katharine Silbaugh (1996) notes that the law's failure to recognise a woman's work within the home as holding a productive value has been explicitly and implicitly justified through the discourses of love, leisure and affection. Therefore, despite its private nature, by no means is a woman's work in the home rendered invisible; rather it is 'subordinated to and dependent upon familial affections' (Silbaugh, 1996: 26).

Nor is a woman's work 'invisible' in the action for wrongful conception, since it is precisely this dimension that becomes the exclusive focus of the courts. Rather than being given productive value, caring work is conceptualised as sitting solely within the province of natural love, affection, care and gratuity. It is only once the caring labour goes beyond 'what women just do', as is typified by the wrongful birth and conception cases involving disabled children, that the law recognises the productive value of women's work in the form of an 'additional' (as opposed to the 'ordinary') award for maintenance. But we might be surprised as to how extensive the nature of that ordinary burden actually is. While Reg Graycar (2002: 207) suggests that others, such as grandmothers, are exempted from taking on the ordinary burden of caring, this caveat no longer applies in the English law of negligence. As the wrongful conception case of *AD v East Kent Community NHS Trust* [2002] EWCA Civ 1872 illustrates, women's caring roles extend well beyond the ordinary burdens of 'motherhood'. In this case, the claimant was a patient detained under the Mental Health Act 1983 in the care of the defendant NHS Trust. She became pregnant while living on a mixed ward, and gave birth to a healthy child. Asserting that her pregnancy was the result of the trust's various failures, including inadequate supervision and the failure to arrange a sterilisation, the claimant sought damages for pain and suffering attendant upon pregnancy and childbirth, the psychiatric trauma caused by her separation from and inability to raise the child, and the additional costs of the child's upbringing, maintenance and education. However, this latter head of damages was sought not for the claimant, but the child's grandmother who, having been granted a residence order, had taken on the role of the child's carer. While *AD* raises numerous issues of considerable interest,[10] of concern here is the court's response to the claim for the substitute cost of care and the question as to whether the grandmother was providing 'caring services' or 'gratuitous care'. In denying the claim for maintenance costs on the basis of *McFarlane*, Cooke J at first instance (*AD v East Kent Community NHS Trust* [2002] EWHC 1890) remarked:

> [B]oth the claimant, to some extent, and her mother, to a greater extent, have the benefits of the child, the value of whose life is incalculable to them. . . . Mrs A, whilst taking on, as a 50-year-old grandmother, a considerable burden in bringing up the child, also receives the great joy and blessing of such a child. . . . Mrs A has taken on a great responsibility, no doubt out of love for her daughter, out of a sense of responsibility for her granddaughter and because of natural ties of family love and affection. It clearly involves considerable sacrifice on her part.
>
> ([27])

But not a compensable sacrifice, since, as the judge concluded, to award the costs of maintenance would have the effect 'of valuing the child to Mrs A as more trouble than she is worth in circumstances where Mrs A, in place of an adoptive parent or foster parent, has voluntarily taken on herself the entire upbringing of the child' ([27]). Despite Mrs A's decision being driven by the 'highest motives', it could not realistically be said 'that she is providing services to the claimant'; rather, 'she is bringing up the child herself in substitution for the claimant' ([34]). And, the language of love, gratuity, voluntary assumption and joy also litters the Court of Appeal's determination of this case. Mrs A, though having given up full-time work for part-time work in order to care for her daughter's child, was not the provider of a 'service', but nevertheless she performed an act deserving of both sympathy and admiration in coming 'to C's rescue and provid[ing] her with the love and care that she needs' ([22] per Judge LJ). So, even when women sacrifice their employment and sources of staple income to care for a child there is *still* no economic value accorded to caring work; quite simply, if it is a 'loss' or a 'risk' emerging from the tort, it was one voluntarily undertaken. And this construction of women is a dominant theme that runs throughout these cases; according to one judge, if a woman were to obtain damages, 'she would happily be in a position whereby she would look after her much loved child at home, yet at the same time in effect would receive the income she would have earned had she stayed at work' (per Laws LJ p 1292 in *Greenfield v Irwin (A Firm) and Others* [2001] 1 WLR 1279). Rather than constituting compensation, this would be the 'conferment of a financial privilege' (p 1292).

But the legal construction of all these women as admirable volunteers is far from innocent. Rather, it is a legal strategy designed to 'absolve the defendant from the legal consequences of an unreasonable risk of harm created by the defendant, where the claimant has full knowledge of both the nature and extent of risk' (Jones, 2002: 591). And the judgments are simply imbued with the language of *volenti non fit injuria* – 'voluntary', 'acceptance', 'assumption' and 'willingness' – as expressions of the individual responsibility for the outcome harm.[11] So, in wrongful conception suits involving healthy children, women are constructed as having made a conscious and 'voluntary' choice to keep the child, as is evidenced by their failure to terminate their pregnancy or place the child up for adoption. In each case, all these women are characterised as having voluntarily run the 'risk',[12] and as having accepted private responsibility for the much 'loved', 'ordinary' and 'natural' consequences of negligence. Quite simply these women are the authors of their own great *fortunes* – only their own actions can be said to 'naturally flow' from the breach – for this is 'what women just do'. In her examination of ideas surrounding what is normal, ordinary or natural, Mayo Moran (2003: 157) observes that these conceptual devices have often been invoked to justify the discriminatory treatment of women, among others. And in the context of the wrongful conception and birth claims, these comments hold equal force. The consequences of negligence are the very ones the female claimants sought to avoid – there is nothing 'natural' about the attribution of responsibility *to* women in such cases. But, the wrongful conception and birth cases are not isolated examples. Such 'commonsense' ideas about the 'natural' essence of femininity are positively thriving – the stereotype of the devoted wife, loving mother and gratuitous homemaker, are frequently told stories in law. As Graycar comments in the context of personal injury awards for loss of sexual function, while a man's loss is primarily characterised as one of 'pleasure', 'it is easier to find references to women getting pleasure and satisfaction from housework than it is to find references to sexual pleasure' (2002: 207). Instead, the loss that women suffer is constructed as that consisting of her (in)capacity to reproduce, since 'the natural consequence of women having sex seems to be having children' (2002: 211). In addition, the devaluation of women's work within the home is well illustrated by the discounting of care given to injured family members; unless an individual has given up paid employment, 'the commercial rate is inappropriate where a relative acts out of love or a sense of duty' (Jones, 2002: 677; *McCamley v Cammell Laird Shipbuilders Ltd* [1990] 1 All ER 854). In these (non-exhaustive) instances the law is systematically articulating women's lack of 'attachment to the paid labour market in view of their childbearing capacity' (Graycar, 1995: 14), and is declaring that women's roles as carer, mother and home-worker, even when negligently brought about, are far from harmful. Rather, according to the law, these are the normal vicissitudes of life for which women are 'naturally' and morally responsible.

The 'Woman in Need'

Standing alongside these two images of undeserving women is the 'Woman in Need'; her situation is so different, so much more compelling, acting to further reinforce the law's decision to deny damages for the costs entailed with raising a healthy child. As Ognall J's dicta in *Jones v Berkshire Area Health Authority* (unreported, 2 July 1986) suggests, this Woman in Need might well reflect upon how fortunate those other women really are; by contrast with her situation, they are not only *better off*, but in some cases, in precisely the position that she longed for:

> I pause only to observe that, speaking purely personally, it remains a matter of surprise to me that the law acknowledges an entitlement in a mother to claim damages for the blessing of a healthy child. Certain it is that those who are afflicted with a handicapped child or who long desperately to have a child at all and are denied that good fortune would regard an award for this sort of contingency with a measure of astonishment.

As we saw from Chapter 3, the courts' response to cases of wrongful conception and birth involving disabled children provides a direct contrast to those involving healthy children; and these two kinds of cases are often played off against one another to illustrate that while some are so blessed by healthy children, 'others have the sorrow and burden of looking after a disabled child' (per Lord Steyn p 165 in *McFarlane*). In these cases, 'our joy at birth would not be unalloyed; it would be tinged with sorrow for the child's disability' (per Lord Millett at [112] in *Rees*). And this narrative of tragedy is a pretty constant feature across the judgments in the reproductive torts for this Woman in Need is an exceptional figure, and who is, unlike others, deserving of a legal response. The birth of an unwanted child for her is not the vicissitudes of life – it is so often a disaster; her accommodation is now rendered unsuitable, she struggles to make ends meet for this child and her existing family, she provides around-the-clock care for her severely disabled child who sometimes presents difficult and challenging behaviour; and so often does she suffer these burdens alone, following strained marriages, which eventually dissolve, or by virtue of disinterested and lazy partners. Similarly, though an exceptional case, such tragedy is also a feature of the account of Karina Rees; here too are we presented with the woman in need. As Hale LJ's account of the claimant in *Rees v Darlington Memorial Hospital* [2002] QB 20, this woman, unlike others, who 'are able to look after and bring up their child', *needs* help:

> [I]n order to be able to discharge the basic parental responsibility of looking after the child properly and safely, performing those myriad essential but mundane tasks such as feeding, bathing, clothing, training, supervising, playing with, reading to and taking to school which every child needs . . . [Able-bodied parents] do not need [help] in order to avoid the risk that the child may have to be taken away to be looked after by the local social services authority or others, to the detriment of the child as well as the parent.
>
> (per Hale LJ p28)

Of course, my criticisms surrounding this 'dichotomous' treatment of health and disability have been well rehearsed; the thrust of my argument was that it is impossible to sustain this difference whatever way one approached the matter. Yet despite the difficulties courts incurred in justifying this difference, the Woman in Need has been constructed as a most exceptional case. And it is her difference from *other* cases which has justified a departure from *McFarlane* and, according to Lord Steyn in *Rees*, the rules of distributive justice:

> While not wishing to endorse everything said in the detailed judgments [of *Parkinson*] . . . I agree with the decision. . . . In such cases normal principles of corrective justice permit recovery of compensation for the costs of providing for the child's needs and care relating to his disability but not for the basic costs of his maintenance.
>
> [35]

It is doubtful that the principles of corrective justice are operating here, for arguably such a conclusion should lead to full, rather than 'additional', damages. Yet while the presence of disability marked out an exceptional case of where a claimant had suffered harm, the view taken was that damages should nevertheless be limited, in light of *McFarlane*, given that those costs related to the ordinary costs of raising a child. In Hale LJ's view in *Rees*, awarding the claimant such additional damages would not overcompensate her, but put her 'in the same position as her able-bodied fellows' (pp 28–9).

In wrongful birth cases, however, such an approach to quantum is arguably (though not straightforwardly) justified. A good illustration as to the problems and promises of such an approach is provided by the case of *Salih v Enfield Health Authority* (1991) 7 BMLR 1. This case arose from a failure of the health authority to diagnose and warn the mother of the danger that the child she was carrying might be affected by rubella syndrome, with the result that she was unable to have the pregnancy terminated. While there was no question as to whether the additional costs of rearing a disabled child would be available, the issue debated at both first instance and in the Court of Appeal was whether the claimant was entitled to the ordinary costs of raising the child. Since the claimants in these cases wanted a healthy child, logically one can assume that they were willing to bear its ordinary costs. But what should a court make of this, in light of the birth of a disabled child, coupled with an abandonment of plans to have further children? The crux of the defendant's claim was that the birth of the disabled child had *saved* the plaintiffs the ordinary costs of bringing up a normal child. At first instance, Drake J rejected the defendant's argument as flawed; noting that while the costs relating to a healthy child would have been willingly incurred, negligence resulted in a severely disabled child that they never wanted. The Court of Appeal, however, concluded differently. In an evocative speech detailing the significant and unwanted repercussions of a severely physically disabled child upon the parents, the family as a whole, and in particular the wife, 'who has had the major care of the child', Butler-Sloss LJ conceded that the issue was 'difficult to evaluate entirely unemotionally'. Nevertheless, perhaps against her better judgment she considered it necessary to 'strip away the emotion from this case and look at the issue in terms of money for heads of damages that can properly be awarded'; and the result of which was a denial of ordinary damages.

There is no doubt that Butler-Sloss LJ was correct as to the motivational distinction between cases of wrongful birth and wrongful conception; in the latter, parents had firmly resolved not to have any further children. But what is open to debate is the assessment of damages resulting from the conclusion that the parents' complaint results not to the birth, 'but rather to the special burdens which the abnormality imposes' (Seymour, 2000: 93). Certainly the objective of damages in tort is to place the injured party, as far as money can do it, into the pre-tort position. But what is that *position* in such cases? No child being born at all, as a result of having the opportunity to terminate – or following termination, a 'replacement' healthy child (which Mrs Salih's later terminated foetus indicated that she would possibly have had)? The carving up of awards in these cases is fairly problematic, for it is questionable how, in either wrongful conception or wrongful birth involving disability, an award of additional damages could be viewed as restorative of the status quo. In wrongful conception cases, additional damages work upon the fiction that claimants are being placed into the same position as parents caring for healthy children; and wrongful birth cases work upon a similar fiction, via the parents' willingness to sustain 'ordinary' costs – they are only harmed insofar as the financial costs exceed those.

The Woman in Need, though indeed exceptional and treated very differently to other cases, is slightly more complex to evaluate because of the manner by which damages have been assessed. No doubt such approaches are capable of justification if one is willing to exercise pure logic (rather than emotion or common sense), or truly thinks that parents are only harmed insofar as most would naturally seek to avoid a disabled (rather than healthy) child. Although constructed as a devoted and tragic character, both deserving and needy, the limitation of damages to those flowing from the disability suggests that other factors are operating in these cases. The judiciary has not, for example, explicitly advocated that these women should mitigate their losses by placing a disabled child up for adoption or by terminating the pregnancy. While policy reasons may preclude advocating adoption in either case, and abortion could not run in wrongful birth cases where the claim turns on the lost opportunity to terminate, the situation in cases involving wrongfully conceived but disabled children is quite different. In such cases a woman's opportunity to access an abortion is that much greater than in the context of bearing a healthy child; by virtue of the 'foetal abnormality' ground under s 1(1)(d) of the Abortion Act 1967, her opportunity exists potentially up to term. Given this, might it not be questionable as to why the courts have not sought to scrutinise the claimant's choices to 'keep the child' as they have in situations involving the births of healthy children? While Mason *et al.* remark that there is 'no legislative basis for such a suggestion which has strong overtones of positive eugenics' (2002: 189), it should be noted that there is no legislative basis for creating a duty (hypothetical or not) to terminate healthy foetuses either. Nevertheless, while the fear of articulating views that could be perceived as eugenicist may well explain why courts do not closely scrutinise the choices of claimants in cases involving disability, possibly the better answer, and one certainly furnished in *Emeh*, is that the presence of disability is usually detected very late into pregnancy. On that basis not only would it appear to be too much to ask of any woman to access such a late abortion, but arguably quite distasteful for any court to scrutinise her failure to do so.

However, what the courts have felt themselves more able to scrutinise (most obviously in cases of wrongful birth) is the woman's prior 'willingness' to take on the burdens and costs that relate to the healthy child *she might have had*; and to set this off against the full costs relating to the birth of an unwanted disabled child. And so too does this theme appear to run in wrongful conception cases involving disabled children; although an exceptional woman, a woman in need, so too do the laws of natural maternity apply to her. If the Woman in Need is harmed, she is not harmed by virtue of having an unwanted child – wouldn't any woman be willing to bear those ordinary costs and burdens? Rather her labour and its productive value, her need for help only becomes apparent when these go beyond 'what women just do', culminating in an 'additional' (as opposed to ordinary) award for maintenance.

Conclusion: Not a choice?

This chapter commenced by briefly considering the ordinary rules of mitigation as they operate in the civil law and noted the anomalous treatment of women in the reproductive torts. By comparison to other contexts where a mitigation enquiry is invoked, the standard imposed in cases of wrongful conception has not merely been an objective one, but, as I suggested, it is one that borders on strict liability. In the absence of a suitable justification for this, for example the existence of insurance, the remaining analysis was dedicated to exploring why courts have imposed this higher standard. Drawing upon Sheldon's (1997) analysis of the parliamentary debates leading up to the Abortion Act 1967, three stereotypes of choosing/non-choosing individuals were located in the narrative of the courts: the self-regarding woman, the natural woman and the woman in need. The first two constructions of choice presented women who had exercised a choice, whether driven by selfish and self-regarding desires or a natural maternal instinct to love and care for a healthy child. Neither of these women is considered by the law to be deserving of a legal response – not only have they chosen the consequences, but this is simply 'what women just do'. Reinforcing these images of undeserving women is the construction of a desperate and needy individual. This woman, by contrast, *does* capture the courts' attention, for her circumstances are so different. She is constructed as isolated and vulnerable, her labour as that much harder, and the outcome of negligence, at least insofar as it does not reject 'ordinary' maternal norms, is so obviously unwanted.

The stereotypes presented by the courts are powerful; they play upon an amalgamation of attributes and circumstances pertaining to both real and imagined women. The facts of the cases *do* reveal the hardship and significant impact on the lives of claimants following the birth of a disabled child; claimants in wrongful birth cases *had* sought the birth of a healthy child; and by virtue of their bringing such claims to court for child maintenance damages, we can safely assume that claimants *have* kept their children. Yet what has been excluded from the courts' construction of these choosing and unchoosing individuals is *more* telling: the courts' failure to enquire into whether these claimants really did choose to keep their children, the repercussions on women's lives in caring for unwanted but healthy children, and how, for claimants in wrongful birth and conception cases, *all* the repercussions flowing from their negligently born children were unwanted. But these images all play upon a powerful and stubborn stereotype:

> [T]here is a strong ideology that through pregnancy and childbirth an enduring bond develops between mother and child which cannot easily be broken. This mystical bond is perceived of as inevitable, and more powerful than any woman can realize in advance. . . . Insofar as the ideology designates women as the natural rearers of children, it has been used to limit women's options outside the home, especially in the workplace, and thus has not been entirely favourable to women. But as a model for how we might want parents to feel about their children, it seems a constructive starting point . . .
>
> (Bartlett, 1988: 333)

The ideology of natural bonds of love and affection is absolutely central to the actions of wrongful conception and birth. It is this dimension that is heavily canvassed by those who most object to parents receiving damages awards for unplanned children – how can a parent be harmed, or a child 'unwanted', when their child is so loved?[13] Of course, there is a grain of truth in such claims – as Tony Weir's illustrations of the 'outrages consequent on *Emeh*' portray, there is no doubt that many of these parents do love their children – and quite readily declare that they would not give them up 'for the world' (Weir, 2000: 131). This issue constitutes the most powerful objection against recovery; and it is not one that is overcome by disputing the universality of this parental love. No doubt many parents will come to embrace and love their *initially* unwanted child. It is *this issue* that is most frequently invoked as a counterpoint for recovery, and it does provide a coherent explanation as to why the courts, and indeed some scholars, see these claims as far less deserving of damages (typically from the cash-strapped NHS) than other clinical negligence claims. After all, how many other victims of clinical negligence are simply delighted with their injuries; and if they had the opportunity to avoid that injury, would they not have chosen to avoid it? Given the critical nature of this question, and my view that the existence of 'love' far from indicates that parents are left *un*harmed, this question will be tackled in due course. Before doing so, however, there is a prior question that needs addressing. In Chapter 6 I take up an issue that the courts and the rhetoric of maternal love has speedily dismissed: whether women who deliberate between terminating a pregnancy, placing a child up for adoption or keeping the child, really do have a choice. Although courts have assumed that decisions to keep healthy children are always welfare-maximising and natural choices for which claimants should inevitably be responsible, without an enquiry as to the reasonableness of such choices, arguably this conclusion can be disrupted; here we might forward that these claimants' decisions were not motivated by love or the exercise of rational choice at all, because neither adoption nor abortion constitute choices. This is, of course, quite different to saying that parents had a difficult choice; the possibility being furnished here is that keeping a child constituted inaction in the face of having absolutely *no* choice. Thus, we might formulate the kind of argument that the pursuers' Counsel advanced in *McFarlane*:

> The parents had no choice ... since it is a part of their culture that parents do not put their children up for adoption ... The parents were also morally opposed to abortion. Therefore it is not reasonable to say that they exercised a choice. Matters were beyond their control from the moment of conception. They did not 'choose' to keep the child.
>
> (p 65)

But can this be right? Does an abortion not constitute a choice? Do women have *no choice* but to continue with their pregnancies? Arguably, if women are incapable of exercising their reproductive autonomy, by choosing to terminate a pregnancy or to place a child up for adoption, then surely it cannot be right to hold them responsible for the consequences that follow; the consequences were, on this view, completely unavoidable. And such an argument seems to provide a suitable rejoinder for Mason's contention that 'it is at least arguable that the exercise of that autonomy involves acceptance of the consequences of the exercise' (2004: 15), for here we would be emphasising that while on the one hand a woman should be entitled to freely choose in matters of reproduction, on the other, the exercise of reproductive choice is an entirely different matter – here she cannot choose. Yet, the problems of these arguments are apparent. First, they seem pretty absurd, given that many women do choose to access precisely these reproductive options. Therefore, it is impossible to say at a general level that women as a class do not choose. But second, and more significantly, such a strategy is arguably dangerous. Presenting reproductive decisions as difficult or impossible for women not only threatens to reinforce the very images of natural motherhood that the courts have invoked ('she had no other choice'), where the 'right' choice for every woman is to continue her pregnancy, but one that represents women as unable to exercise choice, as non-autonomous, non-choosing agents, in need of regulation and control. On the face of it, then, it would seem that there are significant costs entailed in emphasising that a woman has *no* choice.

The construction of choice in the reproductive torts, while problematic, is underpinned by a kind of logic that is difficult to refute. *Our* choice is this: women are either held completely responsible for their 'choices' (even when those don't feel like choices), or viewed as lacking responsible agency given their inability to exercise choice. Neither outcome is desirable. Yet, as the next chapter seeks to illustrate, this representation of choice is not isolated to cases of wrongful conception. Departing from the immediate context of the reproductive torts, we briefly turn to consider 'choice' in the field of reproduction, more generally. As the analysis endeavours to show, while there is an obvious need to exercise extreme caution in theorising what should count as a 'choice', it should also be recognised that the dominant discourse of 'choice' presents us with the same double bind; while a decision to abort or place a child up for adoption for some will constitute a 'choice', if applied to *all*, it risks masking and trivialising the experiences of those who do not, like the claimants in these cases, experience these acts of 'choosing' as constituting a 'choice'.

Notes

1 For detailed examinations of feminist scholarship on the 'Reasonable Man', see in particular, Conaghan (1996); Conaghan and Mansell (1999) and Moran (2003).
2 See also Simons (1997), in which the author provides a detailed exploration of the justifiable criteria and limits of claimant strict responsibility.
3 For a succinct appraisal of the possible risks and side-effects of an abortion at different gestational stages, see Glover (1977: 142–3).
4 The same statistical decline is evident in the UK where a large proportion of adoptions are by step-parents (see Bridge, 1993: 83). The decline might be explained by reference to reproductive technologies and increased desires for genetically related children.
5 Under the eggshell-skull rule, providing that the 'kind' of damage is foreseeable, the defendant will remain responsible even where an injury of a different or unforeseeable type occurs (*Bradford v Robinson Rentals Ltd* [1967] 1 All ER 267).
6 In this case, the defendant stabbed the victim, piercing her lung. She died following her refusal to accept a life-saving blood transfusion on the grounds of her religious convictions as a Jehovah's Witness. Rejecting the defendant's argument that her refusal was unreasonable and broke the chain of causation, Lawton LJ instructed the jury that the stab wound was the operative and substantial cause of death.
7 While courts are shifting towards adopting a slightly more critical stance over medical opinion (see *Bolitho v City and Hackney Health Authority* [1997] 4 All ER 771; *Chester v Afshar* [2004] UKHL 41), their reluctance to find clinical opinion unreasonable through the imposition of a more stringent standard of care include fears of hindering medical progress, encouraging the practice of defensive medicine, imposing a heavy burden upon the NHS through litigation, as well as the judiciary's recognition of its own limitations in acting as an arbiter of scientific perspectives, which though often conflicting, can be reasonably held. Nevertheless, this latter point, as Norrie argues, holds considerable weight in relation to moral perspectives surrounding abortion.
8 For a critical discussion of the standard of care, see further Conaghan and Mansell (1999: 52–62).
9 See Stephen Wilkinson's (2003) full and engaging critique of commodification in the context of commercial uses of the body.
10 Note that this case was decided prior to the House of Lords' determination of *Rees v Darlington Memorial Hospital* [2003] UKHL 52. Therefore, in determining whether a claimant, suffering from mental disability, should be able to make a claim for the costs of care, the courts were bound by *Rees* at Court of Appeal level *and* the House of Lords' determination of *McFarlane*. Despite the possible parallels that could be drawn between *Rees* and *AD* on the basis of disability, there were several complicating factors. First, the claimant would never be in a position to look after the child; these facts served to differentiate *AD* from precedent. Second, while the damages were claimed on the basis of the substitute cost of care, the case did not fall squarely within the principle of *Hunt v Severs* [1994] 2 AC 356, since normally such care is provided directly for the injured claimant. Nevertheless, a

fuller analysis of the wrongful birth cases illustrates that some courts have been willing to interpret these principles in favour of the claimants.
11 *Volenti non fit injuria* has a considerable overlap with contributory negligence and the doctrine of mitigation. Each approach expresses the idea that an individual should take responsibility for her own actions and thereby centralises the claimant's behaviour.
12 A further related point that is not explored here for reasons of space is the gendered construction of risk-taking. As Jenny Steele comments, while men's risk-taking is defined as virtuous, courageous and heroic, risk-taking is less 'valorised for the performance of femininity' (2004: 161). Nevertheless, the point that is being made here is that such reproductive risks are not being constructed as productive of harmful outcomes, but rather beneficial ones.
13 See, for example, Meagher JA's judgment in *CES Superclinics (Australia) Pty Ltd* (1995) 38 NSWLR 47, in which he points to this dimension as giving rise to problems where mothers variously describe their children as loved or unloved, and comments ([10]), 'Does that not indicate that the law has strayed into an area in which it has no business?'

Chapter 6

Reproductive choice, reproductive reality

> Fertile women can stop baby making with Norplant, RU486, or abortion. Infertile couples can still make babies with the help of artificial insemination, *in vitro* fertilisation, donor semen, donor eggs, frozen embryos, and surrogate motherhood. Soon we will be able to exact quality control regarding the health and perhaps the genetic make-up of future children with the aid of genetic screening, genetic engineering, nuclear transplantation, egg fusion, cloning, selective abortion, and *in utero* fetal surgery. A woman can become a mother at age 62. And if experiments in ectogenesis and interspecies gestation prove successful, a woman will be able to become a mother without herself becoming pregnant.
>
> (Peters, 1996: 11)

The human biography is in a state of flux. No longer determined by traditional identities, the *human being* has become 'a choice among possibilities, *homo optionis*' (Beck and Beck-Gernsheim, 2003: 5). Even the most fundamental aspects of daily living are characterised by a plurality of 'choice': life, death, gender, corporeality, identity, religion, marriage, parenthood, social ties – all become negotiable, 'decidable down to the small print' (2003: 5). And from the era of 'choice' emerges an ethic – an ethic of individual self-fulfilment where the 'choosing, deciding, shaping being who aspires to be the author of his or her own life, the creator of an individual identity, is the central character of our time' (2003: 22). But the concept of 'choice' should not fool us here – the notion of self-determination is 'compulsive and obligatory' (2003: xv). So while 'individualisation' heralds the end of 'fixed, predefined images of man' (2003: 5), in the sense that the individual's biography is released from 'given determinations' and placed under the control of the self, it also means being '*forced* to live a more reflective life towards an open future' (Giddens, 1999b). In other words, faced with a plurality of lifestyle choices where 'the signposts established by tradition now are blank', we have 'no choice but to choose' (Giddens, 1991: 82).

'Choice' might well seem too inconsequential a word for what is going on here; for facing an open future with a plurality of choices is not merely a question of 'how to act but who to be' (Giddens, 1991: 81). It means actively 'creating a self-identity rather than simply taking self-identity from a cultural background or traditional form of history' (Giddens, 1999b). And for women this has held the promise of truly liberating consequences; as Beck and Beck-Gernsheim comment, the female biography has undergone an 'individualisation boost' (2003: 55). Tradition and nature, forces that once structured what it was to be 'a woman' – a life bound in domesticity, motherhood and subordination 'in a male dominated universe' (Giddens, 1999b) – are now declining in their impact. Although motherhood remains 'the strongest tie to the traditional female role', the continued subordination of 'nature to human purposes' (Giddens, 1991: 144) serves to disrupt the notion of reproduction as 'fate' or 'natural'. On this view, it seems that reproduction has become 'a variable individual decision' (Giddens, 1991: 221) – a lifestyle choice, as the woman's reproductive biography transforms from 'ascribed' to 'acquired', from 'living for others' to a 'life of one's own' (Beck and Beck-Gernsheim, 2003: 56). The body becomes 'emancipated' (Giddens, 1991: 218) through the transformative power of technology – the power of choice. But increased choice has its consequences, since with the individualisation of choice comes the individualisation of risks. No longer are life's events conceived as attributable to things *that just happen*; rather, failures are located at an individual level, and seen instead as 'consequences of the decisions they themselves have made, which they must view and treat as such' (Beck, 1992: 136). But under this imperative of choice, not only is the individual responsible for the decisions s/he consciously makes, but also for non-decisions, omissions and incapacities (Beck and Beck-Gernsheim, 2003: 25). The individual 'will have to "pay for" the consequences of decisions not taken', even in the absence of alternatives (Beck, 1992: 135).

In matters of reproduction, the significance of this is clear – increased reproductive choice 'comes at a price' (Millns, 2001: 475). The widely held perception that nature can be controlled to suit our needs imposes a burden of responsibility upon individuals, a burden to make 'responsible' choices under the new morality of reproduction. While there are clear dangers that increased choice may 'swiftly evolve into pressure to reproduce' (Millns, 2001: 475), so too can it swiftly translate into a pressure *not* to reproduce. In an era of increased technological control, and increased sentimentalism surrounding children, notions of responsibility have come to take on a much broader meaning:

> The more that safe methods of contraception become available, the more widespread becomes the idea of responsible parenthood. Once this referred to the quantitative aspect: only as many children as you can properly bring up and provide for. Now, with the new possibilities in reproductive medicine and prenatal diagnostics, the concept of responsibility

has been moving in the direction of a qualitative choice that begins before birth or perhaps even before conception.
(Beck and Beck-Gernsheim, 2003: 146)

Women face shifting discourses here; while responsibility is presented as meaning *greater autonomy* (Beck and Beck-Gernsheim, 2003), the traditional norms of maternity have given way to new reproductive norms under which women are *always* confronted with the permanent pain of action. No longer does responsible parenthood simply mean 'intentional parenthood' and 'wanted children' – although it clearly means this too. As 'accidents' transform into 'preventable misfortunes', there is no justification for women to fall pregnant when they crave independent lives. Under the new morality of reproduction, Mary Evans explains, 'a good woman is one who makes effective use of contraception, and sexual relations between unmarried heterosexual partners are acceptable so long as both are 'careful' (2003: 97). Nothing it seems needs to be left to fate; or rather under the notion of reproductive autonomy, nothing *should* be left to fate. The new morality of reproduction, then, is not only 'about the use of technology' (Evans, 2003: 97); it also entails a judgment upon women.

Whether these discourses surrounding 'choice' fairly reflect the reality of women's lives is questionable; the notion that a pregnancy is 'preventable' by virtue of contraception, as Maxine Lattimer comments, 'contradicts realities for women' (1998: 64). Furthermore, the presentation of reproduction as a preventable misfortune in the complete control *of women* conceals 'inequalities of power between men and women' and 'issues of women being responsible for male sexuality' (Lattimer, 1998: 64). But of equal concern, this rhetoric of reproductive choice presents women with a 'double-bind', since:

> They live in a society that constructs motherhood as good and abortion as bad through dominant discourses, but the same discourses assert that babies should be born in the 'right' circumstances. Women are condemned if they do have an abortion, but also if they continue with a pregnancy in culturally unacceptable circumstances that are not 'fair' to the child. Aspects of hegemonic discourses of motherhood condemn single mothers living on state benefits, lone parents and broken homes for being 'unfair' on children, and women who work and leave their children with childminders for not being caring mothers. This is the reality of the contradictory pressures on British women with unplanned or unwanted pregnancies who must make decisions regarding abortion ...
> (Lattimer, 1998: 66)

While these hegemonic discourses present conflicting messages about sexuality, reproduction and motherhood, it is precisely this increasing conflation of 'choice' and 'responsibility *to choose*' that should concern us. Not only are the choices now presented to women so capable of becoming *choice diminishing*, but the very language central to strategies designed to enhance *women's* reproductive freedom is being used *against us* – 'choice' can so easily become anyone's battle cry. We may live in an era of seemingly endless reproductive possibilities, but if women's freedom is to be preserved among them, then there are very good reasons for re-evaluating the political effectiveness and the epistemological foundation of 'A Woman's Right to Choose'.

A (wo)man's right to choose

> For feminists, pregnant women are the best judges of whether abortion is an appropriate response to their pregnancies . . . best able to weigh the relevant factors – the particular consequences of pregnancy in their lives at that time and/or the potential life under the circumstances.
>
> (Bender, 1993: 1263)

> If you exclude yourself from the process, or if you are excluded from the process, I think that's terrible. It's a gap in the child's life which is very difficult to fill later on. I went to everything, all the ultrasound scans. I thought 'To hell with it the rest of my life has to be chucked out.' I was going to have these nine months, it was going to be my time, as well as hers. *Steven, 44, father of one*
>
> (Fathers Direct, 2001: 3)

Foregoing chapters have presented the harms of enforced reproduction and parenthood as ones that are experienced by *women* – by contrast, *men* have been fairly shadowy individuals throughout. For some, this omission will be unforgivable. What about men's choices? What about the construction of paternity that arises in these cases? What about men's involvement in the processes of reproduction and parenthood and the impact upon *their* lives? More suspiciously still, why only raise 'men' in the analysis where it serves to highlight their lack of involvement, their disinterest and their absence? And these are all fair points. The case law in this field readily illustrates that procedures designed to avoid reproduction are not merely performed on women, but also men (vasectomy). Furthermore, in those cases where both parties have brought a claim for wrongful conception, couples, rather than just an individual woman, may well have arrived at the 'joint' decision to abstain from parenthood, or in the cases of wrongful birth, made the joint decision to have a (healthy) child. In those cases, while women must confront a changed life plan as a result of a negligently born child, so too does this apply to men. None of this is denied. While my concern throughout the book has been, and continues to be, with *women*, by no means is this to undermine men or the importance of their contribution to the upbringing and care needed for a child.

That said, it would be a mistake to think that my analysis as to the way that women are harmed through enforced reproduction might therefore have *equal* application to men; in this respect, men are so differently situated. Although men contribute their genetic material to the resulting progeny, for the greater part they *are* fairly distant characters in the processes of reproduction. And while men can certainly take on the primary role of providing hands-on care for a child, it remains the case that more often than not, this burden falls upon women. Without wishing to deny the importance of joint decision making occurring prior to reproduction or the role that fathers can and do play, given the unique decisional responsibility that confronts a woman, *her* choice as to whether or not to continue with a pregnancy must always be paramount.

This does, however, raise important questions around the nature of 'choice'. If women have the right to choose to avoid reproduction via abortion, then why can't men who have no wish for fatherhood also exercise their reproductive choices? If women can choose motherhood, then why can't men demand that women continue with their pregnancies under circumstances where their partner seeks an abortion? What about men's interests in matters of reproduction? Indeed it was precisely this threat of 'interested parties' contesting notions of 'choice' and 'rights' in the area of abortion that led Elizabeth Kingdom to warn that if women have the right to reproduce, 'there is no obvious reason why that right should not be claimed for men too, and on traditional liberal grounds of equality it would be difficult to oppose that claim' (cited in Beveridge and Mullally, 1995: 247).

Recent years have illustrated how the reproductive realm threatens to become a site of increased progenitive contestation; the landscape is changing in the face of quite dramatic changes in reproductive and familial norms. Sex is no longer inevitably tied to procreation, nor is procreation tied to marriage; relationships are no longer endurance contests, but more a matter of choice as divorce rates and different living arrangements illustrate (lone parenthood, cohabitation and stepfamilies). In the light of familial breakdown, increasing emphasis has been placed on the welfare of children and parental responsibility; the role of genetic fathers has been afforded a central role in legislative efforts to entrench their responsibility towards children, not only financially (the Child Support Act 1991), but actively 'during marriage and partnership and after divorce or separation', via the Children Act 1989 and the Family Law Act 1996 (Collier, 2001: 530). And increasingly, the care of a child is presented as not merely matter that can be handled individually, but as a joint enterprise; men's active involvement in the care and upbringing of children is typified by some as not merely desirable, but of critical importance to children's educational and social development (Jack O'Sullivan, *The Times* 23 November 2004). Even donations of gametes, though not giving rise to financial or legal responsibility, give rise to a new sense of social accountability to genetic offspring as the curtain of anonymity is lifted on the identity of those who choose to become donor 'mums' and 'dads'.[1] While 'conventional wisdom' has told us that 'women are interested in sex for procreation, men are interested in sex for pleasure' (Sheldon, 1999: 130), undoubtedly the significance of sex has also dramatically changed in the face of conflicting desires about the welfare of existing and future children. Sexual gratification may only last for moments, but can result in an enduring responsibility for both men and women. Yet if the resulting responsibility is only desired by one party, can it be any wonder that matters of reproduction might end up looking more like a pre-emptive custody battle?

That risk arguably materialised in the context of a challenge to the provisions of the Human Fertilisation and Embryology Act 1990 (hereafter 'the 1990 Act') in the case of *Evans v Amicus Healthcare Ltd and Others (Secretary of State for Health intervening)* [2004] EWCA Civ 727; *Evans v UK* (Application 6339/05, decided March 2006). Here, the courts were confronted with competing claims over stored embryos created from the gametes of a couple, Ms Evans and Mr Johnson (J), who had separated prior to implantation. J, who had agreed for the use of his sperm for this purpose, later withdrew his consent and later wrote to the clinic asking for the destruction of the embryos. Ms Evans, who had agreed to the harvesting of her eggs and the creation of embryos with J's sperm, had done so with the express purpose of retaining the ability to have a child in the future. The (then) couple's decision had followed the devastating news that both of Ms Evans's ovaries would need to be removed owing to the presence of serious precancerous tumours. Ms Evans, who sought to use the stored embryos in order to become pregnant, therefore sought to challenge specific provisions of the 1990 Act, notably Sched 3, which necessitated the destruction of the embryos once one of the parties withdrew their consent to their continued storage. Ms Evans's challenge, which *inter alia* sought a declaration of incompatibility under Arts 8 (the right to respect for private and family life), 12 (the right to marry and found a family) and 14 (freedom from discrimination), also pleaded that the embryos were entitled to protection under Arts 2 (the right to life) and 8. Her action failed in the High Court, the Court of Appeal and in the European Court of Human Rights.

In so many ways this is an incredibly tragic case. These embryos constituted Ms Evans's only chance to have a child to whom she was biologically related; her choice to become a parent would be permanently frustrated by J's choice to withdraw his consent. Yet how to reconcile these competing desires? Undoubtedly, on its facts and the provisions of the 1990 Act, the case could *only* be reconciled in J's favour. The 1990 Act very clearly requires the consent of both parties seeking 'treatment together' under s 6(3) of Sched 3:

> An embryo the creation of which was brought about *in vitro* must not be used for any purpose unless there is an effective consent by each person whose gametes were used to bring about the creation of the embryo

to the use for that purpose of the embryo and the embryo is used in accordance with those consents.

Furthermore, J was entitled, up to the point of 'use' (s 4(2))^2 to vary or revoke that consent under s 4(1) of Sched 3:

> The terms of any consent under this Schedule may from time to time be varied, and the consent may be withdrawn, by notice given by the person who gave the consent to the person keeping the gametes or embryo to which the consent is relevant.

Central to this case was the concept of 'treatment together' under the 1990 Act. The ethos of a 'joint [genetic] enterprise' underpins not only the consent provisions, but the circumstances by which treatment can be provided. On this basis, even if Ms Evans could have shown that J's consent was satisfied or that his withdrawal of consent was invalid, the embryos resulting from the genetic material of both Ms Evans and J could not be implanted unless such services were provided to both parties 'together' (s 28(3) of the 1990 Act). In the context of the parties' estrangement (a circumstance that had not been expressly considered during consultation leading up to the 1990 Act), this would be impossible to show. However, while the verdict in *Evans* 'was entirely predictable given the very clear wording of both the HFEA 1990 and the various consent forms signed at the time the embryos were created' (Sheldon, 2004: 451), and highlights fairly significant flaws with the provisions of the 1990 Act, what is interesting to briefly explore here is how the Court of Appeal sought to reconcile the competing choices/intentions of the parties. J's 'right to choose' to avoid parenthood is certainly rendered fully effective under the terms of the 1990 Act, but what was less clear, as Arden LJ questioned, was the rationale of parliament in requiring such 'joint' consent:

> There are a number of possible reasons for requiring the consent of the genetic father at all stages. It can be said that it is important to involve the male at all stages so as to ensure that he will be involved in the upbringing of the child. No doubt that is a very good idea in principle but the genetic father can equally withdraw his consent after implantation. Moreover, it is not to be assumed that the child cannot properly be brought up without two parents. Another approach might be that the father has some rights of property in his genetic material. But the question posed by this case is, why should he have any right of property in this regard since he would not have had any right of property if sexual intercourse had taken place in the normal course of events?
>
> [88]

On this issue, there is no clear answer; however, as the court explored, one potential rationale for the continuing requirement of a father's consent to storage of his genetic material may relate to the potential 'feelings of guilt or even responsibility, for instance if the mother became unable to look after the child' (per Arden LJ at [89]). The importance of a man's choice is not merely because it can result in legal and financial responsibility; in response to the question as to whether he would feel differently under circumstances where he escaped legal responsibility, J's desire to avoid parenthood was conceptualised as one also motivated by the prospect of an *emotional* responsibility:

> He does not want to know there is a child of his growing up in some other town. So the wider issue arises whether in a world in which many people have come to accept a woman's right of choice as to whether she should have a child or not, the genetic father should have the equivalent right – a right greater than that conferred by nature.... Is it to be supposed that, if a father in this situation some years after the birth of the child met the child, in whom the spark of human life had by then been kindled by his ex-partner, he would be bound to say 'I wish you had never been'? These are difficult questions.
>
> (per Arden LJ at [89])

The notion that men wish to avoid – like women – the significant financial, legal and *emotional* responsibilities that attend parenthood powerfully raises the question as to why the 'Right to Choose' should not be extended to men more generally in matters of reproduction. In the context of the consent provisions of the 1990 Act, a man's autonomy when pitted against a woman's is in one sense rendered 'equal'; a woman can avoid parenthood by withdrawing her consent, as can a man. Both their Art 8 rights in this context are fully invoked:

> The fact is that each person has a right to be protected against interference with their private life. That is an aspect of the principle of self-determination or personal autonomy. It cannot be said that the interference with Mr Johnson's right is justified on the ground that interference is necessary to protect Ms Evans's right, because her right is likewise qualified in the same way by his right. They must have equivalent rights ... The interference with Ms Evans's private life is also justified under Article 8(2) because, if Ms Evans's argument succeeded, it would amount to interference with the genetic father's right to decide not to become a parent. Motherhood could surely not be forced on Ms Evans and likewise fatherhood cannot be forced on Mr Johnson, especially as in the present case it will probably involve financial responsibility in law for the child as well.
>
> (per Arden LJ at [110–11])

Setting aside my own personal difficulties with the case and the tragic nature of a decision that seems inevitable on a reading of the 1990 Act, the pressing issue here is whether the principles raised in this case could have more general application. The Court recognised that while Ms Evans's bodily integrity (private life) is affected, she could not assert her right to a family life with such a future child where the embryo has not yet been transferred to her ([108]). Given this, because the consent provision was intended to 'reverse nature's discrimination' (per Thorpe LJ at [72]), the 1990 Act could only be seen as discriminatory as between 'women who can and women who cannot conceive through sexual intercourse', and not between the two parties in this case who were determined to have equivalent rights. But how far into the processes of reproduction does that equivalency extend? At what point would an attempt to 'reverse nature's discrimination', a 'formal equality' approach, serve to render the parties' choices unequal?

Reversing nature's discrimination

As Arden LJ noted, in normal sexual intercourse 'a man gives his sperm voluntarily but is not thereafter in a position to prevent the consequent birth of a child' ([86]). And indeed, men's past attempts to invoke their autonomy rights against their sexual partners at later points in the reproductive process have proved unsuccessful. The courts at both domestic and European level have proved resistant to attempts to co-opt as is demonstrated by the failure of putative fathers' attempts to gain a decisional stance in the abortion decision (*C v S* [1987] 2 WLR 1108; *Paton v BPAS* [1979] 1 QB 276; *Paton v UK* (1981) 3 EHRR 408). In matters of abortion, the only parties who have the power to interfere with a woman's decision are registered medical practitioners under the terms of the 1967 Act. This, coupled with the foetus being afforded no right of its own until birth and having an existence separate from its mother in English law, would surely render a man's claim that his rights should prevail over that of a woman's, a 'manifestly ill-founded' one (*Paton v UK*).

Yet, there is little room for complacency here either, for it would seem that a possible consequence of men's exclusion from the abortion decision has been the creation of a different argument forwarded by men's advocates: if women have unilateral control over whether or not to continue a pregnancy, it is unfair to hold genetic fathers financially liable for child support. The logic of this claim, as Sally Sheldon explains, is that legal abortion has challenged the 'inevitability of the causal link between sex and procreation and, as such, it is unfair not to allow that this chain may also be broken for men in certain circumstances' (2003: 178). Although generated to challenge the provisions of the Child Support Act 1991, which continues to impose an 'absolute and unreserved responsibility' upon men to provide support for their genetic offspring, of interest here is the emergence of this argument in the broader field of reproduction and its resonance with claims raised in the context of wrongful conception. Akin to mitigation, the men's advocates' argument poses the same hypothetical duty; women are not being asked to terminate their pregnancies; rather, these men seek to extricate themselves from the financial responsibilities where women forego their autonomous *choice* to do so. Of course, this reading of choice seems *compulsive* and *obligatory* – if not downright *threatening* – but perhaps the most disconcerting feature of this rights-based argument is that it is 'made in the language of feminism' (Nolan, 1998: 218). And on traditional liberal grounds of 'equality' it *is* an extremely difficult claim to rebut – unless, that is, we are prepared to say that a woman has no choice but to continue a pregnancy?

'In practice abortion is not a choice'

As a starting point we might employ a legal perspective and point to those jurisdictions where abortion is generally prohibited in order to argue that women have little choice *but* to continue a pregnancy. And in this respect, the jurisdictional competence of the 1967 Act is limited. By contrast with the rest of the UK, its provisions have no application to Northern Ireland where doctors continue to rely on the archaic 'good faith' provision created by the case of *R v Bourne* (1939) 1 KB 687. Here, terminations are only permitted where the continuation of the pregnancy creates a serious risk that the woman will become a 'physical or mental wreck'. But in the absence of guidelines, many women may be uncertain whether they fit within the terms of a permissible abortion (Fegan and Rebouche, 2003: 222). As a result, those seeking abortion services will do so by, 'illegal and often dangerous means or through travel (mostly in secret and at great cost) to clinics in Great Britain' (Fegan and Rebouche, 2003: 227). If there is anything close to 'choice' here, by no means is it a 'free' one.

But even where the 1967 Act does apply, it is arguable that the notion of 'choice' still fails to reflect the reality of abortion provision. Despite the apparent liberal provision of abortion under the Act, as Emily Jackson notes, there is no right to abortion 'even if the grounds in the Act are plainly satisfied' (2000: 470). Women continue to be *dependent* on medical discretion, and will need to convince two non-conscientiously objecting doctors under s 1(1)(a) of the Act that an abortion is necessary.[3] Furthermore, women reliant upon NHS funding may not only encounter hostility and judgmental treatment from medical practitioners, but increasingly significant delays in the performance of a termination *if* permission is granted. And in view of the considerable variations in NHS abortion provision nationwide, accessing such services may well depend on the woman's postcode (Sheldon, 1998: 46), leaving some having to pay for an abortion in the private sector (Jackson, 2000: 471). While these legal and practical obstacles to abortion provision must leave us doubting the reality of 'choice', by no means is this the only concern. What constitutes a choice is rendered more problematic given an analysis of the 'neglected space between discursive constructions and women's actual negotiation of them in their own experiences' (Fegan, 1999: 258).

'Women do not experience abortion as a choice'

> [A]t the heart of this issue is the fact that women generally do not experience the decision to abort as one of choice . . . rather, most women who abort perceive termination as their only viable option.
>
> (Fox, 1998: 82)[4]

Presenting abortion as a matter of choice ignores the fact that most women would rather not be in the position of having to make *that* choice at all. And arguably, it is this dimension of choice that receives less pro-choice 'air-time' – women's *negative* experiences of abortion decision making. Nevertheless, reluctance to engage in such discussion is perhaps understandable, since those holding political opposition to abortion or general designs towards denying women an *active* choice in reproduction so often typify the issue in *primarily* negative terms. As Mary Boyle comments, such discourse was evident in the parliamentary debates leading up to the enactment of the Abortion Act 1967, which presented abortion decision making as: 'inevitably painful and traumatic', 'a decision that women agonize about', 'a decision of despair', 'intolerable' and 'complex' – when by contrast, evidence illustrates that *many* women *do not* find such decisions difficult, particularly when made at an early stage (Boyle, 1997: 104–5). But, nor is the negative construction of abortion simply limited to decision making; increasingly, accounts of abortion itself are typified as not only traumatic, but deeply harmful to women's physical and *mental* health. And for this reason, great caution is required in problematising women's negative experiences, since this latter claim, as Ellie Lee explains, is not only politically driven, but constitutes a significant shift in *pro-life* strategy (2003b: 2).

No longer relying upon moralised grounds of defending 'unborn life' alone, and in stark contrast to previous constructions of women as selfish consumers of 'convenience' abortions, the pro-life movement has sought to deploy an argument based upon 'medical science'. Under this medicalised construction, women are portrayed as the 'victims' of abortion at serious threat of suffering from post-abortion syndrome (PAS).[5] And this reconstruction of abortion politics is extremely powerful. In appearing to centralise women's health, this would seem to situate the pro-life movement as those who are 'truly concerned with women's health and well-being'. Nevertheless, their *real* concern sits not with women's welfare, but in promoting a very different conception of *women's rights* in abortion:

> Where those who argue that legal abortion is an aspect of women's rights place emphasis on women's freedom *from* state interference in their lives,

PAS claimants argue just the opposite; that women's rights require that the state intervene *to protect women* from ending pregnancies through abortion. The rights of women are redefined as the right to be protected by the state from the psychological harm done by abortion, from the actions of doctors who perform abortion, and from women's relatives and friends, who allegedly pressure them to end pregnancies.

(Lee, 2003b: 36)

While the existence and extent of PAS is highly contested, the 'popular consensus' among the medical profession would seem to be that abortions pose few adverse psychological consequences (Lee, 2003c).[6] However, of concern here is that the *foundation* of PAS is far from beneficent, but is political and pernicious. Rather than protecting women's rights, the intention of anti-abortionists is to demonstrate that women 'did not really choose to end their pregnancy' (Lee, 2003b: 2). Instead, women are typified as non-autonomous agents, 'fragile beings who are unable to make choices for themselves and who are not responsible for their actions' (Lee, 2003b: 2). Therefore, the reluctance of feminists to engage in women's experiences surrounding abortion is completely understandable. The concern here, as Eileen Fegan comments, is that negative experiences 'are all too easily captured by anti-choice groups and pathologised into concepts such as "post-abortion trauma syndrome", which in turn threaten the legality and availability of abortion services' (1999: 266). Nevertheless, conceding that women's personal narratives might throw 'complex and inconvenient factors into the political balance' (1999: 265), Fegan argues that listening to these stories has become critically important for feminism as a political movement. Constructing abortion as an accessible and relatively unproblematic medical procedure seems strategically unsatisfactory in the long term since:

> It does not acknowledge or speak to the vast and varied personal experiences of women who may suffer after abortions, yet remain pro-choice in principle and who would make the same decision again.
>
> (Fegan, 2002: 168)

Therefore, while many women report 'feeling fine' about abortion, feel 'very certain' about the decision to terminate, and express 'relief' following the procedure, *negative* accounts of abortion and related decision making *do* exist (Petchesky, 1986: 367; Boyle, 1997: 105). Some women find the decision difficult, and experience feelings of loss, lack of control, ambivalence, anxiety and regret (Harden and Ogden, 1999: 441). While these accounts present conflicting positions, as Mary Boyle (1997) considers, the negative social and legal construction of abortion, combined with women's lack of power in abortion decision making, might well be productive of such negative responses. So, too, might more positive expressions be explained through the power dynamics of abortion legislation.[7] But whatever the influence – whether discourse surrounding reproduction, or cultural, religious and familial commitments, acknowledging the *diversity* of women's experiences means embracing these varying accounts. Given that 'negative accounts' *do* exist, Fegan forewarns that 'a refusal to acknowledge this in feminist and pro-choice literature does not make the issue go away' (1999: 266). Embracing these perspectives, she argues, has become crucial:

> In the absence of a feminist discourse of agency which might enable pro-choice groups to consider ... women's mixed and contradictory emotions surrounding abortion – such as, isolation and relief, pain and anger at bearing the responsibility – women are left to negotiate these experiences through whatever interpretative frameworks – discourses and ideologies – are currently available.
> (Fegan, 1999: 266)

While these conflicting experiences of abortion illustrate the 'mismatch between law and the social realities of women' (Fegan, 2002: 158), how do we reconfigure 'choice' so as to embrace these diverse experiences? If abortion decision making is in some instances subjectively defined as a difficult decision or experienced as a *not-choice*, should these then fail to count as *autonomous* choices? Such an approach is firmly rejected by Sheldon (2003), who comments that while such analyses illustrate that 'choice' is problematic for some:

> [I]t does not deny that many of the women who will terminate pregnancies in Britain ... *will* exercise careful, thoughtful choices. These are women with alternatives (though typically none of them ideal) which are often considered and discussed at length, sometimes in extremely supportive, explicitly pro-choice environments.
> (Sheldon, 2003: 184)

This is beyond question; however, my concern is that the language of autonomous choice not only masks the experience of those women who describe themselves as having no choice, but potentially renders *their* experiences as marginal, and arguably, non-autonomous. Do *these* women not exercise autonomous choice? Nevertheless, suggesting that *these* women do not exercise choice seems to present an unrealistic, if not rather utopian, account as to when autonomy applies as a value. As Marilyn Friedman comments, autonomy is not 'only about choosing a luxurious life from among prosperous options, a life of endless delights. Even the most desperate and tragic circumstances may present someone with different ways to respond' (2003: 26). In this respect, while these women are 'choosing' under less than ideal conditions, which undoubtedly makes it *harder* to choose, if we accept autonomy operates even where options are severely restricted, then these women are still *choosing*. However, while this analytical perspective presents difficult choices and subjectively felt 'no choices' as still counting as instances of autonomous choice, not all readily accept this claim. Some argue that under particular conditions, what might appear to be an act of choosing 'turns out to be an instance of conformity' (Morgan, 1991: 354).

'Women are conforming, not choosing'

Contrary to the view that reproductive technology provides *increased* choice, Kathryn Morgan claims that there are important 'ideological, choice-diminishing dynamics at work', which *structure* women's 'choices' towards the goals of eugenics and perfectionism (1991: 357). Similarly, Barbara Katz Rothman (1988: 14) suggests that technologies such as amniocentesis and selective abortion, surrogacy, embryo transplants and so forth are being used to give the 'illusion of choice'. And, like Morgan, she regards 'choices' as the product of social structures that create needs: 'the needs for women to be mothers, the needs for small families, the needs for "perfect children" – and creates the technology that enables people to make the needed choices' (Rothman, 1988: 14). Further along these lines, however, are those who argue that the 'choices' women make are structured by an 'integrated system of power relations that systematically disadvantages women' (Williams, 1988: 826). Such claims, variably referred to as 'ideological determinism' or 'false consciousness', forward that women buy into their own marginalisation – perpetuate the gendered system themselves – for example, by choosing to leave the workplace to allow them to care for children (Williams, 1988: 826–8). Therefore, when we refer to such actions as 'choices', Joan Williams argues, this is because we are blinded by gender prescriptions, since women have to choose *not* to fulfil their family responsibilities, whereas men do not (1988: 831).

Although well meaning, these views are highly controversial and problematic. As Kathryn Abrams (1990) comments, not only do such claims overlook the complex influences of race, class and sexual orientation, and multi-causal explanations of women's choices, but the suggestion that women are assimilating gendered ideology and playing an active role in their own subordination, actually provides support 'for the position that women lack the capacities for self-determination necessary to give them autonomous control over all spheres of their existence' (1990: 776). And in the context of our current discussion this is an essential point. Interestingly, scholars such as Williams consciously avoid scrutinising decisions to abort or carry to term entirely. As Abrams remarks, this stems not from the impossibility of making such claims, but rather, because the purpose of feminism in this area 'is to protect women's opportunities for choice', and 'any argument which questions the ways in which women choose or impugns their capacities as rational decision-makers seems unaccountably reckless' (1990: 788).

But ideological determinism claims remain 'unaccountably reckless', even when limited to the sphere of domesticity. They ignore to their peril the risk that such arguments might be used to make much broader claims about women's choices. Therefore, considering that the abortion debate is so polarised, and abortion decision making is commonly typified by pro-life groups as both difficult and harmful, *any* claims that 'women do not choose' are arguably at serious risk of spreading into the reproductive field. In this vein, Abrams argues:

> Doubts about the capacity of women to make critical choices . . . have long played a role in the opposition to equality for women. The fact that these arguments no longer occupy the primary ground of political debate does not mean that they have been successfully banished . . . It may be no coincidence that many of the most popular forms of legislation restricting abortion require women to secure the consent of others, rather than allowing the reproductive choices to be made by the women by themselves.
> (Abrams, 1990: 789–90)

And this argument must hold force more generally to our question of 'When does a "choice" count as such?' – asking that question seems inevitably to risk undermining women's agency. So for example, while we might draw a distinction between abortion decisions from decisions to continue a pregnancy, and suggest that the latter does not constitute a choice since it is the product of pronatalist norms or, 'a deep-rooted or a "natural" course of events' (Sheldon, 2003: 184), these arguments hold equal risk to women's agency. Furthermore, as Sheldon comments, such appeals to biology are deeply problematic, since feminists 'have worked hard precisely to establish that motherhood is not the natural or "default" option for women'; rather, arguments reinforcing female stereotypes of maternity are more typically invoked by those who *oppose* abortion rights (Sheldon, 2003: 184). Similarly, appeals to religious conformity and socialisation as rendering not-choices, not only give rise to 'counter-intuitive results' (Sheldon, 2003: 186),[8] but more specifically provide an under-inclusive view of autonomy.[9] In accepting that autonomy applies even in less than ideal conditions, discounting religious motivations would, as Friedman suggests, 'prompt persons to regard a greater number of others as failures at personhood and thereby reduce the number of others they regard as respectworthy' (2003: 23).

So, what is the combined effect of these arguments? As considered earlier, one of the most problematic features of the construction of autonomous choice in wrongful conception actions was its failure to properly consider those who do not experience some reproductive 'choices' as presenting 'true choices'; yet, the arguments advanced above do nothing to undermine that approach – they merely *affirm* it. Under circumstances where abortion decision making is difficult, even highly restrictive, it is concluded that women still make a choice.[10] Similarly, in discounting the claims of ideological determinism, the notion that women might be coerced into tests such as screening for foetal abnormality is also rejected; as Ann Furedi comments, 'women are capable of making hard choices, and for many a difficult decision is preferable to being an ignorant victim of circumstance' (1998: 169). Indeed, it would seem that the dangers of arguing 'no choice' in all of these circumstances inevitably leads us to the conclusion (one that is shared by Sheldon in the context of the men's advocates' argument) that in all but the most exceptional circumstances, women *do* choose to continue a pregnancy; and that conclusion, as Sheldon notes, 'seems to allow no basis for refuting the men's advocates' argument' (2003: 192).

But, at this juncture we should consider quite carefully the impoverished choice that *we* have been presented with, by both the men's advocates' argument and the construction of choice in the reproductive torts: it is one of 'Control versus Freedom' (Brown, 1993: 51).[11] Arguing that women in some circumstances are incapable of 'choice', potentially threatens to articulate that women are less than fully responsible and choosing agents, opening up the way for increased regulation and control. Yet are we satisfied with that choice, when considering that many women experience so little choice when 'deciding' to continue a pregnancy, terminate a pregnancy, undergo screening for foetal abnormality or indeed surrender a child for adoption? How do we even begin to create a 'woman-centred discourse' that allows women an alternative interpretative framework to negotiate these experiences (Fegan, 2002: 170), when we seem irretrievably trapped between 'Control versus Freedom'?

Conclusion

As Beverley Brown argues, the critical framework of 'Control versus Freedom' runs the risk of both promoting and at the same time denying bodily fantasies. In its denial, she argues that this framework 'works to undercut the validity of complex and often ambivalent feelings of women towards their bodies' (1993: 55). The very discourse that we have embraced in the reproductive realm – of freedom of choice and self-determination – seems to exclude those women whose experience of ' "falling pregnant" is yet another instance of a world perceived to be out of their control' (Brown, 1993: 55). In excluding this domain, we have become caught up in a binary logic, 'yes/no, all or nothing, form', a framework that operates so as 'to deny components of guilt or regret in women's feelings' as well as the 'imaginative possibilities' surrounding abortion (Brown, 1993: 56). At the same time this framework may itself promote fantasies:

> These are fantasies in which the foetus is represented as an alien, invading

being, a parasite feeding off its host. Here the self is radically threatened by this being that has penetrated the body's defences, got inside the boundary that marks out 'I' from the world ... This really is individualism.

(Brown, 1993: 57)

As previous chapters have examined, liberal individualist concepts of autonomy treat the body as something to be controlled by the mind, and bodily boundaries as in need of protection from outside invasion; this is the law's way of seeing and understanding human nature. But it is precisely this aspect of 'choice rhetoric' that many find so pernicious; it systematically reconstructs individuals as self-interested, adversarial, single-mindedly pursuing their own vision of the good and, as Fox argues 'facilitates the characterization of the woman who seeks abortion as selfish' (1998: 57). While this framework might reflect the way that *some* women feel about pregnancy, as Brown argues, it serves to exclude those who experience feelings that may alternate with other fantasies (1993: 57). In other words, this framework not only acts to deny such fantasies of complexity, relationality and connection, but casts them 'into the realm of the "irrational" and hence unmentionable' (Brown, 1993: 52).

Should we then, as some suggest, abandon the language of choice in favour of one rooted in women's 'needs'? Indeed, because choice is so open to contestation, represents women as selfish decision makers, and holds little meaning for women who do not experience such choice and control in their lives, perhaps this alternative language will, as Fox suggests, help us to 'frame a vision of justice founded in the needs and realities of women's lives as a building block towards a meaningful vision of equality (1998: 97–9).[12] Such a framework might provide a more forceful expression that true freedom depends:

[N]ot only on the number of adequate alternatives and on the importance these alternatives have for an individual's life plan and the value [s]he – and the society which surrounds h[er] – attaches to them, but also on the question of how difficult it is to realize these alternatives.

(Hildt, 2002: 66)

There is some merit in this approach; appreciating the constraints that individuals confront in making choices is clearly essential if we are committed to embracing and responding to individuals' diverse experiences of reproduction. But how do we construct the linguistic framework of need? How might our claim look? A right or responsibility to have one's needs fulfilled? Or a need to have one's needs recognised? While initially compelling, this alternative language is not wholly convincing, nor does it stand up to closer scrutiny. As Jeremy Waldron rightly points out, the abstract nature of *both* terms renders 'needs' equally open to contestation, since 'they are a dialectical response among a diverse and quarrelsome community of thinkers to the complexity of human life and its problems' (2000: 121). No doubt one could easily reconstruct putative fathers' claims in terms of needs, whether *his* need to realise parenthood, or a 'need' for the recognition of foetal personhood *over* the needs of the mother. Furthermore, 'needs', unlike 'rights', which invoke a duty or responsibility, are not 'straightforwardly prescriptive in the way that rights-talk is' (Waldron, 2000: 121). And this links to a further point – while 'needs' might well sound less adversarial than the liberal conception of the autonomous chooser, if we are pitting our 'needs' against others' 'rights' or 'choices', then it is likely that the language of needs might so easily collapse into equally individualistic language when we seek to give it prescriptive force. Even if we resist that urge, then arguably we risk reinforcing the same problematic stereotypes that have featured so prominently in legal discourse: the woman in need, 'an emotionally weak, unstable (even suicidal) victim of her desperate social circumstances' (Sheldon, 1997: 35) – in need of sympathy and *control*. Therefore, while there may well be room for 'needs' in an alternative framework, by no means is it clear in practice how this would differ in substance from choice-based claims of freedom since:

> This is a political predicament, not a semiotic one: there are no magic words which, if only we could find them, would do everything we want them to do.
>
> (Waldron, 2004: 122)

So, while the language of 'needs' seems to carry less (liberal) baggage than notions of 'choice', it remains as susceptible to a similar liberal reconstruction. Instead, what is required here is a closer examination of the liberal framework that shapes and informs concepts such as 'choice', and a serious rethink as to whether it is *fair* that women are being held responsible for outcomes that they experience as instances of not choosing. Appreciating that there are perils to an argument that creates a *necessary* and *inevitable* link between sex and procreation, as this chapter has sought to illustrate, there are *also* significant costs in arguing that there is no link *at all*. Such an argument can be used as a weapon to represent women's choices as 'easy', affording them with complete and unfettered freedom in the realm of reproduction. Taking up this concern, as the final chapter argues, while 'choice' has seemingly become a double-edged sword for women, both in the context of the reproductive torts and more generally in matters of reproduction, there is no necessary reason why this should be so. In exploring a counterpoint for this construction of choice, we now turn to pose the question: 'Is it inevitable in all situations that he who "chooses" *must* always take responsibility?'

Notes

1 By virtue of the Human Fertilisation and Embryology Authority (Disclosure of Donor Information) Regulations 2004, which came into force in July 2004. Applying only to donations that occur after 31 March 2005, the Regulations require that an applicant – an individual over the age of 18 years who was born through the use of donated gametes – can request detailed information about the donor from the Human Fertilisation and Embryology Authority.
2 For a fuller analysis of this case and discussion as to what constitutes 'use' for the purposes of such treatment services, see Sheldon (2004).
3 As Sheldon (1995) notes, women are unlikely to have advance knowledge of doctors' views and doctors are under no obligation to refer women to non-objecting clinicians.
4 This was also the finding by the Commission of Inquiry into the Operation and Consequence of the Abortion Act (Rawlinson, 1994: 17), 'the decision to have an abortion often appeared to be the only "choice" available to them. Such a decision does not represent a free choice'.
5 As Ellie Lee (2003c) comments, this reframing of the abortion issue as one based on health in reality reflects the limited success of morally based claims.
6 However, see Rawlinson (2004); the Commission found that some of the studies conducted, such as the RCGP/RCOG prospective study, held a number of methodological limitations, which may have affected its conclusions.
7 As Mary Boyle (1997: 106) suggests, women may 'overstate their certainty about their decision, and de-emphasise ambivalence, because they are afraid that otherwise their request for an abortion may be refused.'
8 Here, Sheldon (2003) explains that while a strict Catholic might argue that she has no choice but to continue a pregnancy in conformity with her faith, to recognise this as a not-choice would also render decisions to marry based on faith, as not-choices, while decisions to marry on the basis of tax benefits would.
9 This leads onto the related point as to how easily 'choice' might well translate into a *judgment* over those who break from socialised reproductive norms; as Katherine Franke (2001: 185–6) suggests, it has been so taken for granted that only women who are *not* parents are regarded as having made a non-traditional, unconventional and unnatural choice. By contrast, she argues that the issue of choice switches for lesbians, since they continue to have an identity understood as non-reproductive in nature.
10 Even in the example of women travelling from Northern Ireland to Great Britain for abortions. As Fegan and Rebouche (2003: 228) comment, these women still exercise agency 'through their secret and subversive actions – but only at great psychological, physical and financial costs'.
11 As Brown explains, the 'Control versus Freedom' label stands for 'resistant politics conducted in the name of women'.
12 Marie Fox is fully cognisant of the dangers that attend rejecting the language of choice.

Chapter 7

The moral domain of autonomy

> Margaret Raby killed her husband after a history of abuse which was described by the judge as 'effectively imprisoning . . . [her] and then brainwashing . . . [her] physically, psychologically and sexually.' Margaret Raby testified: 'I loved Keith very much with all my heart and I thought what I could give him, sir, with my love and psychiatric help, we would overcome what he did to me.' She also testified, 'I thought what I could give him – my love, anything he wanted, would [stop the abuse] . . . but it didn't. Later she testified, 'I loved him,' to which the prosecutor replied, 'and he wasn't really a bad fellow, was he?'
>
> (Seuffert, 1999: 212)[1]

Some choices are pretty straightforward, and require no more than a simple selection between two courses of action, which lead to morally neutral outcomes. And indeed, sometimes we are presented with questions which beg an easy choice between 'yes' or 'no', '1' or '0', 'black' or 'white', 'A' or 'not-A'. However, there are junctures in our lives where selection is not only tricky, but perhaps nigh impossible. In the face of a cross-examination, where the witness must 'just answer the question, yes or no?', she might hesitate before answering, or be uncertain of the 'right' response; that is not to say the witness *can't* answer, but in particular circumstances a yes/no response just seems to obscure the 'truth'. And this, Bart Kosko (1994) would suggest, is a mismatch problem. While scientists see their art in terms of black and white, computer programmers in terms of all true and false, this is a rarely afforded luxury, for often in life some things are just grey:

> Statements of fact are not all true or all false. Their truth lies between total truth and total falsehood, between 1 and 0. They are not bivalent but multivalent, gray, fuzzy.
>
> (Kosko, 1994: 8)

Such uncertainty is part of our everyday lives, as it is of law. It explains those moments when we add a qualifier to an initially firm statement: 'but', 'however', or 'well, it's not quite like that'. In law, as Kosko comments, rather than being able to draw a clean line between breach of contract and not breach, or self-defence and excessive force, we soon realise that, the 'lines are curves and you have to redraw them in each new case. Every rule, principle, and contract has exceptions' (1994: 263). So whether we are invoking concepts like reasonableness, foreseeability or indeed, damage, these enquiries require the exercise of judgment, and demand that the issue be determined either way; reasonable/unreasonable, foreseeable/unforeseeable, or damage/no damage. But that is not to say that we can't question *where* those lines are drawn; often that process involves imposing certainty on situations where no such certainty exists. And this is where a 'fuzzy' analytic proves valuable. Not content, like bivalence to 'trade accuracy for simplicity', fuzziness takes a multivalent view and it is never happier than when dealing with uncertainty, degrees, paradoxes and contradiction (Kosko, 1994: 21).

Nevertheless, law trades accuracy for simplicity all the time, enjoying the certainty that binary logic offers: private/public, reason/emotion, and man/woman and so on. This either/or construction serves to delineate law's boundaries and jurisdiction. However, as Finley comments, 'the reductive instance of legal language on a consistent yes/no position, a bottom line simple "answer", denies the possibility of shifting contexts and the need to resort to different lines of argument for different purposes' (1989: 903). And the very reason that law can achieve such 'simple' answers is through attempting to limit the 'emotional' realm. It is this realm that is seen as disrupting, creating uncertainty where there is none, and as Susan Bandes comments, it is conceptualised as encroaching upon the 'true preserve of law: which is reason' (1999: 2). And for some, it is more than an encroachment; emotion is *dangerous* – for Posner, the threat here is of 'rational' judgment being 'distorted by "emotionalism" ', or being utterly overwhelmed by a more 'primitive mode of reasoning' (1999: 311). But despite Posner's views, emotion is very much a part of law; indeed, legal reasoning can depend 'heavily on assumptions about how people are emotionally constituted' (Calhoun, 1999: 218), creating not only 'emotional scripts', which determine the proper place for emotion, of love, jealousy, hate, guilt and their physical manifestation (Calhoun, 1999: 220), but emotional outlaws which:

> [V]iolate emotional scripts in ways that challenge social hierarchies. Welfare recipients who feel resentment rather than gratitude at welfare payments, racial minorities who feel anger rather than amusement at racist jokes, and women who feel discomfort or fear rather than feeling flattered at male sexual banter all experience outlaw emotions. These instances of resentment, anger and fear challenge dominant perceptions of what is going on . . .
>
> (Calhoun, 1999: 223)

Judges 'like to think of themselves as inured to human feeling' (Rosenbaum, 2004: 157), but most will agree that the idea of the impartial and distanced judge is a myth. Law *is* inherently emotional; judges are, after all, humans. The problem is that the myth of impartiality disguises the raw emotions the law is acting upon, and undoubtedly makes harder work of deciphering *which* emotional scripts it deploys in constructing what it means to be a 'reasonable person'. Yet, although our job is made harder, the question of 'how, why and with what and whom, law peoples its world' (Naffine, 2003: 346) has occupied much of our time in this book. Looking beyond the rhetoric of 'healthy children as blessings' and the narrative of tragedy that attends the birth of a disabled child, the primary objective has been to question how law thinks about and represents women's choices in reproduction and to reveal how that thinking informs the drawing of the line between deserving (non-choosing) and undeserving (choosing) claimants. We have questioned where those lines have been drawn, illustrated the law's tendency to act upon stereotypes of 'how women are', and have also seen the resulting costs we pay for this: choice, under its liberal rubric, has become a double-edged sword for women. And, as the last chapter concluded, this rhetoric of choice is not isolated to law, but has come to inhabit the reproductive landscape more generally, presenting *us* with a double bind: one of control versus freedom. Yet strategies employed by feminists to provide theoretical counterpoints have tended to collapse back into the liberal framework, and for good reason. In light of the apparent dangers that *alternative* approaches seem to pose, the strategy has been:

> [T]o construct one feminist Woman who can best serve the purposes of the array of concrete women who stand by her. . . . [A]s rational, self-determining, responsible and mature: as the person best placed to consider the needs of herself and the foetus, and to make the correct decision with regard of whether or not to abort. This should form the basis for demanding a model of law which leaves the decision of whether or not to abort to the individual woman and therefore leaves the maximum amount of space for women's diversity. The feminist Woman, then, will seek to leave maximum space for real and concrete women.
>
> (Sheldon, 1993: 22)

This strategy, I suggest, now needs revision; there is no 'one feminist Woman' who can ever represent or serve the interests of real and concrete women. Any 'Woman' that we design to do this job, would either be too complex to deploy as a 'standard' in practice, or alternatively, will become yet another stereotype serving to mask the experiences of others and minimising the space for real women's voices. The question of 'Which Woman better represents us?', I think, is simply unanswerable. And as this chapter illustrates, feminists are acutely aware of the perils of buying into single constructions, ultimately doubting that either liberal or *relational* representations of female personhood can promote women's interests. So, in light of this, coupled with the dilemma that we have confronted throughout this book, the analysis that follows argues for a different approach. And while the reader might think it slightly odd, given the foregoing, the method that I advocate is an explicitly *relational one*. As the analysis seeks to illustrate, a relational approach, while expressing a 'moral' voice (or an 'ethic of care') is a voice that belongs to *all* of us; it is not an attribute of a particular *kind* of person (or a 'woman') but of *people*. In the context of holding individuals *responsible* for their choices, that moral voice explores the nature of those choices, and questions the context and circumstances under which responsibility might arise. It is an approach, not content like 'distributive justice' to treat all parties as equally situated before the law, but seeks justice through questioning the disequilibrium already existing in society. And significantly, as this chapter endeavours to show, in the context of reproductive choices, that moral voice recognises that while women are confronted with *difficult choices*, that is different to saying that women cannot choose; it recognises that while women are responsible as they navigate difficult choices, that too is different to saying that women should therefore be *held responsible* for those choices – it may be that very necessity to choose that *harms them*. Importantly, this relational approach constructs no single *person*, but what it expresses is far more powerful than any conception of personhood could ever convey: the values of fairness, equality and ultimately, *our care for persons*.

What kind of person?

As we have already seen, liberal ideology and the person of law it expresses is less than popular in feminist thought. Critiques of this liberal conception of legal personhood tend to emphasise its inability to deal with connection, in conceptualising humans as essentially 'discrete, bounded units, beings who come in ones, not twos' (Naffine, 2003: 360). As Naffine illustrates, cases such as *Re A (Children)(Conjoined Twins: Surgical Separation)* [2000] 4 All ER 961, and those concerning pregnant women, largely concern failures of individuation, since under the liberal ideal of autonomy we only 'become persons once we individuate . . . once we separate from our mothers' (Naffine, 2003: 360). A similar point is also expressed by John Harris who suggests that the most striking feature of *Re A* was how the court resorted to pitting the 'welfare of each child "against the other" which clearly resonates with the judicial tradition of conceptualising pregnancy in adversarial fashion' (Harris, 2001: 228). So, if the conception of the rational legal actor is underpinned by a biological assumption, *he* is always 'individuated and therefore sexed (at least in the sense of never pregnant, because this compromises individuation)' (Naffine, 2003: 364). In order to be a truly free autonomous 'rights'-wielding actor under the liberal ideal, one must therefore be individuated, independent, disembodied, self-possessed and self-contained (Naffine, 2003: 364).

As a counterpoint and challenge to the liberal 'separation thesis', Robin West and others have offered the 'connection thesis', a relational account of human existence, which seeks to include precisely those aspects of our lives that the liberal understanding excludes, of dependency, embodiment, emotionality, connection and care. West's stance might be said to be broadly captured by the following:

> Women are actually or potentially materially connected to other human life. Men aren't. This material fact has existential consequences. While it may be true for men that the individual is 'epistemologically and morally prior to the collectivity', it is not true for women. The potential for material connection with the other defines women's subjective, phenomenological and existential state, just as surely as the inevitability of material separation from the other defines men's existential state. Our potential for material connection engenders pleasures and pains, values and dangers, and attractions and fears, which are entirely different from those which follow, for men, from the necessity of separation.
>
> (West, 1988: 14)

Contextual accounts such as West's strongly reflect the arguments of Carol Gilligan (1982), in drawing broad gender distinctions between the 'voices' of men and women. Women, in Gilligan's view, exercise their moral responsibility through relationships, connection, selflessness and care, by contrast with the male pursuit of morality, which defines fairness in terms of individualised justice, objectivity, separation and hierarchy. Nevertheless, while clearly influential, relational accounts provided by Robin West, and others (for example Bender, 1989; Finley, 1989) have not been without their critics either. One criticism to which relational accounts are open is well elucidated by Joanne Conaghan who questions:

> Do not such appeals to a unified female experience make the same false claims to universality that feminists attribute so frequently to men, resulting moreover in the same oppressive consequence, namely, that those who do not share the privileged experience are thereby excluded and their experience denied?
>
> (Conaghan, 1996: 65)

Furthermore, bespeaking the criticisms of many, Joan Williams observes that the danger of relational accounts is that they are 'potentially destructive' (1988: 801), in rehabilitating 'inherently loaded stereotypes' (1988: 821) derived from the 'pre-modern stereotype of woman as the "weaker vessel"', both in physical and intellectual terms (1988: 804). The claim that there is a 'singular' female voice not only runs against the theoretical tide of anti-essentialism (Conaghan, 1996: 67), but that the values attached to the 'female voice', of emotion, caring and moral responsibility, are pernicious. Since it is these values that have traditionally acted to oppress and control women, relational feminism is thus seen by many as creating the potential for it to be 'used as a weapon against women' (Williams, 1988: 813). Indeed, as has been highlighted in earlier chapters, it is this 'universal' and 'contextual' standard as to what is ordinary, normal and natural, which has been used against women in the reproductive torts; and as others illustrate, many have used the same stereotype to argue for the delegitimisation of abortion on 'the grounds that it goes against women's instinct to have babies' (Lee, 2002: 66). Therefore, attempts to undermine the liberal ideal through a more contextualised standard give rise to the danger of reinforcing the very stereotypes we wish to jettison; as Nicola Lacey comments:

> One of the avoidable binds that we have sometimes been caught in, then, is a reassertion of the very stereotypes we are challenging. By getting seduced by the explanatory power of our doctrinal critique, and in our enthusiasm to deconstruct the oppositions which it has exposed, we see them where they may already have been dislodged; we construct them as more seamless than they are. We confirm the stories we say legal doctrine has told, and even begin to believe that they are as powerful as the most sexist man could wish.
> (Lacey, 1998: 205)

If the relational perspective of autonomy is so deeply flawed, holding the capacity to undermine women's agency and personhood under the law, what conception of autonomy are we to be left with? According to Beate Rössler, because women have so often been 'compelled to understand themselves not as independent but as dependent' (2002: 149), a non-relational concept of autonomy appears to be both conceptually coherent and normatively appropriate. And Rössler suggests that it is 'precisely the distinction between a relational and non-relational concept of autonomy that allows a person the possibility of extricating herself from relationships' (2002: 149). So, do we just return back to square one then, content to stick with the liberal vision of autonomy which is, after all, just as 'essentialist', since 'it assumes one standard for everyone' (Monti, 1999: 573)? Or, might there be another way to supply 'a fuller, more realistic account of the legal lives of men and women: to make us appreciate "the rich thicket of reality" '(Naffine, 2002: 79)?

Beyond personhood

Let us think of these extreme accounts of legal personhood as lying upon a spectrum – liberal individualism at one end and relational accounts at the other. Plausibly, what we may be describing is a spectrum of possible accounts of personhood that *could* describe us surprisingly well at different points in our lives. Emotions might fluctuate between either extreme, or sit constantly in the middle; these might vary from hour to hour, from day to day and so on, and be subject to change depending upon our social environment, lifestyle, material living conditions, health, friendships and family – all these aspects of our lives are conditional and often subject to change. One might confront a life event, which changes us quite radically as a person and invokes either the most selfish, self-regarding behaviour, or by contrast, brings out other-regarding behaviour that is grounded in connectivity, selflessness and care. And, of course, one might exercise one's autonomy based on emotions that could be derived from both ends of the spectrum, a confluence of selfish and caring concerns. Arguably, that presents an account of who we are; identities and personalities which are fluid, shifting and changing throughout our individual biographies.

What is being furnished here is *something that we all know*: neither the liberal autonomy ideal, nor the relational account of personhood can ever provide the perfect blueprints that we aspire to. Absent of complexity, no singular account ever will. All that a unitary account can achieve is a two-dimensional view of personhood that necessarily filters out aspects of the human condition – and any comparison of our 'real' complex and emotional selves will inevitably result in contradiction, confusion, or at worst, a failure of personhood at particular times. Consider Hazel Biggs's description of two women's exercise of autonomy in end-of-life decisions:

> They fought for their autonomy to be respected not only so that they might die in a manner and at the time of their choosing, which some would regard as selfish, but also in order to protect those they cared for and spare them the hurt associated with watching them die over a protracted period.
>
> (Biggs, 2003: 298)[2]

As Biggs is acutely aware, constructing the exercise of autonomy as expressed through connection and care holds particular dangers. One of those concerns being, 'how can we be certain that a person is acting autonomously when she is clearly motivated by her perception of the needs of others?' (Biggs, 2003: 298). Here is the first contradiction on a liberal account – doubts immediately surround 'other-regarding', rather than fully 'individuated' behaviour. But, so must we question whether the desires of these women can be understood as being completely immersed in concerns for others under a relational account. As Biggs notes of one of these women, who had asked for the withdrawal of life-sustaining treatment: 'In her view this would be preferable not only for her, but also for those who cared about her' (2003: 293). Therefore, Biggs rightly argues that 'autonomy will be better respected by accepting that people have their own reasons for making decisions, and that for many women the desire to shield their loved ones from the unpleasant experience of their own protracted dying will be *amongst* them' (2003: 298–9). The complex confluence of individual and relational concerns must mean that neither extreme of the spectrum provides a full explanation as to the exercise of these women's autonomy, although relational concerns are certainly strong. Furthermore, recognition that for these women, this was one particular *moment*, an event in their lives is particularly important here. It was the very nature of the situation they confronted that brought 'others' into the decision-making forum – the people that mattered the most at that time to these women, whose lives would otherwise be rendered *incomprehensible* without reference to those who also exercised love, sacrifice and affection for them.

The idea that autonomy is guided by different concerns at different points in one's life, while obvious, is of considerable importance towards any quest for authenticity in structuring the 'ideal' vision of legal personhood. But it does present us with a problem. Even if this 'complex person' creates a space to represent the diversity of individuals, by theorising within the boundaries of liberal and relational thought, are there not dangers to this approach? Arguably, such an approach holds equal pitfalls to which liberal and relational accounts are susceptible, for it embraces them both. Furthermore, such an approach begs serious questions as to how this would be applied in practice. How does the law begin to engage with notions of complexity or complex personhood? What sort of 'ideal' does this produce, and where do we draw the lines when there is conduct that the law cannot condone, excuse or make concessions for? What, for the purposes of law, does a complex person look like? It would seem that reliance upon 'complexity' would not only prove problematic for law, but is potentially a hazardous strategy:

> [I]t may be that the implication of recognising a multiplicity of perspectives and conflicting subject accounts in place of an 'objective' understanding of a particular interaction precludes the articulation of any standard at all, in the sense of operating as a norm, a call for compliance, a prohibition of deviance. Moreover, it is arguable that the same insights render problematic any attempt . . . to articulate a public realm, in the sense of a set of standards which govern community life, because such standards inevitably operate to privilege particular viewpoints and suppress others.
>
> (Conaghan, 1996: 65)

That is the danger; the empty slot that complex personhood leaves open could, as Naffine suggests of the liberal autonomy ideal, be 'filled in certain gendered ways' (2002: 100). While complex personhood seems intuitively appealing, perhaps even liberating, it takes little time to summon up examples as to how 'complex personhood' could work against women once it crossfertilises into areas like domestic violence, sexual assault, rape and sexual harassment, and serve to excuse or justify emotional responses, which we think not only inappropriate, but also harmful. But the second danger of this approach is one that we have already seen in practice; in the context of the reproductive torts, there is no doubt that the Woman of law is *already* complex. She is relational at those times when the law wishes to transform harm into the harm*less*, to *reinforce* her responsibility for events occurring within the 'natural and private' spheres of life, even when brought about by negligence; she becomes the liberal rational self-regarding individual precisely at those times when a relational understanding might promote a better account of the difficult choices that she confronts in the familial and reproductive domain.

We confront an apparent dilemma here. An account of complex personhood seems to reflect what it is to be human – our diversity, our emotionality – and sheds light on the range of moral concerns that explain our actions and choices. It offers a rebuttal for the narrow conception of persons that sits behind liberal and relational ideals; for neither of these is ideal, but only serves to deeply misrepresent who we are. By contrast, the notion of complex personhood is completely unworkable; even if it does offer an account that might better represent decision making in the realm of reproduction. If generally applied, what standard could it possibly promote as to how people should act, or what values they should be guided by? Perhaps the solution is not to search for a 'reasonable woman', but to question whether what the law is asking of women is *reasonable* in this context. Joanne Conaghan advocates such a possibility:

> [I]t may be that the answer to this dilemma lies not in a principled adoption or rejection of the 'reasonable woman' standard but in the careful and pragmatic consideration of its desirability and application in particular contexts. Such a pragmatic and strategically focused approach to its deployment may help to avoid the exclusionary tendencies inherent in the standard and at the same time give recognition to those instances where gender is a dominant interpretive and allocative factor. Moreover, such a focus avoids the 'all or nothing' approach which conventional reasoning compels, in favour of a solution which depends less on the articulation of abstract principle and more on the consequences of concrete application.
>
> (Conaghan, 1996: 66)

Arguably, what is required is that we dispense with ideas of 'personhood' and 'reasonable persons' entirely. Asking the 'reasonableness' question doesn't entail creating a 'person', nor indeed does it require us to create another version of personhood that forms a counterpoint for liberal (or relational) extremes. In the context of the reproductive torts, as we have seen, both models of personhood have thrown up contradiction – a woman who chooses, but does not confront a true choice; a woman who loves her child, yet claims the child to be 'unwanted'. Against such stereotypes of personhood – even those designed to advance women's freedom – that woman can *never* be harmed; her claims will be rendered suspicious, even fraudulent. But to abandon the search for an elusive 'person' standard is not to say that we should also abandon the concerns or standards that relational theorists have advanced. What a relational perspective provides is a close attention to *context*; it highlights those moments where the law has lost its moral compass in attempting to understand human decision making through a narrow (economic) lens based upon values which fail to fit the context – culminating in determinations of reasonableness that twist or exclude other ways of seeing, being, trivialising other moral frameworks, which guide our actions and choices in life. A relational perspective challenges such narrow approaches to humanity: renders visible the broad spectrum of concerns that motivate human decision making; makes understandable what law sees as contradiction; and can explain those instances where individuals are caught between yes/no, black/white and choice/no choice. Significantly, none of this requires that we construct alternative visions of 'ideal personhood'; rather a relational approach simply requires us to focus on context so as to reveal the law's lack of emotional response in adjudging situations in which emotion is so begging.

'Autonomous choice': A relational approach

Chapter 5 argued that as a means of explaining decisions to become a parent or care for a child, the economic model embraced within law not only lacks explanatory power, but seriously misrepresents the nature of intimate relationships. It transforms our so-called 'autonomous' relations with others as proprietary, separate, contractual and voluntary (Brenkert, 1998: 48), thereby excluding love, care, sacrifice, physical nurture, dependency and moral responsibility, as well as other less virtuous values, which may equally inhabit the family home, of anger, jealousy, fear, conflict and guilt (Estin, 1994: 1082). There is little doubt that self-interest can play a role within the family realm, as it can within reproductive decision making. Nevertheless, so many of the values excluded from economic rationality change dramatically the meaning of 'choice' within the reproductive and familial domain. Leaving work to care for a child, or 'choosing' to continue a pregnancy that one would otherwise 'rationally' abort, are not necessarily voluntarily 'chosen' towards the furtherance of one's self-interests. Rather, the exercise of 'choice' within the reproductive and family spheres may be equally understood as driven by a sense of moral responsibility *to others* and conformity with social norms

(Himmelweit, 2002: 235–3). Those supportive of the view that the pure exercise of 'choice' inevitably leads to increased welfare, illustrate nothing other than a respect for the inherent value of 'choice'. By excluding the moral domain and the complexity of human decision making, every individual choice, whether exercised through action or inaction, is assessed as having benefited its owner. Yet, there are many situations that we might confront in life where this would clearly not be true. Sometimes the necessity to make a choice could seem like a double-edged sword – a tragic event, where *none* of the options presented offer any prospect of increased welfare, but rather only its *diminishment*:

> People consent to changes in the world that involve a wide range of market choices, risk pools, and apparent authorities. Wives submit to abusive husbands; employees consent to exploitative and humiliating work environments; consumers consent to sales of defective, dangerous, and over-priced merchandise; women consent to 'date rape' and to sexual harassment on the street and on the job; religious converts submit to directives compelling consensual suicide; subjects in an experiment consent to the dehumanizing, authoritative instruction to electrically shock other human beings. . . . Many of those consensual changes leave both the individual and community not just worse off, but miserable. It is not obvious why we should assume that all of these consensual changes in the world are moral changes on the ground that they promote autonomy.
>
> (West, 1985a: 427)

There is no doubt that the woman who submits to her abusive husband, rather than face 'grinding poverty', exercises rational choice. And, of course, the same must be said of the claimant in wrongful conception who continues a pregnancy rather than face an abortion. Both had choices, both exercised rational choice. But were these women's choices welfare-maximising? Were their choices 'voluntary'? And does the exercise of choice between options render these women better off? These are simply not questions that the court has asked, but has assumed as a matter of 'common sense'. In doing so, the inevitable conclusion generated is one of non-intervention, and therefore, one of full individual and private responsibility for that choice. That we should be dissatisfied with this seemingly inescapable conclusion cannot be overemphasised. As West remarks it is only once we drop the assumptions driven by economics that we can start asking important questions. So, in the case of the abused wife, she comments:

> [W]hy these staggeringly depressing alternatives – an abusive husband, grinding poverty, or an oppressive state – are the only choices we can imagine for an abused wife. If these are in fact her only choices, it is

because we have failed to act. And we will not create or even envision better alternatives until we cease to believe what is surely false: that we are all inexorably rational individuals, that we can never assess the misery of a victimized woman's life better than can the victim herself . . . Until we truly understand that a marriage of terror, no less than a state of terror, is *bad* – even when consensual – we will not be moved to create better alternatives.

(West, 1985b: 1455)

Other authors in the field stress similar points, and the most prominent here is Martha Fineman who argues that the notion of individual choice is all too often used as a justification for ignoring the 'inequalities in existing social conditions concerning dependency' (Fineman, 2004: 42). In doing so, she suggests that we also fail to recognise that 'choice of one's status or position carries with it consequences not anticipated or imagined at the time of the initial decision' (2004: 42). So, although a woman might well 'choose' to become a mother, whether she consents to the risks of foregoing the opportunities entailed in dependency work is more questionable; but even if she does consent to these risks, Fineman (2004: 42) questions, 'should that let society off the hook?'

What these powerful arguments display is a close attention to context – a dimension to 'choice' that is painfully absent from economic thought. Both West and Fineman illustrate that the seemingly inevitable leap from individual choice to individual responsibility is pernicious and flawed. Quite simply, it is far from *inevitable* that autonomy need be read in this way. Stressing this point further, Fineman comments that:

[S]ocial conditions, particularly conditions of oppression, are of far more than individual concern. They are of public concern, in a society that has established norms of justice, incorporating ideals of equality and inclusion.

(Fineman, 2004: 226).

The significance of Fineman and West's analysis cannot be overstated and to some extent, this sheds some light on the dilemma that feminists have confronted in problematising choice in the reproductive domain. Recognising that some women do not experience an abortion as a straightforward act of choice is *entirely different* to saying that she is not a responsible and autonomous agent. Indeed we might say that it is *because* she is taking that decision so seriously – weighing up the moral context of the situation, the impact upon her, upon others – that reinforces her responsibility as an agent. But the point is that there is no necessary relationship between *being a responsible* agent and *being held* responsible – and significantly, this construction of responsibility is central to the law.

Being responsible beings

> [A]ccording to the liberal conception of responsibility we are entitled to hold someone responsible for his or her actions only if he or she could have chosen otherwise.
>
> (Reece, 2003: 217)

As a starting point, it is noteworthy that the law is not so harsh as to hold individuals 'responsible' for *all* their 'choices'. In private contractual disputes, for example, the law recognises a series of 'vitiating' factors, which undermine 'consent'. Take for example the doctrine of economic duress. Here, a contracting party, faced with an illegitimate threat by the other party, may find him/herself presented with a 'choice of two evils'. Neither option presents a realistic way forward, although submitting to the threat in the short-term may present *less* disastrous economic consequences. There is no doubt that the individual has exercised a 'choice', but the question that the law asks is whether *s/he* should be held to, or be made *responsible* for, his/her 'contractual promise' *under such circumstances*. Was his/her 'choice' (or 'consent') made voluntarily? Did *s/he* have a 'reasonable alternative' so as to enforce that contract? Asking these questions is the law's way of policing 'the limits of "fair" bargaining', and bringing into the public domain behaviour that under those circumstances 'trumps the otherwise prevalent norm of non-intervention' (Dalton, 1985: 487). Alternatively, we might consider the provocation defence to murder in the criminal law. Although the successful invocation of this defence merely results in the substitution of a manslaughter verdict for one of murder, it still nicely illustrates the point. In making an excusatory case, as John Gardner comments:

> One needs to argue that, even if one had inadequate reasons to kill, one had adequate reasons to get angry to the point at which one killed. In the term favoured by law, one needs to argue that getting angry to a murderous extent was *reasonable*.
>
> (Gardner, 2003: 160)

Of course the defendant who successfully raises such a defence will still be held *responsible*, albeit s/he will not be held responsible to the fullest extent. Yet despite the law's dispensation, there can be no doubt that the defendant who was provoked to kill still made a choice, and in one sense remains fully responsible, since:

> Like any rational being, the defendants in the cases ... wanted to avoid responsibility in the consequential sense; they wanted to avoid facing the unwelcome moral or legal consequences of their wrongs. But they didn't

want to do so by denying, or casting doubt on, their responsibility in the basic sense.

(Gardner, 2003: 161)

And our examples could multiply in providing illustrations as to when the law makes concessions to human behaviour in the face of an absence of 'true choice'. Nevertheless, what should be emphasised here is that making a 'concession' is not necessarily the same as undermining individual responsibility under the liberal autonomy ideal. Law does not undermine responsibility in the 'basic' sense, but makes concessions to full *legal* responsibility in the 'consequential' sense (Gardner, 2003). And the distinction is important, for the latter constitutes law's recognition of human complexity and subjectivity in particular contexts. To return to Gardner once more, responsibility in the 'basic' sense is, 'the ability to explain oneself, as a rational being. In short it is exactly what it sounds like: response-ability, an ability to respond' (2003: 161).

Yet as we have seen, this contextual and relational enquiry as to the reality of 'choice' is also central to mitigation; it symbolises one of those moments where the law is *willing* to sever the link between agential and consequential responsibility. In contexts where actors are confronted with 'no choices', the law intervenes and makes 'public' the constraints under which individuals must 'choose'; and significantly it makes public the identity of the actor or circumstances, which generated that difficulty of choice. However, in the reproductive field, the law has become suspiciously silent on constraints surrounding choice, even in circumstances where the judiciary provides express acknowledgement that the claimants may have had 'no other choice', or where 'choice' didn't seem like the right word. But, one should ask, are we only talking about 'difficulties' in making a choice – does this really encapsulate the reality of reproduction for all? Rather, it seems possible to argue that there are numerous situations in this context where individuals might face what could be termed a 'tragic question', one where there is no morally acceptable alternative. The significance of this, as Martha Nussbaum explains:

> The tragic question is not simply a way of expressing the fact that it is difficult to answer the obvious question. Difficulty of choice is quite independent of the presence of moral wrong on both sides of a choice. . . . The tragic question registers not the difficulty of solving the obvious question but a distinct difficulty: the fact that all the possible answers to the obvious question, including the best one, are bad, involving serious moral wrongdoing. In that sense, there is no 'right answer'.
>
> (Nussbaum, 2000: 171).

Take, for example, the tragic question that confronts so many women who hold the sole decisional responsibility for making the choice of whether to continue or terminate a pregnancy where genetic testing reveals that the foetus, if born, will be severely disabled. As one genetic counsellor remarked to Barbara Katz Rothman in interview, 'It's a choice between bad and worse' (1988: 216). And as Rothman herself remarks, 'Taking the least-awful choice is not experienced as "choosing", not really. It is experienced as being trapped, caught. She enters into a rational seeking of information and choices, and finds herself trapped in a nightmare' (1988: 181). So, for women who are trapped between the 'choice' of terminating a foetus, or raising the child in societal conditions that still fail to support the needs of disabled individuals, what, then, is the 'right answer'? Or what of the woman in the reproductive torts who had sought to avoid that 'tragic question'? Here she is confronted by the choice of sacrificing her dreams and aspirations by keeping an unwanted child, or of not keeping the child via abortion or adoption, what then is the right obvious answer for her? These women are torn between two moral frameworks, between self-care and care for others.

For the author, this captures the importance of recognising the 'tragic question', it reminds us of 'the deep importance of the spheres of life that are in conflict within the drama and of the dire results when they are opposed and we have to choose between them' (Nussbaum, 2000: 177). In other words, the tragic question reminds us of what matters, the things we deeply care about as humans, and brings to the surface the very real moral framework that underpins and disrupts so many of our 'choices'. Yet, the tragic question is not posed by law within the reproductive torts. Rather, by embracing cost-benefit analysis, 'if anything, it suggests that there is no such question, the only pertinent question being what is better than what' (Nussbaum, 2000: 196). This is not, however, to claim that all women in reproduction will *always* confront 'tragic questions'; nor indeed, that such questions confront individuals with an impossibility of choice. Some women may exercise such choices with considerable ease, and of course, more selfish considerations might underpin that decision, for example, on the grounds that having a child would simply interfere with their life (Bartlett, 1988: 324). But, this cannot speak of all women. As Katherine Bartlett comments of adoption:

> [S]he may conclude that although she longs to keep her child, the child would be better off with an adoptive family. In these circumstances, her decision to place her child for adoption is *an act of self-sacrifice for the welfare of the child.*
> (Bartlett, 1988: 323; my emphasis)

And there is no doubt that similar 'other-regarding' reasoning may equally underpin rational choices to *avoid* adoption or abortion. Similarly, recognising individuals' exercise of autonomy as complex and diverse, that relational connections can both enhance and deter its exercise should also make us rethink the nature of legal and moral responsibility. Here, we might direct our minds to precisely those occasions where individuals get stuck in between 'yes' and 'no' – and question why some individuals come to confront the 'tragic question' in the first place, the conditions of their choosing and, significantly, their responsibility for making that choice. It is at those defining moments, when individuals are torn between two morally unacceptable outcomes, where they do not experience an act of *choosing* as a 'choice', that we *should* question the absence of realistic alternatives, the relational constraints upon individual choice, no matter how 'autonomous' its exercise may have been. Those moments where we feel an acute sense of discomfort and concern for those who lack real choices and feel 'trapped' is *our* moral voice speaking to us. It is a voice that belongs to each and every one of us, and it is our moral responsibility to vocalise our concerns in precisely these kinds of situation.

For the author, this is absolutely central to the actions for wrongful conception and birth. While claimants' decisions to care for healthy and disabled children were certainly the products of 'choice', these were *enforced* choices that presented *them* with a unique decisional responsibility that they never should have had. For a woman who confronts the dilemma of a subjectively felt 'no-choice', a 'tragic question', for example in abortion decision making, whether this dilemma is driven by an emotional perspective of an adversarial fight between a woman and her foetus, or from an emotional 'connection between them' (Gilligan *et al.*, 1985: 38), it is undeniable that it is this very responsibility to choose that *harms* her. In this sense then, the damage in these cases is the creation of that very relationship, the unique decisional responsibility it imposes upon the woman, and the resulting 'sense' of loss of autonomy that results.

Significantly, this perspective of relational harm is one that has been embraced elsewhere; as Gleeson CJ in the Australian case of *Cattanach v Melchior* [2003] HCA 38 stated:

> If they have suffered actionable damage, it is because of the creation of that relationship and the responsibilities it entails.... It was the existence, and the continuation of that relationship that formed the vital link between the potential interference with their financial interests from conception and the actuality of such interference following birth. That relationship is the key to an accurate understanding of the damage they claim to have suffered.... [T]he claim for damages is not limited to expenses that will be incurred as a result of the legal obligation. It extends to expenses that will be incurred as a matter of moral obligation ...
>
> ([26])

The emotional script from which Gleeson CJ reads provides a very different vision of responsibility to that invoked by the English courts; by contrast with the view that the moral obligation to care renders women unharmed and therefore responsible for the 'ordinary' burdens of motherhood, Gleeson CJ locates the damage as emanating from *precisely that moral obligation*.[3] Here there is no talk of 'willingness', 'voluntariness' or 'assumption'. For this judge, the harm is far from ordinary, or 'traditional'. Rather, the harm results from the *negligent* creation of a relationship of dependency, and the loss of autonomy entailed in undertaking the significant moral and legal responsibilities that parenthood imposes on these claimants. Furthering this perspective is Hayne J, presiding in the same court that embraces the complexity of human emotion in conceptualising 'choice':

> That a parent has decided to keep the child (or did not decide not to continue with the pregnancy or to offer the child for adoption) is the premise for debate.... To say that a child is born and not given for adoption as a result of the plaintiff's choice to keep the child *tells only part of the story*. Not only does it ignore the fact of the defendant's negligence, 'choice' is an expression apt to mislead in this field. For some, confronted with an unplanned pregnancy, there is no choice that they would regard as open to them except to continue with the pregnancy and support the child that is born. For others there may be a choice to be made. But in no case is the 'choice' one that can be assumed to be made on solely economic grounds. Human behaviour is more complex than a balance sheet of assets and liabilities. To invoke notions of 'choice' as bespeaking *economic* decisions ignores that complexity.
>
> ([222]; my emphasis)[4]

The analyses of both Hayne J and Gleeson CJ hold considerable value in bringing a different perspective to bear on notions of responsibility and choice in cases of wrongful conception and birth. They are exercising *their* moral voices, bringing an emotional sensitivity to the context of the case before them that has been so lacking in many of the cases we have examined previously. Their judgments provide a richer, contextual account as to how individuals' reproductive autonomy has been set back, and significantly, engage more fully with the question as to what those autonomy interests consist of and how parents' lives have been disrupted. And their judgments must also be seen as holding considerable force in revealing the power of the moral voice that emerges from relational thought. If we consider Hayne J's comment that the notion of parents having a choice to keep the child, 'tells only part of the story' ([222]), his concern was to narrate the complex relational elements that the liberal notion of choice missed, ignored, and excluded.

It is *this* perspective that provides a fuller account of the harms suffered in the actions of wrongful conception and birth; it is a view that directly challenges the logic of the 'Harm Paradox', notably that women are left unharmed as a result of 'choosing' to keep their 'unwanted child'. A relational perspective does not refute that women had a choice to terminate their pregnancies or to place a child up for adoption – those women *did* have a choice. On that narrow view, the resulting harm that a woman suffers is undoubtedly the product of rational choice. However, the conclusion that it is inevitable, fair or reasonable that she be held responsible for those choices is what is challenged here. These were choices that women were *entitled to avoid* and are *harmed* by. To understand this we must enter a different jurisdiction of engagement and be willing to exercise our moral voice.

The woman who 'loves' and therefore stays with her abusive partner, and the woman who resents giving up her dreams and aspirations to care for her unwanted, but perhaps much loved child – neither of these constitutes a situation where we should feel entitled or content to walk away from – indeed those very discourses of love that confuse us may well constitute individuals attempting to 'make sense of their situations in part by positioning themselves within such discourses' (Seuffert, 1999: 226).[5] This is not contradiction. The truth lies within that contradiction in theorising the moral space in between yes and no, choice and no choice. A search for the answer as to why women have been confronted with a Harm Paradox in matters of reproduction and parenthood reveals that we have lost sight of what a relational perspective forcefully tells us: so often in life, it is our sense of moral responsibility, obligation and connection that *harms* us.

Concluding remarks

> The notion that it is an individual choice to assume responsibility for dependency work and the burdens it entails allows us to ignore arguments about our general responsibilities. Choice trumps any perceived inequity and justifies maintenance of the status quo. We ignore the fact that choice occurs within the constraints of social conditions, including history and tradition. Such conditions funnel individual decision making into prescribed channels, often operating along practical and symbolic lines to limit and close down options. Women historically have been identified with the role of mothering, and presumed to have the responsibility for children. Women who choose not to have children are seen as having made a non-traditional, even unnatural choice.
>
> (Fineman, 2004: 41)

From the outset of this book I argued that the reproductive torts held the symbolic potential to *reinforce* the message that the set-back of women's reproductive choices was a real harm, to *enhance* women's reproductive freedom by enforcing higher standards of medical care, and to reflect the reality and diversity of women's lives and the importance of reproductive autonomy within them. However, on reflection there is little doubt that that symbolic power has been lost. Foregoing analysis has illustrated the difficult legal engagement with the concept of autonomy and has highlighted the manner by which these conflict with alternative accounts and understandings that might better resonate with women's sexual and reproductive lives. Aside from occasional glimpses of promise for the invocation of deeper and richer understandings, for the main part there is little doubt that one 'unruly horse' (per Lord Clyde p 100 in *McFarlane v Tayside HB* [2000] 2 AC 59) has dominated the whole proceedings: that of 'public policy'. And, whatever one chooses to call it, legal policy, distributive justice, duty, breach, causation, mitigation, damage, reasonableness, the commuter on the Underground – these reproductive torts reveal that under those various guises, each concept remains quintessentially 'public policy'.

As a means of overriding legal principle, it is unsurprising that 'public policy' has come to acquire 'a bad name in English tort law' (Hoyano, 2002: 883). Although some note that the reasons for 'its tumble from grace remain obscure' (Hoyano, 2002: 883), these are perhaps less difficult to ascertain within the context of the reproductive torts. If, as Lord Nicholls suggested in *Fairchild v Glenhaven Funeral Services Ltd* [2002] 3 All ER 305, the law should be coherent, principled and the basis upon which cases are distinguished, 'transparent and capable of identification' ([36]), then undoubtedly the determination of these reproductive torts falls 'well short of this standard' (Hoyano, 2002: 890). 'Public policy' has not only led to the demise of legal principle in these actions, but appears to have also excluded possibilities of an alternative remedy in contract law, as well as the operation of a human rights-based framework. One might speculate that both Arts 8 and 14 of the European Convention of Human Rights and Fundamental Freedoms 1950[6] could offer considerable scope for argument within these actions, and of course, a contractual remedy easily tackles the issue of purely economic losses, by contrast with tort. However, in this latter respect, as a more detailed analysis of case law would have revealed, not only would such measures only apply to a limited number of claimants, but the appellate courts are equally ill-disposed to a contractual response for these claims in any event (see in particular, *Greenfield v Irwin* [2001] 1 WLR 1279). As Lord Scott had suggested in *Rees*, the same result would be reached, 'whether the claimant was a private patient or an NHS patient' ([113]). And while certainly not dispositive of the potential for human rights argument within these cases, it must also be a matter of some intrigue that in the UK no reported cases in this field have sought to fully engage Convention rights since the passing of the Human Rights Act 1998.[7]

Why, then, should we be worried about the decline of the reproductive torts? There are a number of answers to this question, one of which may be well encapsulated by Mark Lunney's comment that 'the [English] law of negligence in relation to unplanned births appears something of a mess' (2004: 154). Such sentiments, as we have explored in this book, are shared by many; the line of case law running from *McFarlane* through to *Rees* not only illustrates how the courts have stumbled 'from one set of facts to the next', creating a 'formula for confusion and instability in the law' (Cane, 2004: 191), but 'how far negligence law has come adrift of principle' (Hoyano, 2002: 900). Undoubtedly the outcomes of these reproductive torts are difficult, perhaps impossible, to sustain upon conventional legal principle. However, this 'mess' is owing to more than merely doctrinal concerns. Insofar as these cases raise complex ethical and legal issues, as Peter Cane notes, the idea that 'legal principle' can determine whether tortfeasors should be held responsible for the costs of child maintenance might be a 'fairy tale' (2004: 26). Notions of 'fair, just and reasonableness', the principles of distributive justice or the commuter on the Underground do not, in themselves, explain the shift in legal policy illustrated by these cases, nor indeed do they illustrate why we should be concerned by this development. For a fuller explanation, we must look elsewhere.

Throughout this book I have been attempting to make sense of precisely this 'mess'. The majority of my analysis has been devoted to gaining an appreciation as to why *these* specific actions are in decline and, in particular, what assumptions have informed the courts' response that women are left (other than in the most exceptional circumstances) unharmed by the births of unwanted children resulting from clinical mishaps in family planning. While much time has been spent in exploring the (unsatisfactory) legal basis of decisions in the reproductive torts, alongside concerns surrounding the invidious distinctions that have arisen on the basis of health/disability, my main concern has been with how the law of negligence constructs harms and injuries specific to *women*. In assessing how law *thinks* about women, and how that informs 'legal principle', the main thrust of the critique involved an analysis of one core value arising in the courts' deliberations – the concept of autonomy. This concept, though central to my argument as to how women suffer significant and enduring harms through clinical negligence in the reproductive domain, has *also* proved to be central to the courts' conclusion that women are left *unharmed*.

Of course, the concept of autonomy is highly susceptible to differential interpretation – a variety of perspectives will bear down on how that principle is applied in practice. As Engelhardt has noted:

> Autonomy is always exercised in a context. In addition, collaborating with others requires freely giving up some of one's freedom. One must commit oneself along with others to a particular account of human flourishing. In health care, this role of particular moral visions is especially salient: humans disagree about how to understand human sexuality, reproduction, disease, disability, suffering, and death . . . Individuals place these pivotal experiences within radically different, indeed, conflicting and competing moral accounts and narratives. One person's liberation is another's enslavement, and the reverse.
>
> (Engelhardt, 2001: 284)

In the reproductive domain, however, we might have imagined that autonomy would hold a clearer meaning. Laura Purdy, for example, argues that reproductive autonomy means 'the power to decide when, if at all, to have children' (2006: 287). Given this, it would seem that in the reproductive torts at least, where the result of negligence involves the setback of that power to decide, that the concept of autonomy could provide a powerful characterisation of the various ways in which women are harmed. Yet the reliance of the courts upon this value as a justification for outcomes in the reproductive torts illustrated not only how empty and inexpressive this concept can often be, but how it can also serve ends that so obviously *fail* to promote women's reproductive autonomy. Whether described as an assault on bodily integrity, as a frustrated choice, a lost hope, a quantification device, and in particular, as a freedom which *should* be exercised, in all these instances the dominant conception of autonomy appearing in these cases has ultimately boiled down to the value of 'choice'. And this relates to my first argument as to why we should be concerned at the demise of the reproductive torts – how the courts have arrived at the conclusion that women are unharmed. What has guided legal principle in these cases have been flawed and deeply harmful stereotypes of women – the law's understanding of 'how women are', has been premised upon characterisations of self-regarding and maternal women; women who regard abortion or adoption as choices amenable to a straightforward cost-benefit analysis, or women who are so tied to their biology that they are left with no choice (but still a choice) but to keep children born as a result of negligence. It is these assumptions, I argued, which explained the existence of a Harm Paradox: where there is no choice but to choose, where every outcome is a wanted one. And the logic of this paradox is powerful, seemingly inescapable: if women are really harmed by the consequences of negligence, if the prospect of a child was really an unwanted one, why did they not *choose* to avoid its birth? Why should others take responsibility for consequences that were very much chosen? However, these concerns are not isolated to the reproductive torts; I have also sought to demonstrate the broader relevancy of my discussion in exploring general discourses surrounding women's sexual and reproductive lives. Here too do we see the reproductive landscape transforming through the rhetoric of choice; 'others' are asserting their *equal* 'Right to Choose', whether to pursue *their* individual reproductive desires, to undertake or avoid the responsibilities of parenthood, or indeed as we saw with the men's advocates' argument, to simply avoid financial responsibility for 'women's choices'. As I argued in Chapter 6, 'choice' no longer means reproductive 'freedom' for women – it has become anyone's battle cry, one that serves to both diminish women's reproductive freedom, and to entrench women's reproductive responsibility. Yet here too, the liberal language of 'choice' seemed to forward an inescapable premise – after all, if women are entitled to reproductive freedom, why shouldn't this liberty be afforded to *men*? Shouldn't both parties have an *equal* 'Right to

Choose'? All these questions formed the basis of the mess that I sought to explore.

In an era where every aspect of a daily life seems to be increasingly optional, our bodies, destinies and future happiness all seem to hang perilously around the concept of choice. As we enter into an era of 'choice politics', with promises of increased alternatives in public transportation, healthcare and education, 'choice' becomes *the* new political currency where social life can only get better with its increase. And, in many respects this is true; our lives have become increasingly mobilised, our lifestyles increasingly diverse, the market offers a cornucopian supply of goods and services for society to consume, and information now sits at our fingertips – it seems that every dimension of our lives – 'education, career, friendship, sex, romance, parenting, religious observance' (Schwartz, 2004: 3) – is a matter of our selection. So, as a means of enhancing our individual freedom and autonomy, it seems that choice has become a crucial expression of our modern liberty, the crux of the matter – a good in itself. But, as an expression of our freedom, the concept of choice can often contribute to a rather distorted view as to the options *really* available in life, the extent of *control* that we hold over the future and, significantly, *which* choices are open to *whom*. And in the field of reproduction this is particularly true. In avoiding parenthood, there is little doubt that the widespread availability of contraception in this country has allowed many women to exert greater control over their reproductive lives. However, the reliability of methods such as the contraceptive pill is often overstated, leading to the 'prevalent belief that pregnancy is now effectively optional' (Lee and Jackson, 2002: 127). This is simply not true of any method, since as Brazier remarks, 'an infallible contraceptive has yet to be invented' (2003: 262). The reality of many women's lives is that contraceptive failure will leave them reliant upon abortion as the remaining means of regaining control. Yet here, too, the idea that women are presented with unlimited choice is equally troublesome; while for some, abortion decisions are exercised without difficulty, for others abortion is not perceived as a choice at all. And, contrary to wide perceptions of abortion being a matter of individual control – available 'on demand' – a woman's reproductive freedom continues to remain in the hands of *others* from whom she must gain permission. If we *all* live in an 'era of choice', then a woman's right to inhabit this utopian world seems somewhat more qualified.

Qualified or not, none of this was to say that a woman does not choose in matters of reproduction; as earlier analysis illustrates, my conclusion was that women unquestionably *do* choose. However, this relates to my second and most significant concern in relation to dominant discourses surrounding reproduction. Not only does the rhetoric of choice present a double bind for women in the field of reproduction, but it is increasingly being used as a device to increase women's responsibilities for 'choices' – even where these are not *experienced* as exercises of choice at all. What has, among other things, been overlooked by the courts in their engagements with and contestations over choice, are the *conditions* under which women are being required to exercise choice in matters of reproduction. Overlooking these conditions is fairly anomalous in law, and beyond law, morally circumspect. It is simply fallacious to say that we straightforwardly treat uninformed and coerced choices as ones that should necessarily lead to responsibility. We make a *moral* distinction – a moral choice as to when someone is to be held accountable for the exercise of choice under such circumstances. Where a woman must choose between sacrificing her own lifetime interests and sacrificing the interests of another, this is not a choice that we are entitled to walk away from. And in the context of the reproductive torts, this choice was one that a woman was entitled to avoid. There are, then, very good reasons for questioning whether it could ever be fair or reasonable under such conditions to hold a woman fully accountable for the consequences.

However, some understand 'fairness' through a different lens; and rendered particularly suspicious in this context are the principles of 'distributive justice' and 'equal rights' – where all parties are assumed to be equal before the law – but equal in what sense? As Deborah Lupton (1999) has noted, many of the risk-related knowledges and technologies that surround pregnancy and motherhood already place considerable responsibility on women to ensure foetal health, and women who ignore the 'plethora of expert and lay advice' are all too often labelled as 'irresponsible' (1999: 89). Discourses surrounding women's responsibility are often conflicting, since the responsibility to reproduce or abstain from reproduction arises within a much wider social network of potential 'addressees', to one's family, to the putative father, to society, and of course to the unborn child, depending upon its potential future state of health (Beck and Beck-Gersheim, 2003: 146). Yet rarely is one of those addressees the woman herself. The substantial burden of responsibility that women presently confront in matters of reproduction, alongside the 'increasingly inequitable and unequal distribution of societal resources and the corresponding poverty of women and children' (Fineman, 1999: 16), underpin how dangerous it is to assume that all parties are equally situated. It is a blind and partial form of justice – one that has only acted to further privatise responsibility for reproductive risks onto women, even in circumstances where those consequences are brought about through negligence. For the law, these consequences are the 'vicissitudes of life', but for women, this constitutes the law of tort legitimating and trivialising the harm that they suffer as women, if not seeking to convert it 'in the public eye into virtue or public benefit' (West, 1997: 139).

It is, as Maura Ryan suggests, erroneous to say that 'we are free to choose all obligations, and are able to formulate all the conditions of our lives to meet our expectations' (1999: 101). Illustrating that as human beings we are sometimes left with precious few choices that we regard as meaningful does not mean undermining individual autonomy; rather, it emphasises the very real and sometimes difficult conditions under which many of us must exercise choice. And while the sense of responsibility we feel towards others that we love and care for is what can bring great meaning into our lives, it can be precisely those connections that also harm us in varying and sometimes extensive ways. Therefore, in calling for a deeper understanding of harm within these actions, what this ultimately requires is a firm commitment to respecting the value of autonomy, and articulating what it is about 'autonomy' that is so *valuable*. It is essential that our understanding of its worth extends beyond the notion of mere 'choice'. If autonomy is ever to hold any moral *value* or potential in our lives at all, then it must be because our choices are guided towards the aim of human flourishing – or perhaps more simply put, 'to the living of a good life' (McCall Smith, 1997: 30).

Notes

1 The passage discussed by Seuffert is extracted from the judgment of *R v Raby* (Unreported, Supreme Court of Victoria, Teague J, 22 November 1994).
2 Biggs' (2003) discussion centres around the two high profile cases of *R (on the application of Pretty) v DPP* [2002] 1 All ER 1 and *Re B (Adult: Refusal of Medical Treatment)* [2002] 2 All ER 499.
3 For similar emphasis on this notion of responsibility, see also the US judgment of *Troppi v Scarf*, 31 Mich App 240, 187 NW 2d 511 (1971), 258.
4 See also the judgment of Kirby P in *CES Superclinics (Australia) Pty Ltd* (1995) 38 NSWLR 47, who similarly suggests that the argument that parents 'chose' to bring up the child 'has an element of the fictional' and emphasises the parents' legal and moral obligations in raising the child as not being freely chosen ([139]).
5 It is appreciated that there is an extensive and growing body of work that could greatly assist these points, and indeed, Seuffert's analysis (1996) among others (see Goodrich, 1995; Naffine, 1994) holds significant value in its careful linking of law's repression of the jurisdictions of love and emotion with the traditional legal conceptions of women as functions of property.
6 Arts 8(1) and 14 of the European Convention for the Protection of Human Rights and Fundamental Freedoms 1950 provide respectively that: 'Everyone has the right to respect for his private and family life, his home and correspondence'; 'The enjoyment of the rights and freedoms set forth in this Convention shall be secured without discrimination on any ground such as sex, race, colour, language, religion, political or other opinion, national or social origin, association with a national minority, property, birth or other status.'
7 Note that Buxton LJ in *Greenfield* dismissed the potential application of Art 8(1) on substantive grounds by reference to the Commission's decision in *Andersson and Kullman v Sweden* (application no 11776/85) 46 DR 251 (see in particular pp 1288–9), since the Human Rights Act 1998 had not been enacted at the time of the trial decision, and therefore could not be raised on appeal. It is, however, noteworthy that Lord Millett's discussion of the conventional award in *Rees* hints at a human rights-based approach where he suggests that personal autonomy: '. . . is an important aspect of human dignity, which is increasingly being regarded as an important human right which should be protected by the law' ([123]).

Bibliography

Abel, R (1981), 'A Critique of American Tort Law', 8 *British Journal of Law & Society*, pp 199–231.
—— (2006), 'General Damages are Incoherent, Incalculable, Incommensurable, and Inegalitarian (But Otherwise a Great Idea)', 55 *DePaul Law Review*, pp 253–327.
Abrams, K (1990), 'Ideology and Women's Choices', 24 *Georgia Law Review*, pp 761–801.
Annandale, E (2001), *The Sociology of Health and Medicine: A Critical Introduction*, Cambridge: Polity.
Ashe, M (1988), 'Law-Language of Maternity: Discourse Holding Nature in Contempt', 22 *New England Law Review*, pp 521–59.
Atiyah, PS (1997), *The Damages Lottery*, Oxford: Hart Publishing.
Atkins, S and Hoggett, B (1984), *Women and the Law*, Oxford: Blackwell.
Bailey, R (1996), 'Prenatal Testing and the Prevention of Impairment: A Woman's Right to Choose?', in Morris, J (ed), *Encounters with Strangers, Feminism and Disability*, London: The Women's Press.
Bandes, S (1999), 'Introduction' in Bandes, S (ed) *Passions of Law*, London: New York University Press.
Barnes, C, Mercer, G and Shakespeare, T (1999), *Exploring Disability*, Oxford: Polity.
Bartlett, J (1994), *Will you be Mother? Women who Choose to Say No*, London: Virago.
Bartlett, K (1988), 'Re-Expressing Parenthood', 98 *Yale Law Journal*, pp 295–340.
Beatson, J (2002), *Anson's Law of Contract*, Oxford: OUP.
Beauchamp, T and Childress, J (1994), *Principles of Biomedical Ethics*, Oxford: OUP.
Beck, U (1992), *Risk Society, Towards a New Modernity*, London: Sage Publications.
—— and Beck-Gernsheim, E (2003), *Individualization, Institutionalized Individualism and its Social and Political Consequences*, London: Sage Publications.
Belcher, A (2000), 'The Not-Mother Puzzle', 9 *Social & Legal Studies*, pp 539–56.
Bender, L (1989), 'Changing the Values in Tort Law', 25 *Tulsa Law Journal*, pp 759–773.
—— (1993), 'Teaching Feminist Perspectives on Health Care Ethics and Law: A Review Essay', 61 *University of Cincinnati Law Review*, pp 1251–76.
Bergum, V and Bendfeld, M (2001), 'Shifts of Attention: The Experience of

Pregnancy in Dualist and Nondualist Cultures', in Tong, R (ed), *Globalizing Feminist Ethics, Crosscultural Perspectives*, Oxford: Westview.

Bernstein, A (2001), 'Motherhood, Health Status and Health Care', 11 *Women's Health Issues*, pp 173–84.

Beverage, F and Mullally, S (1995), 'International Human Rights and Body Politics', in Bridgeman, J and Millns, S (eds), *Law and Body Politics: Regulating the Female Body*, Aldershot: Dartmouth.

Biggs, H (2003), 'A Pretty Fine Line, Death, Autonomy and Letting It B', 11 *Feminist Legal Studies*, pp 291–301.

Block, N (1984), 'Wrongful Birth: The Avoidance of Consequences Doctrine in Mitigation of Damages', 53 *Fordham Law Review*, pp 1107–25.

Bordo, S (1993), *Unbearable Weight*, Berkeley, CA: University of California Press.

Boyle, M (1997), *Re-Thinking Abortion, Psychology, Gender, Power and the Law*, London: Routledge.

Brazier, M (2003), *Medicine, Patients and the Law*, London: Penguin Books.

Brenkert, G (1998), 'Self-Ownership, Freedom and Autonomy', 2 *The Journal of Ethics*, pp 27–55.

Bridge, C (1993), 'Changing the nature of adoption: law reform in England and New Zealand', 13 *Legal Studies*, pp 81–102.

Bridgeman, J and Millns, S (1998), *Feminist Perspectives on Law, Law's Engagement with the Female Body*, London: Sweet & Maxwell.

Brown, B (1993), 'Bodily Oppositions/Controlling Fantasies', in Bridgeman, J (ed), *Body Politics: 'Control versus Freedom', The Role of Feminism in Women's Personal Autonomy*, University of Liverpool: Feminist Legal Research Unit.

Buchanan, A, Brock, D, Daniels, N and Wikler, D (2000), *From Chance to Choice, Genetics & Justice*, Cambridge: CUP.

Budgeon, S (2003), 'Identity as an Embodied Event', 9 *Body & Society*, pp 35–55.

Calhoun, C (1999), 'Making up Emotional People: The Case of Romantic Love', in Bandes, S (ed), *Passions of Law*, London: NYUP.

Cane, P (1997), *The Anatomy of Tort*, Oxford: Hart Publishing.

—— (2004), 'Another Failed Sterilisation', 120 *Law Quarterly Review*, pp 189–93.

Canguilhem, G (1991), *The Normal and the Pathological*, New York: Zone Books.

Carroll, L (1998), *Alice's Adventures in Wonderland and Through the Looking-Glass*, London: Penguin Books.

Chamallas, M and Kerber, L (1989), 'Women, Mothers, and the Law of Fright: A History', 88 *Michigan Law Review*, pp 814–64.

Clarke, L and Roberts, C (2002), 'Policy and rhetoric: The growing interest in fathers and grandparents in Britain', in Carling, A, Duncan, S and Edwards, R (eds), *Analysing Families, Morality and Rationality in Policy and Practice*, London: Routledge.

Colebrook, C (2000), 'Incorporeality: The Ghostly Body of Metaphysics', 6 *Body & Society*, pp 25–44.

Collier, R (2001), 'A Hard Time to Be a Father?: Reassessing the Relationship Between Law, Policy, and Family (Practices), 28 *Journal of Law and Society*, pp 520–45.

Comment (1995), '*Walkin v South Manchester HA* [1995] 4 All ER 132', *Journal of Personal Injury Litigation*, pp 236–8.

Conaghan, J (1996), 'Tort Law and the Feminist Critique of Reason', in Bottomley,

A (ed), *Feminist Perspectives on the Foundational Subjects of Law*, London: Cavendish Publishing.
—— (1998), 'Tort Litigation in the Context of Intra-Family Abuse', 61 *MLR*, pp 132–61.
—— (2002), 'Law, harm and redress: a feminist perspective', 22 *Legal Studies*, pp 319–39.
—— (2003), 'Tort Law and Feminist Critique', 56 *Current Legal Problems*, pp 175–209.
—— and Mansell, W (1999), *The Wrongs of Tort*, London: Pluto.
Cooke, J and Oughton, D (2000), *The Common Law of Obligations*, London: Butterworths.
Dalton, C (1985), 'An Essay in the Deconstruction of Contract Doctrine', 94 *Yale Law Journal*, pp 997–1114.
Davies, M (2001), *Textbook on Medical Law*, London: Blackstone Press.
Deech, R (1998), 'Family Law and Genetics', 61 *MLR*, pp 697–715.
Dick, P (1968), *Do Androids Dream of Electric Sheep?* London: Millennium.
Dickens, B (1990), 'Wrongful Birth and Life, Wrongful Death Before Birth, and Wrongful Law', in McLean, S (ed), *Legal Issues in Human Reproduction*, Dartmouth: Aldershot.
Diduck, A (1993), 'Legislating Ideologies of Motherhood', 2 *Social & Legal Studies*, pp 461–85.
Dixon, C (2004), 'An unconventional gloss on unintended children', 153 *NLJ*, pp 1732–33.
Donnelly, M (1997), 'The Injury of Parenthood: The Tort of Wrongful Conception', 48 *Northern Ireland Legal Quarterly*, pp 10–23.
Douglas, G (1991), *Law, Fertility & Reproduction*, London: Sweet & Maxwell.
Douzinas, C and McVeigh, S (1992), 'The Tragic Body: The Inscription of Autonomy in Medical Ethics and Law', in McVeigh, S and Wheeler, S (eds), *Law, Health & Medical Regulation*, Hants: Dartmouth Publishing.
Editorial (1998), 'Health care and the human body', 1 *Medicine, Health Care and Philosophy*, pp 103–5.
Eisenstein, Z (1988), *The Female Body and the Law*, London: University of California Press.
Engelhadt, T (2001), 'The Many Faces of Autonomy', 9 *Health Care Analysis*, pp 283–97.
Estin, A (1994), 'Love and Obligation: Family law and the Romance of Economics', 36 *William & Mary Law Review*, pp 989–1087.
Evans, M (2001), 'The "Medical Body" As Philosophy's Arena', 22 *Theoretical Medicine*, pp 17–32.
—— (2003), *Love, an unromantic discussion*, Cambridge: Polity.
Fathers Direct (2001), 'Father Facts: What Good are Dads?', accessed 22 October 2006, www.fathersdirect.com/index.php?id=3&cID=111.
Fegan, E (1999), '"Subjects" of Regulation/Resistance? Postmodern Feminism and Agency in Abortion-Decision Making', 7 *Feminist Legal Studies*, pp 241–73.
—— (2002), 'Recovering Women: Intimate Images and Legal Strategy', 11 *Social & Legal Studies*, pp 155–83.
—— and Rebouche, R (2003), 'Northern Ireland's Abortion Law: The Morality of Silence and the Censure of Agency', 11 *Feminist Legal Studies*, pp 221–54.

Feinberg, J (1984), *Harm to Others*, Oxford: OUP.
Fineman, M (1999), 'Cracking the Foundational Myths: Independence, Autonomy and Self-Sufficiency', 8 *American University Journal of Gender, Social Policy and the Law*, pp 13–29.
—— (2004), *The Autonomy Myth*, London: The New Press.
Finley, L (1989), 'Breaking Women's Silence in law: The Dilemma of the Gendered Nature of Legal Reasoning', 64 *Notre Dame Law Review*, pp 886–910.
Fitzpatrick, P (1997), 'Distant Relations: The New Constructionism in Critical and Socio-Legal Studies', in Thomas, P (ed), *Socio-Legal Studies*, Dartmouth: Aldershot.
Fitzpatrick, T (2001), 'Contributory negligance and contract – a critical assessment', 30 *Common Law World Review*, pp 255–271.
Fleming, J (1992), *The Law of Torts*, Sydney: Law Book Co.
Fox, M (1998), 'A Woman's Right to Choose? A Feminist Critique', in Harris, J and Holm, S (eds), *The Future of Reproduction*, Oxford: Clarendon Press.
Franke, K (2001), 'Theorising Yes: An Essay on Feminism, Law and Desire', 101 *Columbia Law Review*, pp 181–208.
Friedman, D, Hechter, M and Kanazawa, S (1994), 'A Theory of the Value of Children', 31 *Demography*, pp 375–401.
Friedman, M (2003), *Autonomy, Gender, Politics*, Oxford: OUP.
Furedi, A (1998), 'Wrong but the Right Thing to Do: Public Opinion and Abortion', in Lee, E (ed), *Abortion Law and Politics Today*, London: Macmillan Press.
Furedi, F (1999), *Courting Mistrust: The Hidden Growth of a Culture of Litigation in Britain*, London: Centre for Policy Studies.
—— (2003), *Culture of Fear*, London: Continuum.
Galligan, T (1999), 'The Tragedy in Torts', 5 *Cornell Journal of Law and Public Policy*, pp 139–83.
Gardner, J (2003), 'The Mark of Responsibility', 23 *Oxford Journal of Legal Studies*, pp 157–71.
Giddens, A (1991), *Modernity and Self-Identity: Self and Society in the Late Modern Age*, Cambridge: Polity.
—— (1999a), 'Risk and Responsibility', 62 *MLR*, pp 1–10.
—— (1999b), 'Runaway World: the Reith Lectures Revisited', London: 1999–2000 Director's Lectures, accessed 23 September 2006, www.bbc.co.uk/radio4/reith1999/.
Gilligan, C (1982), *In A Different Voice: Psychological Theory and Women's Development*, Cambridge, Massachusetts: Harvard University Press.
—— (1985), 'Feminist Discourse, Moral Values and the Law – A Conversation', 34 *Buffalo Law Review*, pp 11–87 (with discussants, DuBois, E, Dunlap, M, MacKinnon, A and Menkel-Meadow, C).
Glover, J (1977), *Causing Death and Saving Lives*, London: Penguin Books.
Goodrich, P (1995–96), 'Law in the Courts of Love: Andreas Capellanus and the Judgments of Love', 48 *Stanford Law Review*, pp 633–75.
Graycar, R (1995), 'Damaged Awards: The Vicissitudes of Life as a Woman', 3 *Torts Law Journal*, pp 1–21.
—— (1997), 'Hoovering as a Hobby and Other Stories', 31 *British Columbia Law Review*, pp 17–35.

—— (1998), 'The Gender of Judgments: Some Reflections on "Bias"', 32 *The University of British Columbia Law Review*, pp 1–21.

—— (2002), 'Sex, golf and stereotypes: measuring, valuing and imagining the body in court', 10 *Torts Law Journal*, pp 205–21.

—— and Morgan, J (1996), ' "Unnatural rejection of womanhood and motherhood": Pregnancy, Damage and the Law, A note on *CES v Superclinics (Aust) Pty*', 18 *The Sydney Law Review*, pp 323–41.

—— and Morgan, J (2002), *The Hidden Gender of Law*, Sydney: Federation Press.

Grosz, E (1994), *Volatile Bodies, Toward a Corporeal Feminism*, Bloomington, IN: Indiana University Press.

Grubb, A (1985), 'Failure of Sterilisation – damages for "wrongful conception"', 44 *Cambridge Law Journal*, pp 30–2.

Hale, B (2001), 'The Value of Life and the Cost of Living – Damages for Wrongful Birth', 7 *British Actuarial Journal*, pp 747–63.

Harden, A and Ogden, J (1999), 'Young women's experiences of arranging and having abortions', 21 *Sociology of Health & Illness*, pp 426–44.

Harris, D, Campbell, D and Halson, R (2002), *Remedies in Contract & Tort*, London: Butterworths LexisNexis.

Harris, J (2001), 'Human Beings, Persons and Conjoined Twins: An Ethical Analysis of the Judgment in *Re A*', 9 *Med L Rev*, pp 221–36.

Heller, J (1961), *Catch 22*, London: Corgi Books.

Hensel, W (2005), 'The Disabling Impact of Wrongful Birth and Wrongful Life Actions', 40 *Harvard Civil Rights Civil Liberties Law Review*, pp 141–95.

Herbert, A (1936), *Uncommon Law*, London: Methuen & Co.

Hildt, E (2002), 'Autonomy and freedom of choice in prenatal genetic diagnosis', 5 *Medicine, Health Care and Philosophy*, pp 65–71.

Himmelweit, S (2002), 'Economic theory, norms and the care gap, or why do economists become parents?', in Carling, A, Duncan, S and Edwards, R (eds), *Analysing Families, Morality and Rationality in Policy and Practice*, London: Routledge.

Hoyano, L (2002), 'Misconceptions about Wrongful Conception', 65 *MLR*, pp 883–906.

Hudson, A (1983), 'Refusal of Medical Treatment', 3 *Legal Studies*, pp 50–9.

Hyde, A (1997), *Bodies of Law*, Chichester: Princeton University Press.

Jackson, A (1995), 'Action for Wrongful Life, Wrongful Pregnancy and Wrongful Birth in the United States and England', 17 *Loyola of Los Angeles International & Comparative Law Journal*, pp 535–613.

—— (1996), 'Wrongful Life and Wrongful Birth', 17 *The Journal of Legal Medicine*, pp 349–81.

Jackson, E (2000), 'Abortion, Autonomy and Prenatal Diagnosis', 9 *Social & Legal Studies*, pp 467–94.

—— (2001), *Regulating Reproduction*, Oxford: Hart Publishing.

—— (2002), 'Conception and the Irrelevance of the Welfare Principle', 65 *MLR*, pp 176–203.

—— (2005), *Medical Law, Text, Cases and Materials*, Oxford: OUP.

Jones, M (2002), *Textbook on Torts*, Oxford: OUP.

Judicial Studies Board (2004), *Guidelines for the Assessment of General Damages in Personal Injury Cases*, Oxford: OUP.

Karpin, I (1992), 'Legislating the Female Body: Reproductive Technology and the Reconstructed Woman', 3 *Columbia Journal of Gender and Law*, pp 325–49.
Kennedy, I (1981), *The Unmasking of Medicine*, London: George Allen & Unwin.
Keywood, K (2000), 'More than a Woman? Embodiment and Sexual Difference in Medical Law', 8 *Feminist Legal Studies*, pp 319–42.
Kosko, B (1994), *Fuzzy Thinking, The New Science of Fuzzy Logic*, London: Flamingo.
Kuhn, T (1996), *The Structure of Scientific Revolutions*, London: University of Chicago Press.
Lacey, N (1998), *Unspeakable Subjects, Feminist Essays in Legal and Social Theory*, Oxford: Hart Publishing.
Lattimer, M (1998) 'Dominant Ideas versus Women's Reality: Hegemonic Discourses in British Abortion Law', in Lee, E (ed), *Abortion Law and Politics Today*, London: Macmillan Press.
Lawson, A (1996), 'The Things We Do For Love: Detrimental Reliance in the Family Home', 16 *Legal Studies*, pp 218–31.
Lee, E (2002), 'Psychologizing Abortion: Women's "Mental Health" and the Regulation of Abortion in Britain', in Morris, A and Nott, S (eds), *Well women, the gendered nature of health care provision*, Aldershot: Ashgate.
—— (2003a), 'Tensions in the Regulation of Abortion in Britain', 30 *Journal of Law and Society*, pp 532–53.
—— (2003b), *Abortion, Motherhood and Mental Health*, New York: Aldine de Gruyter.
—— (2003c), 'The Context for the Development of 'Post-Abortion Syndrome', accessed 23 September 2006, www.prochoiceforum.org.uk/psy_coun9.asp.
—— and Jackson, E (2002), 'The Pregnant Body', in Evans, M and Lee, E (eds), *Real Bodies, A Sociological Introduction*, Hampshire: Palgrave.
Levine, P and Steiger, D (2001), 'Abortion as Pregnancy Insurance', accessed 23 September 2006, http://irm.wharton.upenn.edu/F01-Levine.pdf.
Lunney, M (2004), 'A Right Old Mess: *Rees v Darlington Health Authority* [2003] 3 *WLR* 1091', 1 *UNELJ*, pp 145–55.
Lupton, D (1999), *Risk*, London: Routledge.
Lury, C (1998), *Prosthetic Culture: Photography, Memory and Identity*, London: Routledge.
MacKenzie, C (1992), 'Abortion and Embodiment', 70 *Australian Journal of Philosophy*, pp 136–55.
Mackenzie, R (1999), 'From Sanctity to Screening: Genetic Disabilities, Risk and Rhetorical Strategies in Wrongful Birth and Wrongful Conception Cases', 7 *Feminist Legal Studies*, pp 175–91.
Macklem, T and Gardner, J (2001), 'Provocation and Pluralism', 64 *MLR*, pp 815–30.
Maclean, A (2000), 'McFarlane v Tayside Health Board: A Wrongful Conception in the House of Lords', 3 *Web JCLI*, accessed 23 September 2006, http://webjcli.ncl.ac.uk/2000/issue3/maclean3.html.
—— (2004), 'Distributing the Burden of a Blessing', 3 *Journal of Obligations & Remedies*, pp 23–45.
Mahendra, B (1995), 'Thrown to Woolf', 145 *NLJ*, pp 1375–76.
Mark, D (1976), 'Liability for Failure of Birth Control Methods', 76 *Columbia Law Review*, pp 1187–204.

Markesinis, B and Deakin, S (1999), *Tort Law*, Oxford: OUP.
Mason, J (1990/1998), *Medico-Legal Aspects of Reproduction and Parenthood*, Aldershot: Ashgate.
—— (2000), 'Unwanted Pregnancy: A Case of Retroversion?', 4 *Edinburgh Law Review*, pp 191–206.
—— (2002), 'Wrongful Pregnancy, Wrongful Birth and Wrongful Terminology', 6 *The Edinburgh Law Review*, pp 46–66.
—— (2004), 'A Turn-up Down Under: McFarlane in the Light of Cattanach', 1:1 *Script-ed*, pp 1–18, accessed 23 September 2006, www.law.ed.ac.uk/ahrb/script-ed/docs/mason.pdf.
——, McCall Smith, R and Laurie, G (1999/2002), *Law and Medical Ethics*, London: Butterworths LexisNexis.
McCall Smith, A (1997), 'Beyond Autonomy', 14 *Journal of Contemporary Health Law & Policy*, pp 23–39.
McDonagh, E (1996), *Breaking the Abortion Deadlock: From Choice to Consent*, New York: OUP.
Mee, J (1992), 'Wrongful Conception: The Emergence of a Full Recovery Rule', 70 *Washington University Law Quarterly*, pp 887–914.
Meyer, D (2000), 'The Paradox of Family Privacy', 53 *Vanderbilt Law Review*, pp 527–95.
Millns, S (2001), 'The Human Rights Act 1998 and Reproductive Rights', 54 *Parliamentary Affairs*, pp 475–94.
Milsteen, J (1983), 'Recovery of Childrearing Expenses in Wrongful Birth Cases: A Motivational Analysis', 32 *Emory Law Journal*, pp 1167–97.
Monti, G (1999), 'A reasonable woman standard in sexual harassment litigation', 19 *Legal Studies*, pp 552–79.
Moran, M (2003), *Rethinking the Reasonable Person*, Oxford, OUP.
Morell, C (2000), 'Saying No: Women's Experiences with Reproductive Refusal', 10 *Feminism & Psychology*, pp 313–22.
Morgan, D (1990), 'Abortion: the unexamined ground', *Criminal Law Review*, pp 687–94.
—— (2001), *Issues in Medical Law and Ethics*, London: Cavendish Publishing.
Morgan, J (2004), 'Tort, Insurance and Incoherence', 67 *MLR*, pp 384–401.
Morgan, K (1991), 'Women and the Knife: Cosmetic Surgery and the Colonization of Women's Bodies', in Sherwin, S and Parish, B (eds), *Women, Medicine, Ethics and the Law*, Aldershot: Ashgate.
Morris, A (2004), 'Another fine mess ... The aftermath of *McFarlane* and the decision in *Rees v Darlington Memorial Hospital NHS Trust*', 20(1) *Professional Negligence*, pp 2–16.
—— and Nott, S (1995), 'The Law's Engagement with Pregnancy', in Bridgeman, J and Millns, S (eds), *Law and Body Politics, Regulating the Female Body*, Aldershot: Dartmouth.
Morris, J (1991), *Pride Against Prejudice*, London: The Women's Press.
Mullender, R (2003), 'Tort, Human Rights, and Common Law Culture', 23 *Oxford Journal of Legal Studies*, pp 301–18.
Mullin, A (2002), 'Pregnant bodies, pregnant minds', 3 *Feminist Theory*, pp 27–44.
Mullis, A (1993), 'Wrongful Conception Unravelled', 1 *Med L Rev*, pp 320–35.
Murphy, J (1994), 'Some ruminations on women, violence, and the criminal law',

in Coleman, J and Buchanan, A (eds), *In Harm's Way, Essays in Honor of Joel Feinberg*, Cambridge: CUP.

Naffine, N (1994), 'Possession: Erotic Love in the Law of Rape', 57 *MLR*, pp 10–37.

—— (1998), 'The Legal Structure of Self-Ownership: Or the Self-Possessed Man and the Woman Possessed', 25 *Journal of Law and Society*, pp 193–212.

—— (2002), 'In Praise of Legal Feminism', 22 *Legal Studies*, pp 71–101.

—— (2003), 'Who are Law's Persons? From Cheshire Cats to Responsible Subjects', 66 *MLR*, pp 346–67.

Nedelsky, J (1989), 'Reconceiving Autonomy: Sources, Thoughts and Possibilities', 1 *Yale Journal of Law and Feminism*, pp 7–36.

—— (1997), 'Embodied Diversity and the Challenges to Law', 42 *McGill Law Journal*, pp 91–117.

Nesse, R (2001), 'On the difficulty of defining disease: A Darwinian perspective', 4 *Medicine, Health Care and Philosophy*, pp 37–46.

Norrie, K (1988), 'Compensation for Wrongful Birth: An Examination of the Principles Governing a Physician's Liability in Scots Law for the Failure of a Family Planning Procedure', unpublished PhD thesis, University of Aberdeen.

Norton, F (1999), 'Assisted Reproduction and the Frustration of Genetic Affinity: Interest, Injury, and Damages', 74 *New York University Law Review*, pp 793–843.

Nussbaum, M (2000), 'The Cost of Tragedy: Some Moral Limits of Cost-Benefit Analysis', in Adler, M and Posner, E (eds), *Cost-Benefit Analyses*, London: University of Chicago Press.

Orr, S and Miller, C (1997), 'Unintended Pregnancy and the Psychosocial Well-Being of Pregnant Women', 7 *Women's Health Issues*, pp 38–46.

O'Sullivan, J (2004), 'The answer is so simple. Just ask Dad', *The Times*, 23 November.

Peppin, P (1996), 'A Feminist Challenge to Tort Law', in Bottomley, A (ed), *Feminist Perspectives on the Foundational Subjects of Law*, London, Cavendish Publishing.

Petchesky, R (1986), *Abortion and Women's Choice*, Northeastern University Press.

Peters, T (1996), 'Multiple Choice in Baby Making', 16 *Word & World*, pp 11–23.

Petersen, K (1996), 'Wrongful Conception and Birth: The Loss of Reproductive Freedom and Medical Irresponsibility', 18 *Sydney Law Review*, pp 503–22.

Phillips, C (2001), 'Re-imagining the (Dis)Abled Body', 22 *Journal of Medical Humanities*, pp 195–208.

Pomeroy, J (1992), 'Reason, Religion and Avoidable Consequences: When Faith and the Duty to Mitigate Collide', 67 *New York University Law Review*, pp 1111–56.

Posner, R (1999), 'Emotion versus Emotionalism in Law', in Bandes, S (ed), *Passions of Law*, London: New York University Press.

Priaulx, N (2006), 'Beyond Health & Disability: Rethinking the "Foetal Abnormality" Ground in Abortion Law', in Biggs, H and Horsey K (eds), *The Human Fertilisation and Embryology Act 1990: Reproducing Regulation*, London: Routledge-Cavendish.

Prosser, W (1971), *Handbook of the Law of Torts*, St Paul: West Publishing Co.

Purdy, L (1997), 'Babystrike!', in Nelson, H (ed), *Feminism and Families*, New York: Routledge.

—— (2001), 'Medicalization, Medical Necessity and Feminist Medicine', 15 *Bioethics*, pp 248–61.

—— (2006), 'Women's reproductive autonomy: medicalisation and beyond', 32 *JME*, pp 287–91.

Quick, O (2002), 'Damages for Wrongful Conception', *Tort Law Review*, pp 5–10.

Rackley, E (2006), 'Difference in the House of Lords', 15 *Social & Legal Studies*, pp 163–85.
Radcliffe-Richards, J (1999), 'Abortion on grounds of foetal abnormality', in Biggs, H and Lee, L (eds), *Abortion, Ethics and the Law*, Canterbury: University of Kent.
Radin, M (1987), 'Market-Inalienability', 100 *Harvard Law Review*, pp 1849–932.
Radley-Gardener, O (2002), 'Wrongful Birth Revisited', 118 *The Law Quarterly Review*, pp 11–15.
Rawlinson, Lord (1994), 'The Physical and Psycho-Social Effects of Abortion upon Women', London: A Report by the Commission of Inquiry into the Operation and Consequence of the Abortion Act.
Read, J (2000), *Disability, The Family and Society, Listening to Mothers*, Buckingham: Open University Press.
Reece, H (2003), *Divorcing Responsibly*, Oxford: Hart Publishing.
Reichman, A (1985), 'Damages in Tort For Wrongful Conception – Who Bears the Cost of Raising the Child?', 10 *Sydney Law Review*, pp 568–90.
Richardson, J (2004), 'Feminist perspectives on the law of tort and the technology of risk', 33 *Economy and Society*, pp 98–120.
Ripstein, A (1999), *Equality, Responsibility and the Law*, Cambridge: CUP.
Robertson, G (1978), 'Civil Liability Arising from "Wrongful Birth" Following an Unsuccessful Sterilization Operation', 4 *American Journal of Law and Medicine*, pp 131–156.
Rogers, W (1985), 'Legal Implications of Ineffective Sterilization', *Legal Studies*, pp 296–313.
—— (2002), *Winfield and Jolowicz on Tort*, London: Sweet & Maxwell.
Rosenbaum, T (2003), *The Myth of Moral Justice*, New York: HarperCollins.
Rössler, B (2002), 'Problems with Autonomy', 17 *Hypatia*, pp 143–62.
Rothman, B (1988), *The Tentative Pregnancy, Prenatal Diagnosis and the Future of Motherhood*, London: Pandora Press.
Rúdólfsdóttir, A (2000), ' "I Am Not a Patient, and I Am Not a Child": The Institutionalization and Experience of Pregnancy', 10 *Feminism & Psychology*, pp 337–50.
Ryan, M (1999), 'The Argument for Unlimited Procreative Liberty: A Feminist Critique', in Robertson, J, Berry, R and McDonnell, K (eds), *A Health Law Reader*, Durham, NC: Carolina Academic Press.
Ryan, S (1994), 'Wrongful Birth: False Representations of Women's Reproductive Lives', 78 *Minnesota Law Review*, pp 857–909.
Samuel, G (2001), *Law of Obligations and Legal Remedies*, London: Cavendish Publishing.
Savulescu, J (2001), 'Is current practice around late termination of pregnancy eugenic and discriminatory? Maternal interests and abortion', 27 *JME*, pp 165–71.
—— (2002), 'Is there a "right not to be born"? Reproductive decision-making, options and the right to information', 28 *JME*, pp 65–67.
Schwartz, B (2004), *The Paradox of Choice*, New York: HarperCollins.
Scott, R (2003), 'Prenatal Screening, Autonomy and Reasons: The Relationship Between the Law of Abortion and Wrongful Birth', 11 *Med L Rev*, 265–325.
Seuffert, N (1999), 'Domestic Violence, Discourses of Romantic Love and Complex Personhood in the Law', 23 *Melbourne University Law Review*, pp 211–40.

Seymour, J (2000), *Childbirth and the Law*, Oxford: OUP.
Sheldon, S (1995), 'The Law of Abortion and the Politics of Medicalisation', in Bridgeman, J and Millns, S (eds), *Law and Body Politics: Regulating the Female Body*, Aldershot: Dartmouth.
—— (1997), *Beyond Control, Medical Power and Abortion Law*, London: Pluto Press.
—— (1998), 'The Abortion Act 1967: A Critical Perspective', in Lee, E (ed), *Abortion Law and Politics Today*, London: Macmillan Press Ltd.
—— (1999), '*Re* Conceiving Masculinity: Imagining Men's Reproductive Bodies in Law', 26 *Journal of Law and Society*, pp 129–49.
—— (2003), 'Unwilling Fathers and Abortion: Terminating Men's Child Support Obligations?', 66 *MLR*, pp 175–94.
—— (2004), 'Revealing cracks in the "twin pillars"?', 16 *Child and Family Law Quarterly*, pp 437–52.
—— and Wilkinson, S (2001), 'Termination of Pregnancy for Reason of Foetal Disability: Are There Grounds For A Special Exception In Law?', 9 *Med L Rev*, pp 85–109.
Sherwin, S (1998), 'A Relational Approach in the Politics of Health', in Sherwin, S (ed) *The Politics of Women's Health, Exploring Agency and Autonomy*, Philadelphia: Temple University Press.
Silbaugh, K (1996), 'Turning Labour into Love: Housework and the Law', 91 *Northwestern University Law Review*, pp 25–86.
Simons, K (1997), 'Contributory Negligence: Conceptual and Normative Issues', in Owen, D (ed), *Philosophical Foundations of Tort Law*, Oxford: OUP.
Smith, S (2004), *Contract Theory*, Oxford: OUP.
Stapleton, J (1988), 'The Gist of Negligence', 104 *The Law Quarterly Review*, pp 213–38.
—— (1995), 'Tort, Insurance and Ideology', 58 *MLR*, pp 820–45.
—— (2001), 'Legal Cause: Cause-in-Fact and the Scope of Liability for Consequences' 54 *Vanderbilt Law Review*, pp 941–1009.
Steele, J (2004), *Risks and Legal Theory*, Oxford: Hart Publishing.
Strangeways, S (2003), 'You could have had abortion: Law Lord', *UK Newsquest Regional Press – This is The NorthEast*, 17 October 2003.
Stychin, C (1998), 'Body Talk: Rethinking Autonomy, Commodification and the Embodied Legal Self', in Sheldon, S and Thomson, M (eds), *Feminist Perspectives On Health Care Law*, London: Cavendish.
Symmons, C (1987), 'Policy Factors in Actions for Wrongful Birth', 50 *MLR*, pp 269–306.
Talbot, C and Williams, M (2003), 'Kinship Care', 33 *Fam Law*, pp 502–7.
Thomas, C (2002), 'The "Disabled" Body', in Evans, M and Lee, E (eds), *Real Bodies, A Sociological Introduction*, New York: Palgrave.
Vehmas, S (2002), 'Parental responsibility and the morality of selective abortion', 5 *Ethical Theory and Moral Practice*, pp 463–84.
Waldron, J (2000), 'The Role of Rights in Practical Reasoning: "Rights" versus "Needs" ', 4 *The Journal of Ethics*, pp 115–35.
Watson, N (1998), 'Enabling Identity: Disability, Self and Citizenship', in Shakespeare, T (ed), *The Disability Reader*, London: Continuum.
Weir, T (2000), *A Casebook on Tort*, London: Sweet & Maxwell.
—— (2001), *Tort Law*, Oxford: OUP.

West, R (1985a), 'Authority, Autonomy and Choice: The Role of Consent in the Moral and Political Visions of Franz Kafka and Richard Posner', 99 *Harvard Law Review*, pp 384–428.
—— (1985b), 'Submission, Choice and Ethics: A Rejoinder to Judge Posner', 99 *Harvard Law Review*, pp 1449–56.
—— (1988), 'Jurisprudence and Gender', 55 *University of Chicago Law Review*, pp 1–72.
—— (1997), *Caring For Justice*, London: NYUP.
Whitfield, A (1998), 'Actions Arising from Birth', in Kennedy, I and Grubb, A (eds), *Principles of Medical Law*, Oxford: OUP.
—— (2002), 'The fallout from *McFarlane*', 18 *Professional Negligence*, pp 234–47.
Wilkinson, S (2003), *Bodies for Sale*, London: Routledge.
Williams, J (1988), 'Deconstructing Gender', 87 *Michigan Law Review*, pp 797–845.
Witting, C (2002), 'Physical Damage in Negligence', 6 *Cambridge Law Journal*, pp 189–208.
Wong, S (1998), 'Constructive Trusts Over the Family Home: Lessons to be Learned from other Commonwealth Jurisdictions?', 18 *Legal Studies*, pp 369–90.
Wyndham, J (1955), *The Chrysalids*, London: Penguin Books.

Index

Abel, R. 125, 126
abortion 6, 7, 22, 85–6, 105–9; as pregnancy insurance 122–3; choice and 101–5, 137–8, 143–4, 150–6; 171–2, 181–2; conceptual basis of 22, 43, 85–6; conscientious objection and 97; delays 151; disability of child and 54, 55, 59, 64–8, 174–6; fathers and 145, 149–50; grounds for legal 82–3, 85–6; mitigation doctrine and 12, 91–109, 116–19; on demand 86, 96, 182; post-abortion syndrome (PAS) 151–2; reasonableness and 117, 118; regulation of 22–3, 43, 85; representations of women and 121–2, 157; self-regarding woman and 123; shifting attitudes towards 96, 118, 143; time-limits and 55, 59, 65, 86, 93; women's negative experiences of 151–3; *see also* foetus; mitigation; reproduction
Abrams, Kathryn 154, 155
Ackner, L. J. 97
Adoption, mitigation and 81, 91, 96, 99, 100, 104, 108, 116–17, 118, 131, 135, 138, 139, 156, 175, 177, 181
Annandale, E. 37
Arden, L. J. 147, 148, 149
Ashe, Marie 41
assumption of responsibility 2, 60, 61; *see* duty of care
Atiyah, P. S. 16, 31, 33
Atkins, Susan 8, 15, 21
Auld, Lord 25
autonomy 13, 18–19, 22–3, 40–1, 42–3, 77, 78–82, 88, 161–4, 178–84; beyond personhood 166–70; conventional award and 3, 73–7; extension of concept of harm and 32–3; limits of 13, 66–8; loss of 8–11, 70–2, 76, 176–7; maternal 119; parental 64–8, 99; relational approach 9–10, 18, 40–2, 43–5, 49, 56, 78, 79–81, 164, 165–6, 167–8, 170–8; responsibility and 173–8; self-determination 22, 23, 141, 148, 154, 156; what kind of person 164–6; value of 9, 11, 13, 78–81; women's 10, 23, 24, 67, 78, 81, 82, 85, 110, 119, 143–4, 164, 168, 178, 181–2

Bailey, R. 54
Bandes, Susan 162
Barnes, C. 54, 65
Bartlett, Katherine 35, 137, 175
Beatson, J. 116
Beauchamp, T. 9
Beck, U. 141, 142, 143, 183
Beck-Gernsheim, E. 141, 142, 143, 183
benchmarking (gender, religious, sexual, ethnic, physiological) 53
Bender, Leslie 85, 124, 144
Bernstein, Amy 10
Biggs, Hazel 167–8
Bingham, Lord 73, 77, 89
blame culture 31
blessing, child as: 1, 3, 5, 6, 7, 8, 12, 72, 77, 80, 90, 163; disabled children 57–9, 61, 62, 75, 163; women as recipients of 130, 132
Block, N. 108
bodies, construction of 18–24; *see also* women
Bordo, S. 18
Boyle, Mary 151, 152, 159
Brazier, Margaret 93, 97, 119, 182

198 Index

breach of duty 16, 87, 90, 91, 109, 110, 114, 118
Brenkert, G. 170
Bridgeman, J. 40
Brooke, J. 24, 60, 61, 100
Brown, Beverley 156–7, 159
Buchanan, A. 54
Budgeon, S. 19
Butler-Sloss, L. J. 134
Buxton, Lord 28, 29, 127

Calhoun, C. 162
Callaghan, J. 96
Cane, Peter 71, 91, 180
Canguilhem, Georges 53–4
caring burden 8, 10–11, 54, 55, 58, 65, 68–71, 76, 136; as price of parenthood 3, 28, 58; as a gratuitous activity 126, 129–30, 131; disabled child and 54, 56, 58, 60, 64–9, 70, 79; healthy child and 11, 69–70; value afforded to 126–7, 129–31
Cartesianism 19, 36, 41, 48, 127
causation, doctrine of 3, 12, 31, 90–1, 92, 100, 108, 110–11, 179; claimant, intervening act of 111; contributory negligence 31, 111, 115, 140; *novus actus interveniens* 12, 91, 92, 94, 97; *volenti non fit injuria*, and 111
Chamallas, M. 38
child maintenance award *see* damages
childlessness 15, 50
children: abortion and existing 22; assumption that most women want 26, 35, 128–32, 136; burdens of 8, 10–11, 54, 55, 58, 65, 68–71, 76, 136; capacity to bear 16, 35, 51; celebration of 1, 3, 5, 6, 7, 8, 12, 72, 77, 80, 90, 163; desire to avoid 7, 12, 28, 34, 35, 85; disabled 7, 10, 12, 53–83, 88, 93, 121, 129, 132–7, 163, 176; inability to have 5, 15, 38, 50, 132; protection of 16; qualitative/quantitative choices concerning 54; value afforded to 6
Childress, J. 9
clinical negligence 137, 180; NHS Redress Bill and 90; reproductive torts and 6, 77, 79, 89–90, 110, 137, 179–80
choice 10, 82, 121, 137–9, 141–4, 156–8, 182–4; abortion and 101–5, 137–8, 150–6; absence of 138, 153, 154; conformity instead of 154–6; context

and 164, 170; difficult 93, 156, 164, 169, 174, ; double-edged nature of 82, 156–8, 163, 171, 182–4; economic construction of 122–8, 181; freedom of 39, 64 (*see also* reproductive freedom); judicial conceptualisation of 74, 78, 88–110, 116, 121–2, 135, 138–9; male dominance over reproductive 11; men and reproductive 144–50; mitigation and 81, 88; qualitative/quantitative 54, 152; relational approach to 170–8; reversing nature's discrimination 149–50; self-regarding woman and 122–8; woman's right to choose 144–9, 181; *see also* autonomy
Clyde, Lord 2, 3, 28, 99, 102, 103, 104, 179
Colebrook, Claire 19, 169
Collier, R. 145
commodification theory 125–6
comparisons, problem of making 53; healthy child versus disabled child 12, 58, 64, 68; mitigation contexts 116, 136; *see also* infertility
Conaghan, Joanne 4, 5, 32, 35, 36, 38, 46, 100, 114, 126, 128, 165, 166, 168
conformity 154–6
conjoined twins 164
consent 18
consortium 21
construction: bodies 18–24; *see also* reasonable woman, constructions of; women
contextual approach *see* relational autonomy
contraception 6
contract law 31, 49, 87, 90, 111, 121, 162, 173, 179
contributory negligence 31, 111
conventional award 3, 73–7; *see also* damages
Cooke, J. 87, 88, 116

Dalton, C. 173
damage/compensable harm 2, 5, 11, 13, 16–17, 26–30, 32–9, 43–5, 49, 91, 109–10, 121, 162, 176–7; choice and 100, 104–6, 108; *see also* harm; personal injury
damages: additional child maintenance award relating to disability 57, 59, 59–64, 68, 72, 73, 75, 77, 129, 133–6;

claim by child, *see* wrongful life; conventional award 72–7, 184; gendered nature of 37–8, 132; ordinary child maintenance award 1, 8, 12, 39, 59, 72, 73, 88, 91, 92, 100, 102, 105, 136; pain and suffering 1, 13, 17, 24, 28, 34, 49, 86, 125, 130; purpose of 126, 134; *see also* mitigation

Davies, M. 93, 98

Deakin, S. 16, 35

decommodification perspective 125–6

Deech, R. 54

defensive medicine 89, 139

Denning, Lord 86, 97, 120

Dickens, Bernard 7

Diduck, A. 15

disability 54; abortion and 54, 55, 59, 64–8, 174–6; emerging dichotomies 56–9; health and 53–83; negative representations of 54–5; 57–9, 70–1, 73–4, 79, 122, 132–3; parental interests argument 54–6, 64–8, 79, 88

disease, meaning of 37; *see also* normality; personal injury

distributive justice 3, 4, 5, 8, 11, 12, 56, 60, 71, 72, 73, 74, 79, 102, 108, 133, 164, 179, 180; criticisms of 61–2, 71; equality and 5, 120, 183

Dixon, Clare 72

doctors *see* medical profession

Douglas, G. 64–5

Douzinas, C. 82

dualism, Cartesian 19, 36, 41, 48, 127

duress, economic 173

duties, maternal 122

duty of care 14, 16, 26, 61–2, 96–7; breach of 16, 87, 90, 91, 109, 110, 114, 118; child maintenance damages and, 2, 11, 60, 61, 62, economic interests and 5; existence of 5, 14, 26; 'fair, just and reasonable', and 2, 12, 57, 60, 180; policy and 100, 179, 180; *see also* negligence

economic duress 173

economic loss: categorisation as 8, 14, 29, 30, 58, 63, 126; liability for 2–3, 13, 32, 179

economic theory: influence on tort law 124–6; family 123–8; models of decision-making 122–5, 170–1, 177; women's work and 9–10, 128–32

eggshell skull rule 117–18

Emotion: autonomy and 42, 43, 45, 167, 169; emotional repercussions/harms 58, 65, 68, 69, 71, 76, 79, 125, 126, 177; emotional scripts 162–3, 176; exclusion of 41, 77, 134, 135, 162, 177; law and 77, 162–3, 170; men and 19, 148; reason versus 19, 162; women and 19, 20, 42, 121, 128, 158, 166, 176; *see also* relational approach

end of life decisions 167–8

Engelhadt, T. 180

equality, 22, 33, 157, formal 120, 145, 149; relational approach and 164, 172; reproduction and 11, 51, 155; substantive and procedural 33, 164, 172; *see also* inequality

essentialism 166

Estin, Ann 123, 124, 170

Evans, Mary 19, 143

family: as 'private' and 128–9; economic theory and 123–8

fathers 144–9; abortion and 149–50

Fegan, Eileen 151, 152, 153, 156, 159

Feinberg, J. 4

feminism: abortion and 86, 123, 144, 152–3, 154, 155, 163–6; autonomy and 42; approach to reproductive torts 17, 23, 43, 45–8, 58; appropriating the language of 150; bioethics and 82; choice and 150, 154, 172; family as 'private' critique and 128–9; gendered harm and 5, 38, liberal ideology and 42, 163–4, 168; relational accounts and 40, 165–6

feminist legal theory, legal personality and 163–6, 168–9, 172, reasonable man and 113–5; torts and 32, 114

Fineman, Martha 79, 128, 172, 178, 183

Finley, Lucinda 129, 162

Fitzpatrick, Peter 35

Fitzpatrick, T. 90

Fleming, J. 35

Foetus: as separate entity 20, 22, 23, 24, 176; as subject of protection 15, 16, 20, 22; conceptual absence of 44, 45, 127; decisional responsibility arising from 40, 48, 127; disabled 22, 55, 59, 65, 82, 93, 135, 175; legal status of 149; maternal connection to 40, 41, 45, 48, 127, 176; maternal/foetal conflict 24;

moral status of 66; *see also* abortion; reproduction
Fox, Marie 151, 157, 159
Franke, Katherine 159
fraud 94
Friedan, Betty 51
Friedman, Marilyn 123, 153, 155
Furedi, Ann 156
Furedi, Frank 32–3

Galligan, Thomas 124, 125
Gardner, J. 114, 173, 174
gender, centralising 5, 40, 58, 115, 169; neutrality 37, 38, 80, 100, 121
gendered harm 5, 131; gendering of judgment 113–15; *see also* women
genetic diagnostic techniques 54
Giddens, Anthony 14, 35, 141, 142
Gilligan, Carol 51, 165, 176
Gleeson, C. J. 176–7
Graycar, Reg 5, 7, 47, 114, 117, 121, 129, 131, 132
Grosz, Elizabeth 19, 21, 22
Grubb, Andrew 93, 94

Hale, Baroness 4, 39, 44–7, 60, 62, 63, 69, 70, 80, 98, 133
Hand, Learned 124, 125
harassment 5, 31, 169, 171
Harden, A. 152
harm: concept of 4–8, 13, 16, 33, 49; disability and 56–9, 54–6, 64–8, 79, 88; extension/stretching of concept of 31–3, 38–43, 48; economic 8, 14, 29, 30, 58, 63, 126; emotional 43, 45, 48, 58, 65, 68, 69, 71, 76, 79, 125, 126, 177; feminist characterisation of 45, 47; gendered 5, 43; harm*less* 5, 11, 16, 28, 36, 56, 64, 70, 78, 81, 88, 169; intangible 10, 58, 75, 125; *orthodox* injuries 31–8; paradigm shifts 43–7; paradox 81, 86–90, 109–10, 177–8, 181; personal injuries 4, 16; physical 2, 8, 13, 16, 27, 28, 29, 32, 36, 40, 44; pregnancy as 16–18, 24–31, 33–8, 48, 49; psychological 32, 44, 45, 152; relational 10, 45, 48; specific to women 5, 40, 48, 169, 180; tortious characterisation of 4–8, 15–18; *see also* damage/compensable harm
Harris, John 164
Hayne, J. 177

Hensel, W. 70
Herbert, Alan 113
Hildt, E. 54, 157
Himmelweit, S. 123, 124, 171
Hoggett, Brenda 8, 15, 21
Holmes, Oliver Wendell 67
home, interests in 129
homosexuality 37
Hope, Lord 2, 3, 13, 27, 39, 57, 73, 99, 100, 101, 103, 104, 108
horse analogy, relevancy of 106, 108
Hoyano, Laura 30, 61, 62, 72
Hudson, A. 95
human rights 31, 179, 184
Hutton, Lord 73
Hyde, Alan 19, 20

impartiality 46–7; myth of 163
individualism 40, 157, 166
industrial injuries 31
inequality 22, 33, 120, 149, 155, 157; *see also* equality
infertility 5, 15, 38, 50, 132
injury *see* harm/damage; personal injury
insurance 120

Jackson, Anthony 7–8, 70–1, 86, 87, 104
Jackson, Emily 6, 7, 9, 23, 26, 65, 89, 150, 182
Jones, M. 131, 132
judges: claim to objectivity 114; deference to medical profession 11, 23, 139; emotion and 163; gender of 46–7, 114–15; reproductive torts and 70, 90, 101; role of 14, 90, 97; stories told by 7, 100; subjective views of 4, 36; underwear worn by 114–15

Karpin, I. 22
Kennedy, Ian 37
Kerber, L. 38
Keywood, K. 19
Kingdom, Elizabeth 145
Kirby, J. 77–8
Kosko, Bart 161, 162
Kuhn, T. 45

Lacey, Nicola 21, 36, 166
Lattimer, Maxine 143
Lawson, Anna 129
Lee, Ellie 85–6, 151, 152, 159, 182
legal profession 31

Levine, Philip 122–3
life plan, disruption of 58, 80, 144, 157
life, sanctity of 7, 97
love: choice and 178, 184; commodification of 125; emotional scripts and 162; family as jurisdiction of 128, 129; judicial emphasis upon 7, 12, 87, 100, 104, 106, 108, 122, 137, 140, 169–70; mother's 130–2, 136, 137, 178, 184
Lunney, Mark 63, 76–7, 179
Lupton, Deborah 183

McCall Smith, A. 82, 184
McCall Smith, R. 9
McDonagh, Eileen 36, 39, 50
MacKenzie, Catriona 40–1
Mackenzie, Robin 9, 11
Macklem, T. 114
Maclean, Alisdair 7, 8, 57
McVeigh, S. 82
Mahendra, B. 37
Mansell, Wade 4, 100, 114, 126
marital rape 21
Mark, D. 108
Markesinis, B. 16, 35
Mason, J. K. 5, 9, 17, 27, 46, 60, 64, 72, 81, 86, 88, 96, 98, 99, 104, 105, 138
May, Lord 29
Meagher, J. A. 108
medical profession: conscientious objection under Abortion Act 1967 and 97; deference to 89, 95, 151; paternalistic control by 11; power of 22, 23, 37, 85, 151, 159; wrongful conception/pregnancy and 2, 8, 11, 89
Mee, Jennifer 7
Miller, C. 41
Millett, Lord 2, 3, 5, 7, 10, 14, 28, 39, 46, 57, 71, 73, 74, 76, 99, 101–2, 104, 105, 108, 132
Millns, S. 40, 142
Milsteen, Jeff 88, 93, 96, 97, 118
mitigation doctrine 87–91; avoidance of consequences language 108–9; choice and 101–5, 174; duty to take steps and 87, 91, 96, 97, 98, 150; early discovery of pregnancy and 93, 94; horse analogy and 106–8; late discovery of pregnancy and 93, 94, 95, 135; mitigation ethic 90–1, 150; policy and 179; reasonableness and 115–16, 120; wrongful birth and 110; wrongful conception and 91–109, 115–17, 118–20; wrongful conception and rejection of 88, 98–101, 109–10, 115, 136
Monti, G. 166
Moral: acrimony over abortion 95, 118–19; convictions and termination 95, 117–19, 138, 172; dilemma 45, 172, 174–5, 176; dimension 18, 40, 44, 97, 98, 128, 169, 170, 172, 174–5, 183, 184; domain, exclusion of 124, 127–8, 170, 171, 174–5, 177; ethos 3–4; foetal status 66; judiciary and morality 3–4, 7–8, 11, 49; and legal fault 120; moral voice 51, 164, 170, 176, 177, 178; reproduction, morality of 142–3; repugnance 3, 5, 57, 114, 183; responsibilities 43, 45, 48, 51, 107, 132, 165–6, 170, 173, 175, 176, 177–8
Moran, Mayo 114, 131
Morell, C. 15
Morgan, Derek 9, 11, 23, 54
Morgan, Jonathan 5, 117, 120, 121
Morgan, Kathryn 154
Morris, Anne 15, 17, 22, 77
Morris, J. 55
motherhood: as chronic 10; choosing 145; costs of 8, 10, 70; constructions of 15–16, 122, 130, 138, 142, 143, 155; enforced 48, 177; relational autonomy and 9; responsibilities entailed in 48, 183; *see also* women; caring; moral responsibilities
Mullender, R. 36
Mullin, A. 20, 39
Mullis, Alistair 16, 24, 26, 51, 120
Murphy, J. 33

Naffine, Ngaire 18, 19, 21, 82, 128, 163, 164, 165, 166, 168
National Health Service (NHS) 77, 89–90, 110, 137, 139, 150
natural woman construction 128–32; *see also* women
Nedelsky, Jennifer 42, 46–7
need, woman in 132–6; *see also* women
negligence, law of 11, 13, 16, 29, 30, 31–3, 34, 35, 44, 59, 67, 72, 76, 77, 79, 87, 89–90, 114, 118, 120, 124, 125, 130, 137, 179–81; *see also* clinical negligence

negligence, contributory 31, 111, 115, 140
Neill, Lord 25
Nesse, Randolph 37
Nicholls, Lord 73, 179
Nietzsche, Friedrich 20
Nimmo Smith, Lord 94
normality 37, 53–4, 76, 90
Norrie, Kenneth 93, 96, 119
Norton, Fred 10, 88
Nott, Susan 15, 17, 22
Nourse, Martin 60
novus actus interveniens 91, 92, 94, 97
Nussbaum, Martha 174, 175

objectivity, legal 7, 37, 100, 104, 105, 110, 114, 115–16, 118, 123, 125, 136, 165, 168,
Ogden, J. 152
Ognall, J. 132
Orr, S. 41
O'Sullivan, Jack 145
Oughton, D. 87, 88, 116

pain and suffering: damages 1, 13, 17, 24, 28, 34, 49, 86, 125, 130; foetal interests argument and 54
Pain, J., Peter 6
paradigm shifts 43–7
parental interests argument 54–6, 64–8, 79, 88
parenthood, *see* motherhood; fathers
Park, J. 92, 93
paternalism 11
personal injury 14, 16, 24, 25, 27, 31, 37, 49; compensatory damages for 19; defining 37–8, 49; framework and exclusion of emotional harms 38, 40–3, 49; mitigation doctrine and 87, 95; wrongful pregnancy as 2, 8, 12, 16, 17, 24–31, 36–45; *see also* harm
Petchesky, R. 152
Peters, T. 141
Petersen, K. 98
Phillips, C. 54
Plato 20
Pomeroy, Jeremy 90, 115–16
Posner, R. 162
post-abortion syndrome (PAS) 151–2
pregnancy, as personal injury 1, 13, 16, 24–31, 38–47, 49; duty to prevent 2, 61; failure to diagnose 28; as instance of harm stretching 31–8, 49; as invasion of bodily integrity 28; natural event 2, 27; as physical event 39, 42; separate from child-rearing 3, 9, 12, 39, 85–7, 127; as unproblematic category 17, 30, 38–9; as unwanted 36, 39; *see also* abortion; women
pregnancy, models of: as adversarial 164; as connected 137; as emotional journey 40–2, 48; as episodic 39, 143; as harmful when unwanted 16, 39, 40; as illness/impairment 22, 25, 43–4; as physical event 19, 20–1, 41, 127; as preventable 143, 182; relational perspective 40–9, 70, 177–8; as separate entities 20–1, 22, 44–5, 127, 164; as valued for product 20; as women's work 15, 20; *see also* abortion; women
pregnancy, risk: abortion as insurance 123–4; insurance 120; privatisation of 171, 183
Priaulx, N. 55
Priestly, J. A. 105, 108
progenitive contestation 145–9
Prosser, William 118
provocation 173
psychiatric harm 26, 32
public policy 1, 6, 14, 179
Purchas, L. J. 92
Purdy, Laura 10, 21, 44, 50, 181

Quick, O. 50

Raby, Margaret 161
Rackley, Erika 51
Radcliffe-Richards, J. 65
Radin, Margaret 124, 125, 126
Radley-Gardener, O. 29
rape 36; marital 21
rationality 18–19, 21, 124, 162
Rawlinson, Lord 159
Read, Janet 68
reasonable man/person standard 95, 113–15, 116, 163, 169
reasonable woman, constructions of 113–39; on being responsible 115–20; natural woman 128–32; responsible women 121–2; self-regarding woman 122–8; woman in need 132–6; *see also* women
Rebouche, R. 159

Reece, H. 173
Reichman, Anna 94
relational approach 9–10, 40–8, 56, 69–71, 80, 164–78
religious beliefs 95, 97, 107, 117–8, 139, 153, 155
reproduction: conflicting messages surrounding 142–4, 182–3; diverse experiences of 56; medical control of 22, 23, 24, 85; men's rights in 21, 144–50; medicalisation of 9, 43, 151; morality of 142, 143; as preventable 143, 182; reproductive freedom 54, 55, 81, 144, 178, 181; risk and 54; *see also* pregnancy risk; technological advance and 35, 82, 141–2; women's identity and 85, 142; *see also* abortion; autonomy; choice; harm; women
responsibility: autonomy and 81–2, 142–4, 156–8, 170–2; for child maintenance costs 11, 61; decisional, in reproduction 40–1, 48, 82, 85, 145, 183; distinction between responsible agency and consequential responsibility 173–4, 183; fathers and 145–6, 148, 149–50; growth of tort and individual 32–3, 48; moral 170, 176, 178, 184; parental and caring 10, 56, 57, 58, 68, 70; relational approach to 164, 170–2; reproductive 44–5, 142, 145–6; shifting legal 90–1, 98, 101, 102, 108, 111, 120, 128, 169, 171, 178, 181; women and 88, 98, 101, 127, 130–1, 133, 142–3, 153, 165–6, 169, 172, 176, 181, 183; *see also* assumption of responsibility; duty of care
Richardson, Janice 120
Ripstein, Arthur 104, 118
Robertson, G. 91, 108
Roch, Lord 25
Rogers, W. V. H. 25, 26, 87, 95
Rosenbaum, T. 163
Rössler, Beate 166
Rothman, Barbara Katz 154, 175
Rúdólfsdóttir, A. 18, 21
Ryan, Maura 85, 183
Ryan, S. 6

Samuel, Goeffrey 87
sanctity of life 6, 97
Savulescu, J. 58, 65
Scarman, Lord 36

Schwartz, Barry 53, 182
Scott, Lord 73, 105, 106–8, 179
Scott, Rosamund 66
self-determination 22, 23, 141, 148, 154, 156; *see also* autonomy
self-regarding woman 122–8; *see* women
Seuffert, N. 178
sexuality 21, 37
Seymour, John 88, 94, 98, 134
Sheldon, Sally 22, 55, 65, 82, 83, 86, 89, 121–2, 123, 136, 146, 147, 149, 150, 153, 155, 156, 159, 163
Sherwin, Susan 9
Silbaugh, Katharine 129
Slade, L. J. 93, 94, 95, 98
Slynn, Lord 2, 12, 27, 39, 99, 102, 104
Smith, S. 91
Stapleton, J. 16, 89
Steele, Jenny 140
Steiger, Douglas 122–3
Stephenson, L. J. 96
sterilisation 1, 25, 26, 27, 30, 45, 50, 51, 60, 62, 73; failed sterilisation and availability of abortion 86, 92, 94, 95; failure to arrange 130; injunctions to prevent 22; as injurious 96; of intellectually disabled 67
Steyn, Lord 3–4, 5, 6, 7, 13, 14, 28, 30, 36, 39, 60, 73, 98–9, 100, 102, 104, 108, 119, 132, 133
Strangeways, S. 105
Stychin, Carl 22, 23
Symmons, C. 6

Talbot, C. 117
termination of pregnancy *see* abortion
Thomas, C. 54
Thorpe, L. J. 149
Toulson, J. 57
trespass 16

universality 5, 90, 114, 137, 165, 166

vasectomy 2–4, 6, 12, 22, 26–7
Vehmas, S. 68
vicissitudes, of life 13, 132, 183; *see also* damage/compensable harm
volenti non fit injuria 111, 131, 140

Waldron, Jeremy 157–8
Waller, L. J. 63, 69, 92, 93
Watson, N. 54

Weir, Tony 31–2, 33, 48, 137
West, Robin 17, 40, 48, 165, 171–2, 183
Whitfield, Adrian 26, 100
Wilkinson, S. 55, 83
Williams, Joan 82, 154, 165, 166
Williams, M. 117
Witting, Christian 16, 29, 33–6, 38
Women: autonomy of 10, 23, 24, 67, 78, 81, 82, 85, 110, 119, 143–4, 164, 168, 178, 181–2; constructions of, abortion debates 121–2, 157; construction of, reproductive torts 3, 28, 58, 122–36; construction of domestic work undertaken by 3, 9–10, 28, 58, 126, 128–32; harms specific to women 5, 40, 48, 169, 180; medical control of 22, 23, 24, 85; regulation/construction of women's bodies 18–24; reproduction and identity of 85, 142; responsibility of 88, 98, 101, 127, 130–1, 133, 142–3, 153, 165–6, 169, 172, 176, 181, 183; violence towards 161, 171–2; *see also* foetus; motherhood; as personal injury; pregnancy, pregnancy, models of; reproduction

Wong, Simone 129
wrongful birth cases 50, 75, 144; construction of women in 129–36; distinction between wrongful conception and 58–9, 61, 75; distinctive treatment from healthy child cases 58, 75, 134–5; failure to diagnose foetal abnormality 134; failure to diagnose pregnancy 28; mitigation and 110, 135
wrongful conception cases 1–4, 12, 16, 24; autonomy and *see* autonomy; characterisation of harm 5–8; choice and 101–5, 121, 122–8, 137–9; definition of problem 11–13; disability and 56–82, 174–6; extension of concept of harm and 33–43, 48; harm paradox 85–90, 109–10, 177–8, 181; mitigation doctrine and 91–109; paradigm shifts 43–7; parental interests argument 54–6, 64–8, 79, 88
wrongful life cases 7, 11, 14, 96–7, 111–12
wrongful pregnancy *see* pregnancy, as personal injury